THE ISLAMIC WORLD
A HISTORY IN OBJECTS

THE ISLAMIC WORLD
A HISTORY IN OBJECTS

LADAN AKBARNIA

VENETIA PORTER

FAHMIDA SULEMAN

WILLIAM GREENWOOD

ZEINA KLINK-HOPPE

AMANDINE MÉRAT

Thames & Hudson

The British Museum

Contents

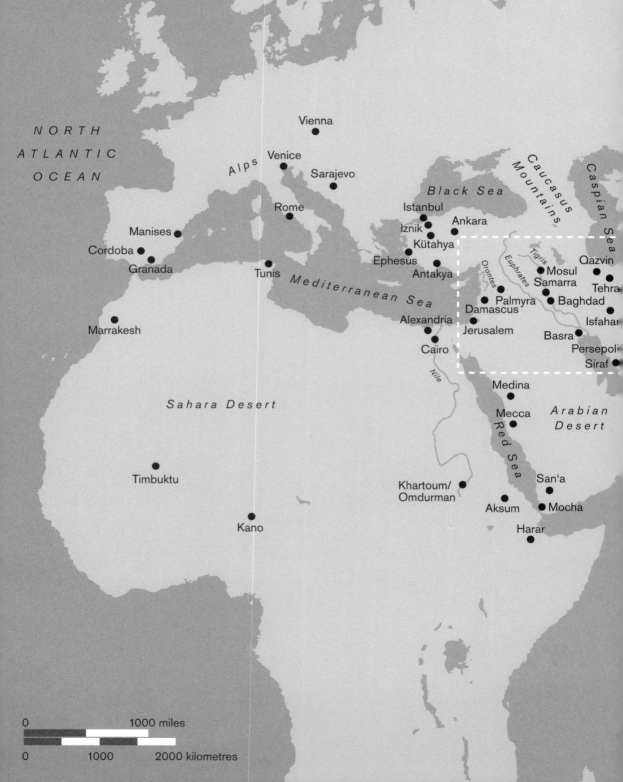

The Islamic World
From the lifetime of the Prophet to the present

NORTH
ATLANTIC
OCEAN

Vienna

Alps

Venice

Sarajevo

Black Sea

Caucasus Mountains

Istanbul

Rome

Ankara

Caspian Sea

Manises

Iznik

Cordoba

Kütahya

Mosul

Qazvin

Granada

Ephesus

Tigris

Samarra

Tehran

Tunis

Antakya

Orontes

Euphrates

Baghdad

Mediterranean Sea

Palmyra

Marrakesh

Damascus

Isfahan

Alexandria

Jerusalem

Basra

Persepolis

Cairo

Siraf

Nile

Medina

Sahara Desert

Mecca

Arabian Desert

Red Sea

Timbuktu

Khartoum/
Omdurman

San'a

Kano

Aksum

Mocha

Harar

0   1000 miles

0   1000   2000 kilometres

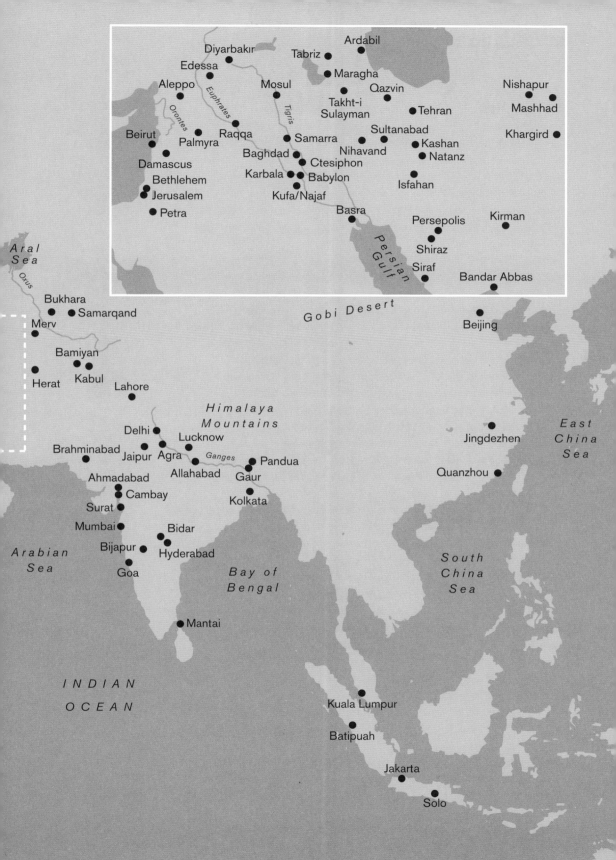

Introduction

Islam has played a significant role in great and multifaceted civilizations stretching from West Africa to the Malay Archipelago. The broad aim of this book is to acquaint the reader with the material culture of these diverse regions. Conveyed through objects housed in the British Museum, the narrative unfolds across media, geography and time, right up to the present day. From clay tiles and cooking pots to golden vessels and fine silks, these works together communicate the extraordinary richness of a world of encounters. Providing insights into artistic patronage and the exchange of ideas, they show us how people lived, how they saw themselves and others, and what they valued.

The Islamic 'world' is not linked to a specific time or place, but rather to a wider concept of contexts significantly impacted by the presence of Islam as a faith, political system or culture. The term 'Islamic art', which is often used to describe many of the works appearing in this book, has been avoided for its limitations. As a field that has existed only since the 19th century, Islamic art remains an artificial concept imposed upon the material culture of an enormous area. This book, however, does embrace the looseness of the catch-all term, exploiting the great degree of diversity contained in a broader spectrum of works, places and ideas. For this reason, the reader should not be surprised to encounter a 17th-century Persian painting of the Queen of Sheba in proximity to a 10th-century Egyptian tombstone, a 20th-century Ghanaian textile, or a contemporary Javanese shadow puppet. The hope is that these juxtapositions will encourage an examination and appreciation of both similarities and differences across time and space.

Such associations have been made possible by the global connections enabled by Islam. These allowed for the movement of artisans, objects and ideas over thousands of miles, beyond areas that would ordinarily be considered 'Islamic'. Even before the first revelations of Islam in around AD 610, Mecca was a centre of trade and worship on the Arabian Peninsula; with the coming of Islam and the *hajj* pilgrimage to Mecca, it became the heartland of the Islamic world (**1**). The centripetal force of the holy city created a place in which people from across that world would meet. Meanwhile, the rise of empires gave fresh vigour to ancient cities such as Damascus and Istanbul, and created cosmopolitan centres such as Baghdad, Cairo (**2**), Samarqand, Isfahan (**3**) and Delhi. These became nexuses for the dissemination of various strands of culture where different peoples – from Arabs and Iranians to Ethiopians and Chinese – could exchange goods and ideas. The 'Islamic' region between the Pyrenees and the Pamir mountains became a vast clearing-house, its position in the midst of Asia, Africa and Europe making it a centre for the refinement and diffusion of everything from royal iconography and mathematics to ceramic technology and coffee.

1. Shadia Alem (Saudi Arabian, b. 1960), *In God's Eye*
At the heart of the sanctuary, or *haram*, at Mecca is the Ka'ba. Muslims believe it was built by the Prophet Ibrahim and his son Isma'il. During the time of *hajj* and other times of the year including Ramadan, the month of fasting, thousands of people flock to Mecca in devotion to their faith. The 12th-century traveller Ibn Jubayr (d. 1217) describes his awe as they reached Mecca at night: 'from all sides voices were loud in invocation humbly beseeching God to grant them their requests'.

2010

2. Islamic Cairo: the 14th-century mosque complex of Sultan Hasan and other Mamluk monuments

The traveller Ibn Battutah (d. 1368) visited Cairo in 1329. He described Cairo, known as Misr, as 'the mother of cities and seat of pharaoh the tyrant, mistress of broad provinces and fruitful lands, boundless in multitude of buildings, peerless in beauty and splendour, the meeting place of comer and goer, the stopping place of the feeble and strong.'

3. Masjid-i Imam (formerly Masjid-i Shah), Isfahan

Popularly described as 'half the world', Isfahan became the capital of the Safavid dynasty in 1598 under Shah Abbas I (r. 1587–1629). The Masjid-i Imam (Imam's Mosque), begun in 1611 under Shah Abbas and completed under his successor, Shah Safi I (r. 1629–42), was the congregational mosque conceived as part of the ruler's new royal square. Celebrated for its stunning and colourful tile revetment, it remains one of the most visited sites in Iran today.

Inspired by the works in the British Museum collection, this book naturally is concerned with objects and the ways in which they illuminate the past. We are not primarily concerned with history or religion, although these represent significant elements within the narrative; here, the attention falls on material culture, by which we mean any objects that reflect human activity, from the everyday to 'works of art'. The aim is to avoid a narrow focus on items produced for the elite and the distorted image that follows from such an approach. Taking into account the entire spectrum of production – from imperial ateliers to cottage industries – we hope to favour a holistic view of the societies that produced and possessed the objects presented. Such an approach by no means excludes art entirely; it celebrates, for example, achievements such as the arts of the book and also considers the modern world through contemporary art and the ways in which it reflects both past and present.

The objects illustrated in this book represent the British Museum's Islamic collections, which form the basis for the selection and its ensuing narratives. Without claiming to be encyclopaedic in nature, the works featured here provide an overview of cultural production in an area stretching from Nigeria to Indonesia and from the early centuries AD to the present day.

The great variety of the collection owes much to those who have bequeathed objects to the British Museum over the last two and a half centuries, as well as to gifts and purchases throughout the years. Although there have been far too many to name all of them here, a brief overview of the most prominent donors will give an idea of the people who created this unique assemblage. The first, and arguably most influential, was Sir Hans Sloane, whose vast collection was donated to the nation upon his death in 1753, becoming the nucleus of the British Museum. Included among his collection were Persian amulets and an astrolabe made for the Safavid ruler Shah Sultan Husayn (r. 1694–1722). The number of Islamic objects remained relatively small until the mid-19th century, when Augustus Wollaston Franks – a curator and the first Keeper of British and Medieval Antiquities and Ethnography (1866–96) – added over three thousand pieces, transforming the representation of objects pertaining to the Islamic world. The personal connections cultivated by Franks ensured that bequests of Islamic objects continued to be made long after his death in 1897. More than 600 ceramic wares, including some of the finest glazed Islamic pottery in the world, came from the collection of Frederick Du Cane Godman (d. 1919), Franks's friend and a former Trustee of the British Museum, donated by his daughter Edith in 1982. More recently, between 2011 and 2015, Leila Ingrams (d. 2015) generously donated and bequeathed around 900 largely 20th-century objects, textiles and banknotes from across Africa and the Yemen, collected first by her parents on their various diplomatic postings in the 1920s to 1940s, and later by her. Purchase funds such as the Brooke Sewell Permanent Fund and CaMMEA (Contemporary and Modern Middle Eastern Art) have enabled the continued growth of the Museum's world-class holdings and allowed the collections to expand in their scope to modern and contemporary works of art. It is also worth mentioning the generous donations by Middle Eastern and Central Asian governments, including significant gifts of 20th-century objects and textiles from the Ministry of Tourism of the Sultanate of Oman (2010) and the Ministry of Foreign Affairs of the Republic of Tajikistan (2015).

The immense range of objects covered in this volume and the narratives they embody echo to some extent the works and stories to be found in the British Museum's Albukhary Gallery of the Islamic World, which opened in 2018. The thematic approach of the book, however, allows the reader to jump from one topic to another at his or her will, while the chronological order (supplemented by timelines with key dates) helps to provide a sense of historical context.

The first chapter charts the rise of Islam within the milieu of the Late Antique world, where elements from other cultures were reused, reassembled and rethought as part of a grand cultural synthesis that was to impact on the wider development of visual culture, the story of writing and the transmission of scientific knowledge. Chapter 2 considers Islam and the diversity of Muslim faith, especially the ways in which it has created and inspired aspects of material culture; it also explores the shared cultures (such as prophets and holy places) of the Abrahamic faiths in the Islamic world. Following this, the book moves into more straightforwardly chronological territory. Chapter 3 tours the period between about AD 750 and 1500, ranging from the great palace-city of Samarra in Iraq to the splendours of Cairo, Tabriz, Herat and Granada (**4**). The fourth chapter continues this approach for the period 1500 to 1900, with a particular focus on the 'Gunpowder Empires' – the Ottomans, Safavids and Mughals (**5**) – that dominated the Islamic world at this time, but also including two key regions that are often ignored in general surveys: Africa and Southeast Asia. Chapter 5, once again thematic rather than chronological, explores the literary and musical traditions of the Islamic world, including shadow puppets, the arts of the book, and musical instruments. The sixth and final chapter brings the reader up to the present day, looking at the Islamic world from the end of the great empires onwards, through, on the one hand, the eyes of contemporary artists and, on the other, the unnamed artisans whose works illuminate these turbulent times.

In its kaleidoscopic diversity, the Islamic world is perhaps better described as an idea rather than a region, and one which defies easy explanation. We hope and expect that this book will lead to more questions than the answers we have tried to provide. At the very least, the selection and discussions of the works presented in the volume are intended to shed light on the peoples and cultures they represent, as alluded to by the Iranian calligrapher Dust Muhammad in an Arabic verse included in his preface to an album assembled for the Safavid prince Bahram Mirza (d. 1549) in Tabriz:

'*Our works point to us: gaze after us at our works.*'

(WG/LA/VP/FS)

4. The Alhambra

Built on a mountain spur overlooking the city, the 'Red Fortress' (*al-hamra*) is a vast palace complex that was the home of the Nasrid sultans (1320–1492). The Andalusian poet Ibn Zamrak (d. 1392) evocatively described its glories:

I am a garden graced by every beauty:
see my splendour, then you will know my being…
The palace portico, so beautiful
It bids to rival heaven's very vault….

5. The tomb of the Mughal emperor Akbar at Agra

The construction of this monumental structure of red sandstone and white marble began in 1604 in Sikandra, Agra, while Akbar (r. 1556–1605) was still alive, and was completed between 1612 and 1614 by his son, the emperor Jahangir (r. 1605–27). Located on the roofless upper story of the tomb, Akbar's marble cenotaph remains eternally open to the sky, the sun and the moon, an arrangement that has been linked to the Mughal fascination with light and its symbolism as well as to the final verse of the Persian inscription found on the entrance gate to the tomb:

May his [Akbar's] soul shine like the rays of the sun and the moon in the light of God.

Timeline

1200 BC–AD 275	Sabean kingdom (capital Marib, Yemen)
c. 300 BC–AD 106	Nabatean kingdom (capital Petra, Jordan)
27 BC–AD 476	Roman Empire (capital Rome, Italy)
c. AD 100–940	Aksumite kingdom (capital Aksum, Ethiopia)
224–651	Sasanian Empire (capital Ctesiphon, Iraq)
260–74	Queen Zenobia rules Palmyra, Syria
330–1453	Byzantine Empire (capital Constantinople, Turkey)
c. 500	Invention of chess, probably in northern India
570 or 571	Birth of the Prophet Muhammad and purported 'year of the elephant'
610	Muhammad begins to receive the Qur'anic revelation through the Angel Gabriel
622	The emigration (hijra) to Medina and start of the Muslim lunar calendar
632–61	Rule of Rashidun caliphs from Medina
634	Battle of Ajnadayn, Palestine (Byzantine forces defeated)
636	Battle of Qadisiyya, Iraq (Sasanian forces defeated)
637	Muslim armies capture Jerusalem
639	Conquest of Egypt under the commander Amr ibn al-As (d. 664)
661–750	Rule of the Umayyad caliphs from Damascus
685–705	Reign of Umayyad caliph Abd al-Malik, builder of the Dome of the Rock in Jerusalem (691) and the Great Mosque in Damascus (715)
750	Abbasid Revolution and foundation of Baghdad
1022	Death of Ibn al-Bawwab, creator of the 'six scripts'

1 A history of histories

Islam emerged as a world religion in 7th-century AD Arabia. It was revealed to the Prophet Muhammad (c. AD 570–632) in a cave outside the Arabian city of Mecca in around 610 and these revelations were to form the holy book of Muslims, the Qur'an. The people of Mecca did not accept the new faith at first and, in 622, Muhammad migrated to the oasis town of Yathrib, later known as Medina. This decisive event, and the new calendar that came with it, is known as the *hijra*, meaning migration or flight, and this is where Islamic history begins. The *hijra* is a 12-month lunar calendar, with years of 354 or 355 days, so it does not run concurrently with the Gregorian calendar and years AH (*anno Hegirae*, 'in the year of the *hijra*') do not convert into exact years AD.

The Prophet Muhammad belonged to the Arab tribe of Quraysh. The Quraysh were custodians of the sacred site of the Ka'ba in Mecca, believed to have been built originally by the Prophet Abraham. Mecca lay adjacent to the great trade route that crossed from the Yemen up to the Mediterranean, and the Quraysh were heavily involved in this trade. On the eve of Islam, the lands of the Middle East were controlled by two major powers: the Sasanians (AD 224–651), who ruled from their capital at Ctesiphon (2) over present-day Iran and Iraq and whose sphere of influence extended across to Central Asia and Arabia; and the Byzantines, who controlled territories including Syria, Palestine, Egypt and Asia Minor, and whose capital was Constantinople (later known as Istanbul). In a short space of time, the adherents of the new religion of Islam were to achieve extraordinary military success. The Sasanians were swept away entirely, and within a few decades the Byzantine Empire was reduced to its strongholds in Asia Minor. By the mid-7th century, the new Islamic empire stretched from Spain to Central Asia.

From the dams and temples of the Yemen to the hieroglyph-covered walls of myriad monuments in Upper Egypt, the physical remains of ancient civilizations formed an inherent part of the world of the new conquerors. Superstition and legend were often associated with these ancient places. The 3rd-century BC Pharos of Alexandria, for example, a marvel that continued to function as a lighthouse well into the 14th century, was believed to have

LE PHAROS.
Cette Tour fut battie de marbre blanc dans lille de pharos aupres de lenbouchure du nil par protomee philadelphe qui donne pour cela 2.80000 Ecus on y mettoict la nui des flamboux pour seruir comme de lanter aux nauigeans

1. The Pharos of Alexandria
Built by the king Ptolemy II
(r. 285–246 BC), the Pharos
of Alexandria was considered
one of the seven architectural
wonders of the world. It stood
on the small island of Pharos
opposite the eastern harbour
of Alexandria. It was believed
to have talismanic powers, with
a treasure hidden in its base
and a mirror at its summit that
could burn hostile ships by
concentrating the rays of the sun.

c. 1660
Engraving by Jacques Picart after
Maarten de Vos
Height 17.2 cm, width 21.8 cm
1856,0112.303

foundations made of glass in the shape of a giant crab (**1**); and Babylon (**3**), one of the great cities of the Mesopotamian region, founded in around the 18th century BC, was said to have been built by the giant Biyurasib. The polymath historian Ibn Khaldun (d. 1406) had a deep nostalgia for the past: 'The Yemen where the Arabs live is in ruins, except for a few cities. Persian civilization in Arab Iraq is likewise completely ruined. The same applies to contemporary Syria. Formerly the whole region between Sudan and the Mediterranean had been settled. This fact is attested by the relics of civilization there, such as monuments, architectural sculpture, and the visible remains of villages and hamlets.' Despite the architectural legacies, the loss of which Ibn Khaldun bemoans, and which in many cases sank without trace and were only rediscovered many centuries later, the customs and practices of the peoples residing in this vast region were to become an integral part of the cultures of Islam and they played an active role in terms of language, religion, art and architecture. As the

33. CTESIPHON IN THE SUBURBS OF BAGHDAD. ٣٣ ـ ايوان كسرى فى ضواحى بغداد

Muslim conquerors pushed into the former territories of the Byzantine and Sasanian rulers, they brought back quantities of booty, crowns, thrones and other symbols of submission, displaying many of these items in the Ka'ba at Mecca. The sheer quantity of objects of high quality that had been made under Sasanian and Byzantine rule circulating in the early Islamic era must have had a significant impact on the artistic styles and iconographies of the time, and indeed this influence is clearly evident on a variety of objects newly made for Muslim patrons.

In this chapter, which we have called a 'history of histories', we examine the world that the early Muslims encountered; through the objects presented, we see explicitly how the symbols of power and the artistic legacies of the ancient world were transmitted and re-envisioned under new patronage. We consider how existing knowledge, in the sciences particularly, was revered, developed and eventually transmitted to Europe; how trade and discovery brought numerals and chess to the Arab world; and how Arabic, a script that also had much earlier beginnings, became the signifier of the new culture and quickly transformed into a method of communication and a means of artistic expression in itself. We also examine other elements of the new 'Islamic' visual culture, how they developed and how they were informed by debates into what was or was not permissible within the tenets of the new religion. (VP/FS)

1 | 1 Arabia Felix and Aksum

Ancient Yemen – known in the Roman world as Arabia Felix – grew rich on the trade in incense from as early as the 1st millennium BC. Precious aromatics were transported by camel across the Arabian Peninsula and on to the Mediterranean port cities, from where they were shipped to Europe and elsewhere (**1**). This was a journey of many months covering nearly 3,000 km, made worthwhile by the enormous demand for the traders' high-value product. The legendary sun-worshipping Queen of Sheba (**2**) came from the Yemen, and the story of her visit to King Solomon is told in both the Old Testament and the Qur'an (27:536). When she arrives, much to her surprise, her throne has been magically brought to her host's palace. The people of the Yemen were among the first to receive Islam, and the Prophet Muhammad was said to have had a special fondness for them.

The Christian empire of Aksum in northeast Africa was a major power in Arabia in the Late Antique and early Islamic period. In the 6th century AD, Kaleb (r. c. 500–25), the *negus* (ruler) of Aksum (**3**), sent his general Abraha into Yemen, where he set up his own state. Later writers report that Abraha constructed the cathedral of San'a as a rival to the pagan religious centre at Mecca, and that he led an army that included war elephants against the city, aiming to destroy the Ka'ba, which, prior to Islam, had been the centre for local cults. This event is referred to in the Qur'an *sura* (or chapter) 105, *al-Fil* or 'The Elephant' (**4**). The year in which this occurred was subsequently known as the 'Year of the Elephant' and was popularly held to be the year (570 or 571) in which Muhammad was born. (VP/WG)

This page
1. Incense burner
Incense burners, such as this example from Yemen, were placed in temples and bear dedications to particular gods. The Sabean inscription here mentions the male deity Athtar, who was worshipped in all of the South Arabian kingdoms.

2nd century AD
Found in al-Sawda, Yemen
Limestone
Height 40 cm, width 22 cm, depth 22 cm
1887,0629.21

Opposite above
2. The Queen of Sheba
In this Qazvin-style painting, the Queen of Sheba, known in Arabic literature as Bilqis, reclines by a stream, and gazes at the hoopoe who holds in its beak a rolled letter from its master, Solomon. Bilqis is shown wearing a remarkable robe that incorporates representations of a hoopoe and other birds and animals.

c. 1590–1600
Iran
Single-page painting mounted on a detached album folio
Height 16.1 cm, width 22.6 cm
Bequeathed by Sir Bernard Epstein, Bart, 1948,1211,0.8

3. Coin of King Kaleb

This coin features the bust of Kaleb, the *negus* of Aksum, on both sides, along with Greek inscriptions stating 'King Kaleb, son of Thezenas'. Kaleb's military expedition into Yemen may have brought Ethiopian forces into conflict with pre-Islamic Mecca.

c. 500–25
Aksum, Ethiopia
Gold
Diameter 19mm
1910,1207.1

4. Star tile

This tile bears Qur'anic inscriptions around its edge, including the verses of *sura* 105, 'The Elephant', which are believed to refer to the destruction of Abraha's army outside Mecca:

In the name of God, the Merciful, the Compassionate. Do you [Prophet] not see how your Lord dealt with the army of the elephant? Did He not utterly confound their plans? He sent ranks of birds against them, pelting them with pellets of hard-baked clay: He made them [like] cropped stubble.

c. 1300–25
Kashan, Iran
Stonepaste painted in blue and lustre over an opaque white glaze
Diameter 22.5 cm
Bequeathed by Miss Edith Godman, G.487

1 | 2 Petra and Palmyra

The names of two great cities of ancient Arabia still have major resonance in the modern world: Palmyra in Syria and Petra in Jordan. Their remains continue to entrance all who visit them. The *raison d'être* for both was that they played key roles in ancient trading networks. Palmyra, known in the Arabic sources as Tadmur, was said to have been founded by Solomon. By AD 20 it had been annexed by Rome, and a statue of the emperor Tiberius (r. 14–37) was placed in the temple of Bel. The city, fabled for its queen, Zenobia (r. *c.* 260–74), was captured by Muslim forces in 634. In the mid-19th century it was also the home of the fascinating aristocratic Englishwoman Jane Digby, who had fallen in love with a nobleman of Palmyra, Sheikh Medjuel el Mezrab. Living between Damascus and Palmyra, she wrote that she preferred 'the wide boundless desert to the cooped up town life'.

Petra, capital of the Nabateans (*c.* 300 BC–AD 106), was described by the poet John William Burgon (d. 1888) as the 'rose-red city half as old as time'. For the Syrian poet Adonis (*nom de plume* of Ali Ahmed Said, b. 1930), author of the *Petra tablets*, it was a place to 'Salute the rocks of the Jinn, the graves of the obelisks'. Carved out of rock, this dramatic desert city developed and survived because of its extraordinary system of irrigation and its position astride trade routes between Arabia and the Mediterranean. Like so many ancient sites, it declined gradually following the Arab conquests; as an exotic place it was visited by the Mamluk sultan Baybars (r. 1260–77) and was 're-discovered' by the Swiss explorer Johann Ludwig Burckhardt in 1812. Once news of this extraordinary city spread, it captured the imagination of western artists and travellers including the Scottish painter David Roberts (**1**).

1. Petra, from the series *The Holy Land* by David Roberts
Royal Academician David Roberts (1796–1864), well known for his beautiful paintings of monuments and landscapes of the Middle East, visited Petra in 1839 and drew the city extensively. Here we see some of the famous rock-cut tombs at the site.

1842
Tinted lithograph with hand-colouring by Louis Haghe after David Roberts
Donated by Campbell Dodgson, 1915,0706.41

Palmyra lies in an oasis some 200 km north of Damascus. The vast architectural complex includes temples, a great colonnade, baths and Byzantine churches. During Zenobia's reign, the inhabitants of the city numbered over 200,000. They spoke a dialect of Aramaic and used a script known as Palmyrene, which is inscribed on the statue of the young man (**2**). Following the Arab conquest, the city continued to prosper, but it declined dramatically after its takeover by the Central Asian conqueror Timur (or Tamerlane) in 1400. Sadly, the extensive archaeological remains of Palmyra suffered massive damage in 2015 at the hands of Daesh (so-called Islamic State) as part of the Syrian Civil War, which started in 2011. (VP)

Many a place have I seen, but nought
Have I seen so beautifully founded and built as Palmyra.
A place entirely chiselled of stone:
When one looks at it, it fills one with awe….
(Wuhayb ibn Mutarraf al-Tamimi)

2. Palmyrene funerary stela
The Palmyrenes buried their dead in elaborate mausolea. This young man, named in the inscription as Ma'nai son of Larhibola, holds a bunch of grapes in his right hand and a dove in his left. His hairstyle and costume, typical of the style of Palmyrene boys shown in depictions, exhibit a mixture of Parthian and Roman influences, resulting from Palmyra's position at the crossroads of different cultures.

150–200 BC
Limestone
Height 36.8 cm, width 27 cm, depth 13 cm
1889,1012.4

1 | 3 The Byzantines and the vine scroll

The Byzantine Empire emerged out of the eastern half of the Roman Empire following the decline of Imperial Rome in the 4th century AD. The emperor Constantine declared Constantinople (later Istanbul) his capital in the year 330. Christianity was the state religion. The Arabs succeeded in wresting control of Syria and Palestine from the Byzantine emperor at the decisive battle of Ajnadayn, west of Jerusalem, in 634, inaugurating Arab rule of what were to become known as the western Islamic lands. The Byzantines retreated to Asia Minor where, among other things, they became the Christian state most exposed through trade, alliance and battle to the Islamic world. It was only in 1453 that the Ottoman sultan Mehmed the Conqueror (r. 1444–81, with interruptions) was able to capture Constantinople, turning the church of Hagia Sophia, built by the Byzantine emperor Justinian (r. 527–65) and the most significant monument of Christendom, into a mosque.

In building their mosques, the early Muslims often chose sites that were already sacred – the late 7th-century Umayyad mosque of Damascus, for example, had previously been a Byzantine basilica and, before that, the site of a temple of Jupiter. Mosques were also built on top of Sasanian fire temples. They also reused material, including columns and capitals, from the buildings they found around them (**1**). The vine scroll, typical of Byzantine architectural decoration, went on to permeate late Sasanian art and transform itself into one of the main styles of ornament during the Islamic era (**2–4**). (VP)

1. Corinthian capital
This Byzantine capital, displaying vegetal ornament, was found in Jerusalem at the site of the Haram al-Sharif (a raised platform on which the Dome of the Rock and the mosque of al-Aqsa are situated), where earlier architectural elements were reused in the Islamic period.

Byzantine, c. 5th–6th century
Jerusalem
Limestone
Height 33 cm, width 51 cm, depth 28 cm
Donated by the Palestine Exploration Fund, 1903,0220.4

2. Architectural ornament

A fragment from the magnificent Sasanian palace at Ctesiphon, south of Baghdad, which was extensively decorated in stucco with vegetal ornament and painted frescoes.

6th century AD
Ctesiphon
Plaster
Width 43 cm, height 30 cm
Donated by Staaliche Museen zu Berlin, 1937,0219.1

3. Bone plaque

This ornamented bone plaque dates to the Umayyad period and belongs to a category of objects used for decorating furniture or receptacles associated with Alexandria. The design was carved onto the convex side of an animal bone and the motif demonstrates continuity with Byzantine-period examples. Known as *nabati* (from the Arabic for plant, also known as arabesque), this style was to become one of the main features of ornament in Islamic lands and the Mediterranean basin (see p. 42).

Umayyad period, *c.* 8th century AD
Egypt
Bone
Height 14 cm, width 4.7 cm
1896,0523.4

4. Flask (detail)

Intertwining vegetal scrolls enclosed in a medallion, on a late 13th-century flask. In a further refinement, on either side of the medallion the tops of the stems have been turned into animal heads known as *waq-waq* (see p. 42).

Late 13th century AD
Probably Syria or Egypt
Gilded and enamelled glass
Length 23 cm, height 23.2 cm, width 15.2 cm
Bequeathed by Felix Slade, 1869,0120.3

1 | 4 Textile traditions in Egypt

Egyptian weavers were renowned for their skills throughout the Mediterranean and Near Eastern worlds, and the region's long-standing tradition of textile production dates back to the 4th millennium BC.

Thanks to Egypt's dry climate and a change in burial practices in the Late Antique period, clothing and textile furnishings have been preserved and excavated in abundance in cemeteries, offering a comprehensive picture of the fashions and production techniques of the past. Textiles were mainly woven in linen, the long-established and favoured Egyptian fibre, as well as wool. Silk was much more expensive and precious and was reserved for luxurious garments produced under imperial monopoly from about AD 560.

Woven on vertical and warp-weighted looms, mainly in plain weave and embellished with techniques such as tapestry and brocade, textiles were produced both in domestic contexts and workshops, some of which were commissioned by the Coptic Church and monasteries.

During the 1st millennium AD, the main item of clothing worn by men, women and children alike was the tunic, following Roman fashions. Hangings, curtains and furniture covers were also produced as soft furnishings for Egyptian homes. The iconography on Egyptian textiles of this period is varied, reflecting Egypt's political and religious contexts at the time. It includes mythological, vegetal, animal and geometric motifs inherited from the Greco-Roman classical repertoire, along with Christian or Sasanian-inspired imagery from the ancient Near East (**1–3**). (AM)

1. Stela of Apa Pachom
From the 2nd century AD, Egyptians were no longer mummified, but buried in their daily clothes and wrapped in furnishing textiles. Tombstones such as this one were used to mark their graves. The deceased, Apa Pachom, whose name is recorded in Coptic (the latest stage of the Egyptian language, written in a modified Greek script), is depicted in prayer with a Christian cross on either side of his head. He wears a tunic decorated with geometric patterns, and is surrounded by a frieze of scrolling grapevines springing out of Greek vases, a motif inherited from classical imagery.

6th–7th century AD
Saqqara, Egypt
Limestone
Height 57 cm, width 44 cm, depth 14 cm
1911,0617.16

2. *Tabula*, or square tapestry ornament

In Late Antiquity, the tunic commonly worn in Egypt was woven in a single T-shaped piece, which was then folded and sewn along the edges. It was decorated with tapestry ornaments, such as this one on the knees and/or the shoulders. The quadruped and vine leaf motifs seen here derive from classical imagery of the Greco-Roman god Dionysius, and similar vegetal friezes are found on Roman and North African mosaics.

c. 5th–6th century AD
Akhmim, Egypt
Linen and wool
Height 27 cm, width 19 cm
1887,0402.109

3. Furnishing textile fragment

While the Arab conquest of Egypt brought significant political and religious change, it does not appear to have caused a rupture in either technology, iconography or artistic production. As far as the textile industry is concerned, the main fibres and weaving techniques continued in use until at least the 10th century. Late Antique imagery such as the vine scroll, sometimes combined with birds and quadrupeds, was still commonly found on early Islamic and Fatimid fabrics.

c. 11th century AD
Egypt
Linen and silk
Height 22 cm, width 22 cm
1992,0518,0.2

1 | 5 Sasanian fire altars and *senmurv*s

Let us pass round the golden cup Persia has decked with diverse images;
Khusraw in their midst and at the sides antelopes pursued by riders armed
with bows. Abu Nuwas (d. 813)

The Sasanian Empire (AD 224–651), which succeeded that of the Parthians
(247 BC–AD 224), controlled a vast region that included present-day Iran,
Iraq, Central Asia and Eastern Arabia. Its state religion was Zoroastrianism,
developed from the teachings of the Ancient prophet Zoroaster, and its holy
book was the Avesta. Central to the Zoroastrian faith is Ahura Mazda, the
'Creator of All', the 'Lord of Wisdom', and belief in the ritual fire (**1**).

The Sasanians were prodigious patrons of the arts; magnificent objects
– textiles and metalwork in particular – were produced for the court, the
silverware often decorated with scenes of feasting and hunting. Following
the Arab conquests, the metalworking traditions of eastern Iran and the
provinces of Tabaristan, Khurasan and Khwarazm were sustained well into
the 8th and 9th centuries (**2**, **3**). Iconographic elements of pre-Islamic Iran,
the most popular example of which was the *senmurv*, also continued to
appear in architectural decoration and on early Islamic objects (**4**, **5**). With the
head of a dog, lion's paws and a bird's tail, and first mentioned in the Avesta,
the *senmurv* is a beneficent creature known for his service to mankind as a
distributor of seeds. (VP)

1. Ceramic bowl
The bowl is decorated with
a fanciful representation of a
fire altar, a stand on which the
sacred fire used in Zoroastrian
rituals is placed. Among the best
preserved from the Sasanian
era are the twin stone altars at
the site of Naqsh-i Rustam, near
Persepolis. They also form part
of the iconography of Sasanian
coins, appearing regularly on the
reverse (see p. 33).

9th century AD
Iraq
Tin-glazed earthenware with
designs in cobalt blue
Diameter 21.5 cm, height 7 cm
1923,0725.1

2. Silver dish
The banqueting scene here was
inspired by earlier Sasanian silver
vessels featuring Dionysius, the
god of wine.

c. 7th–8th century AD
Tabaristan
Silver gilt with relief decoration
Diameter 19.7 cm
Bequeathed by Sir Augustus
Wollaston Franks, 1963,1210.3

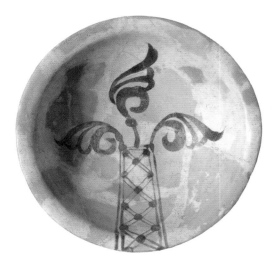

3. Silver bowl

The multi-armed goddess Nana was popular in the province of Khwarazm in Central Asia. In a late survival of a pre-Islamic calendar, this bowl bears a date of 700 in the Khwarazmian era, equivalent to AD 658.

Dated AD 658
Khwarazm, Uzbekistan
Silver with repoussé and engraved decoration
Diameter 12.4 cm, height 4.6 cm
1877,0820.1

4. Plaque

This *senmurv* would have formed part of an elaborate frieze on the facade or interior of a villa.

7th–8th century AD
Chal Tarkhan, northern Iran
Stucco
Height 16.9 cm, width 19.3 cm
1973,0725.1

5. Ewer

The shape of this ewer, with a thumb-rest in the form of a leaf, is derived from classical antiquity. On both sides is a medallion containing a *senmurv* in profile, its lion's paw raised.

9th century AD
Iraq or Iran
Cast brass with relief decoration
Height 29 cm
Brooke Sewell Permanent Fund, 1959,1023.1

1 | 6 The glassmaker's art

Schools of craftsmen in lands newly conquered by Islam did not cease their work with the end of the Sasanian and Byzantine eras; they simply adapted, using their artistic skill and the same technical abilities to create desirable objects for their new patrons. An example of this continuity can be seen in the glass of the early Islamic period: the techniques of sandwich, mosaic and trailed glass came from the Roman and Byzantine world, while cut and moulded glass were extensively developed in Sasanian workshops (**1–5**). (VP)

1. Glass bottle
Sandwich glass was a Roman innovation, but the technique was also practised in the Islamic era in Syria. This bottle was free blown and the gold decoration applied as leaf, with details scratched through. The body was then encapsulated by a second layer of glass. Delicate blue dots were also placed between the classically inspired plant forms.

9th–10th century AD
Probably Syria
Gilded and enamelled glass
Height 14.5 cm, maximum diameter 10.4 cm
1978,1011.2

2, 3. 'Millefiori' glass bowl and tile fragment

The ancient technique of fusing together slices of cylindrical glass canes, known as mosaic or 'millefiori' glass, produced a brilliant colourful effect. This technique, particularly popular in the Roman era, was briefly revived in the early Islamic period. The tile fragment illustrated here was found with others at the site of the Jawsaq al-Khaqani, the palace of the Abbasid caliph al-Mu'tasim (r. 836–42) at Samarra, in present-day Iraq. These glass tiles were likely to have formed panels on the walls. The bowl, which might have been a cosmetic palette or possibly a decorative architectural element, may also be associated with Samarra, although its findspot is unknown.

9th century AD
Iraq
Bowl: diameter 7.5 cm; tile fragment: height 7.6 cm, maximum width 4.7 cm, thickness 0.8 cm
Donated by the Oriental Ceramic Society, 1973,0623.1, Victoria and Albert Museum C.742-1922

4. Glass bowl

The technique of wheel-cutting was perfected by Iranian glassmakers during the Sasanian era, but it continued to be employed by glassmakers for their new Muslim patrons. The vegetal designs on this piece echo the abstract style found in the other arts of the period. It was probably made at Nishapur, a known centre of glass production during the 9th–10th centuries.

9th century AD
Iran, probably Nishapur
Blown and wheel-cut glass
Height 9.5 cm, diameter 15 cm
Brooke Sewell Bequest, 1966,0418.1

5. Donkey-shaped glass flask

The application of delicate glass trails to a glass object was a technique originally associated with Byzantine Syria. Hot trails of glass, the consistency of molasses, were used to create openwork structures and vessels, such as the one shown here, and are generally known as cage flasks. Playful in form, animal shapes were very popular. This donkey appears to carry a large basket on its back.

7th–8th century AD
Syria
Height 12 cm, width 12 cm, depth 6 cm
1913,0523.115

1 | 7 Coins: history in miniature

Nowhere can the transition from the Sasanian and Byzantine worlds be better seen than through coinage. The earliest Islamic coins were copies of the gold and bronze coins of the Byzantine Empire, including the *solidus* (**1**), and the silver *drachms* used by the Sasanians (**5**). The name for the Islamic gold coin, the *dinar,* derived from the Roman *denarius* while the silver coin, the *dirham*, came from the Greek term *drachma*.

In a series of transformations, the Byzantine coin of the emperor Heraclius (r. 610–41) lost its Christian imagery. The representation of the cross on steps turned into a simple pillar (**2**) and the Arabic text of the Profession of Faith (*shahada*) would replace the Latin inscription. In the year AH 76 (AD 695/6), the representation of the Byzantine emperor and his sons was replaced entirely by the single figure of the caliph Abd al-Malik (r. 685–705) in traditional Arab robes holding a sword (**3**). The *dirham* underwent similar transformations: the silver coin of Khusraw II (r. 590–628) (**5**), with his portrait on the obverse and the representation of the Zoroastrian fire altar on the reverse, replaced some of the Pahlavi inscriptions with Arabic (**6**).

In AH 77 (AD 696/7), experimentation with figural designs came to an end, replaced thenceforth by legends entirely in Arabic (**4, 7**). These proclaimed the message of Islam, emphasizing the uniqueness of God on the obverse, and controverting the Christian doctrine of the Trinity on the reverse, stating: 'God is one, He is eternal, He begets not nor is He begotten.' The weight for gold coinage was changed from the Byzantine 4.55 g to 4.25 g, the *mithqal*, a standard maintained for centuries. Such coins became the staple unit for trade across the Mediterranean and beyond in the medieval era. (VP)

1. Gold *solidus* of Heraclius
The emperor Heraclius (r. 610–41) is represented here with his two sons. It was his armies that lost Syria, Palestine and Egypt to Muslim forces.

Minted in Constantinople
Diameter 1.9 cm
1904,0511.319

2. Gold *dinar*
Imitating the Byzantine *solidus*, this *dinar* maintains the three figures on the obverse, but the representation of the cross on steps on the reverse has become a simple pillar and the Latin inscription is garbled. Although there is no mint name, such coins were probably struck at Damascus in about AD 691 and are known as 'Arab-Byzantine'.

Diameter 1.9 cm
1904,0511.320

3. Gold *dinar*

On the obverse of this coin, dated AH 76 (AD 695/6), the caliph Abd al-Malik (r. 685–705) wears traditional Arab garments and holds a sword. Around the edge is the Profession of Faith (*shahada*): 'There is no god but God; Muhammad is the messenger of God.'

Diameter 1.8 cm
Donated by Prof. Philip Grierson, 1954,1011.2

4. Gold *dinar*

In AH 77 (AD 696/7), the caliph Abd al-Malik decreed that, henceforth, coins would bear only inscriptions and that these should state unequivocally the essence of the message of Islam.

Minted in Damascus
Diameter 1.9 cm
1874,0706.1

5. Silver *drachm*

This is the typical style of Sasanian coins struck by Khusraw II (r. 590–628) at the Bishapur mint in AD 626.

Diameter 3.2 cm
1920,0515.239

6. Silver *dirham*

Coins in this style are known as 'Arab-Sasanian'. They adapt the form of the coins of Khusraw II by adding the name of the Umayyad governor al-Hajjaj ibn Yusuf (d. 713), who played a vital role in the monetary reform of the caliph Abd al-Malik. This coin was struck at Bishapur in the year AH 76 (AD 695/6).

Diameter 3 cm
Bequeathed by Dr Charles Davies Sherborn, 1935,0303.20

7. Silver *dirham*

In AH 79 (AD 698/9), two years after the same had happened for gold coins, the Arab-Sasanian style for silver coins was abandoned in favour of Arabic inscriptions.

Minted in Damascus
Diameter 2.7 cm
1846,0523.14

1. Inscribed boulder

Representations of horses and camels have been scratched onto this rock; in between are three phrases in the Safaitic script used by nomads of the Syro-Arabian desert. They read:

By Banat son of Baraqat and he pastured [the animals].

By Simam son of Sunay son of Ha-Malik son of Harb is the hinny [offspring of a male horse and female donkey].

By Hani'at son of Nks are the drawings.

1st–2nd century AD
Found in Jordan
Basalt
Height 34 cm, width 36 cm
Donated by Sir Frederick Palmer,
1931,0820.1

2. The ciborium of Maitre d'Alpais

Around the top of this ciborium (a cup to hold the Eucharist) is a band of repeating Arabic letter forms. Based on a style of script known as floriated *kufic*, it is composed of a series of units probably repeating the word *Allah* (God). Such 'Arabic' inscriptions found their way into Western art and appear in architecture too (an example of which is the 12th-century church at Le Puy-en-Velay near Limoges).

c. 1200–25
Limoges, France
Copper alloy, gold, enamel and glass
Height 12 cm, diameter 16.2 cm
Donated by Hon. Mrs Upcher,
1853,1118.1

Writing and scripts

Until the beginning of Islam, Arabic was predominantly a spoken language with a strong oral tradition. There were informal writings on rock made by nomads of the Syro-Arabian desert (**1**), but the Arabic script as such only begins to be encountered in Southwest Arabia and Syria in a handful of stone inscriptions dateable to the 5th and 6th centuries AD. The script used in these texts is a form of Aramaic used by the Nabateans (see p. 22), and research has shown how the letter forms changed over time to become a script recognizable as Arabic. It was the revelation of the Qur'an to the Prophet Muhammad in the early 7th century that provided the impetus for the development of the script. There was a strong need to write down the words of God in order to preserve them and it is at this point that the remarkable story of the Arabic script begins. The religious association of Arabic gave the script a unique significance; it led, almost immediately, to a conscious beautification of the script and elevated the status of the calligrapher.

Over time a series of different styles of script were developed to copy the Qur'an. The earliest was the *ma'il* (sloping) style, used to copy the first Qur'ans in the late 7th century. This was followed by the angular *kufic* style (**3**, **5**), named after the city of Kufa in Iraq, one of the earliest dated examples of which is the gold coin of Abd al-Malik struck in AH 77 (AD 696/7), illustrated on p. 33. By the 10th century, not only was *kufic* becoming more elaborate and therefore less legible, but also there was a proliferation of cursive scripts being employed for personal correspondence to meet the needs of merchants and bureaucrats. A calligrapher and vizier at the Abbasid court, known as Ibn Muqla (d. 940), was tasked with standardizing the scripts. This initiative and the work of a later calligrapher, Ibn al-Bawwab (d. 1022), resulted in what are known as 'the six calligraphic styles' (*al-aqlam al-sitta*), in which a rigorous system of proportion was used to write a variety of cursive scripts used for different contexts; this still forms the basis of traditional calligraphy today. The styles include the rounded script, *naskh* (**6**), and *thuluth* for the writing of monumental inscriptions. One of the major contributions of Persian calligraphers was *nasta'liq*, the 'hanging' script perfected by the calligrapher Mir Ali Tabrizi (d. 1446) and predominantly used for the writing of poetry (see pp. 38–39). Other regions developed their own characteristic styles: Ottoman chancery documents were written in a script known as *diwani* (see p. 158), while the script used by Chinese Muslim calligraphers is known as *sini* (see p. 149).

The scripts were written on parchment and later paper with the reed pen or *qalam* – the same material that had been used centuries before for pressing cuneiform letters into clay. But many other types of material could be inscribed – from stone to pottery and tiny seals – and each required a unique skill. As inscribed Islamic objects found their way to Europe in the early medieval period, the shapes of the words began to be echoed in the patterning on a variety of objects, including the important early 13th-century Limoges enamel, the ciborium of Maitre d'Alpais (**2**).

The arrival of paper in the 8th century from China revolutionized communication and helped Arabic to become the language and script of the empire's administration. Books on literature and science were extensively produced under the Abbasid caliphs of Baghdad and elsewhere, and reading and writing became widespread. The script was adapted to write Persian, Ottoman Turkish (until Atatürk's reforms in 1928), and a number of the languages of Africa and the Malay world. To accommodate the new languages, a range of symbols was added to the 28 letters of the Arabic alphabet. (VP)

3. Stone inscription

This marble panel is one of four now in different collections that originally made up a cenotaph that was subsequently taken apart and the backs recarved. The outer face, probably carved in the 9th century, consists of the beginning of the *basmala*, 'In the name of God, the Merciful, the Compassionate'. The text is in *kufic* script, some of the letters terminating in elegant leaf forms. The back has been turned into a funerary inscription in a simpler form of *kufic* script:

In the name of God, the Merciful, the Compassionate, this is the tomb of Muhammad ibn Fatik Ashmuni who died in the month of Jumada II in the year 356 (AD 967). God is our sufficiency.

'Ashmuni' indicates that the deceased came from Ashmun (or Ashmunein), in the Nile delta.

9th and 10th centuries
Egypt
Marble
Height 45 cm, length 76 cm
1975,0415.1

4. Amulet-seal

The inscription here, in mirror writing, states 'My trust is in my creator' and repeats the name Ali in reference to the son-in-law of the Prophet Muhammad. He was one of the 'Rightly Guided' (*Rashidun*) caliphs (r. 656–61), and first of the Shi'a imams.

c. 14th–15th century
Bloodstone
Diameter 2.3 cm
OA+.14259

5. Tombstone with *kufic* inscription

To lay out the inscription across the 12 lines on this tombstone, the letter cutter created a grid, the outlines of which are visible. The script, typical of the 9th–10th centuries, is in the angular *kufic* style, subtly embellished by small wedge shapes at the tops of the letters. The Arabic does not contain diacritical marks, which makes reading difficult since several of the letters are the same shape (in later Arabic these are distinguished by dots above or below the letters).

The text follows a formula, beginning with the phrase known as the *basmala* (*bismillah al-rahman al-rahim*, 'In the name of God, the Merciful, the Compassionate') and continuing 'In God one finds consolation from every misfortune and the largest misfortune is the loss of the Prophet Muhammad, may God bless him.' The next part gives the name of the deceased, Ya'qub, son of Abdallah, and the Profession of Faith (*shahada*), stating that he 'testifies that there is no god but God alone, He has no companion and that Muhammad is His servant and His apostle, may God bless him.' The final two lines give the date of death in the month of Dhu'l-Qa'da in the year AH 244 (February–March AD 859).

Dated AD 859 (AH 244)
Egypt
Marble
Height 55 cm, width 42 cm
Donated by the Egypt Exploration Fund, 1891,0701.1

6. Tombstone with *naskh* inscription

Cursive script had been used for writing on a variety of objects from pottery sherds to papyri from the early Islamic period. For ease of reading, the vizier Ibn Muqla (d. 940) regularized the script creating a series of standard styles including *naskh*, which began to be used extensively. This tombstone comes from the Red Sea island of Dahlak. It is carved so that its *naskh* inscription stands proud of the background and is in the shape of a *mihrab* (niche) with a hanging lamp at the top. The text includes prayers to the Prophet Muhammad and verses from the Qur'an (51:15–19): 'As to the righteous, they will be in the midst of gardens and springs, taking joy in the things which the Lord gives them, because, before, they lived a good life.' In bold script are the words 'This is the tomb of the cultured man' and his name: Isa ibn (son of) Ahmad ibn Muhammad ibn Ibrahim ibn Yusuf ibn Hamid ibn Yahya al-Makki. He died in the evening on the 29th day of the month of Safar AH 584 (28 April, AD 1188), a Friday. Unusually for the period, the letter carver also gives his name, Abd al-Rahman ibn Abi Harami al-Makki. Both came from Mecca, as indicated by their names.

Dated AD 1188 (AH 584)
Dahlak, Eritrea
Basalt
Height 65 cm, width 31 cm (max)
Donated by W.D. Campbell, 1928,0305.1

1. Ghani Alani (Iraqi, b. 1937),
Untitled

Among the most famous poems of the pre-Islamic era were the *Mu'allaqat*, seven epic poems believed to have hung on the walls of the Ka'ba at Mecca, the sacred building at the heart of the sanctuary. Not transcribed until the Islamic era, these poems, which evoke the life of the desert, are still learnt today across the Arab world. The text here is written in *thuluth* script, in different directions as though a calligraphic exercise. To be read completely, therefore, the calligraphy needs to be turned 180 degrees while reading. The text consists of the last part of the *mu'allaqa* of Zuhayr ibn Abi Sulma (d. 609). The cistern, or watering place referred to in the first line is likely to be an allusion to the poet's tribe's (or his own) 'pool' of virtue.

He, who drives not invaders from his cistern with strong arms [weapons], will see it demolished; and he, who abstains ever so much from injuring others, will often himself be injured.

Whenever a man has a peculiar cast in his nature, although he suppose it concealed, it will soon be known.

How many men dost thou see, whose abundant merit is admired, when they are silent, but whose failings are discovered, as soon as they open their lips!'

Half of man is his tongue, and the other half is his heart: the rest is only an image composed of blood and flesh.

1993
Black ink on paper
Height 60 cm, width 50 cm
Brooke Sewell Permanent Fund,
2003,0328.0.3

Opposite below

2. Inscribed dish

This dish features, on four lines in *kufic* script, a verse by the Hijazi poet Muhammad ibn Bashir al-Khariji (d. *c.* 718), who wrote poetry for the Umayyads and was known for his love poetry in the Hijazi style. The verses are included in the anthology of Arabic poetry, the *Hamasa*.

If you accept things manfully, then be sure all will be for the best, however long it takes.

c. 8th–9th century AD
Iraq
Earthenware, relief moulded and painted under a transparent glaze
Diameter 21.6 cm
1963,0424.1

3. Lidded Iznik bowl

In cartouches around this vessel are verses by the poet Hayali (d. 1557) in *nasta'liq* script, of which these are the first lines:

*The beautiful creatures of this
   world know not what beauty is,
Just as the fish in the sea know
   not what the sea is.
O pious one! Do not tell of
   hellfire to the tavern-goers,
For they are people who live
   for today and know not of
   tomorrow's grief.*

c. 1550–80
Iznik, Turkey
Stonepaste, painted under a
transparent glaze
Height 37 cm, diameter 26 cm
Bequeathed by Miss Edith
Godman, G.139.a–b

4. Star tile

Persian verses feature on the border of this tile:

*Last night the moon came into
your house, filled with envy
I thought of chasing him away.
Who is the moon to sit in the
same place as you.*

Late 13th century
Iran, probably Kashan
Stonepaste, painted in lustre and
blue on an opaque white glaze
Height 20.2 cm, width 20.4 cm
Bequeathed by John Henderson,
1878,1230.561

1 | 9 Islamic visual culture

Both the concept of 'Islamic art' and its field of study were generated largely by Western European scholarship in the 19th and early 20th centuries. Some of the earliest exponents developed romanticized notions and theories of what constituted the 'essence' or 'identity' of Islamic art. For the French Egyptologist and architect Émile Prisse d'Avennes (d. 1879), it was an Arab distaste for nudity that led to a desire to 'dress' their material culture with decoration and ornament. In contrast to European art, Islamic visual culture was essentialized by many as a purely decorative tradition that was deeply opposed to figural imagery. Such stereotypes have long been shaken off, even though they resurface from time to time.

Four recognizable visual idioms or types of ornament from the Islamic world have traditionally been recognized, especially in the West: epigraphic (use of writing), geometric (shapes and symmetry), floral and vegetal (both naturalistic and abstract) and figural (people and animals). These elements may appear in isolation or in combinations (**1**). Decoration is heightened with the use of colour, symmetry, repetition, luminosity (e.g. the use of gold or shimmering glazes), abstraction of figural and non-figural designs, and all-over patterning that often blurs the distinction between foreground and background. The meanings behind particular patterns and motifs are much debated in scholarship.

1. Portrait of Shah Jahan
This accession painting of the 36-year-old Mughal emperor Shah Jahan (r. 1628–58) shows him holding a royal seal engraved with the regnal year 1 (i.e. 1628) and his illustrious titles, 'King of the World, Ever victorious King of Kings, and Second Lord of the Astral Conjunction'. The style of painting produced in Shah Jahan's royal workshops was less spontaneous and experimental than that of his predecessors. The favoured subject matter in Shah Jahan's reign was the stiff, formal portrait, particularly of himself, commissioned to assert his imperial aims and political legitimacy. This painting, combining geometry, calligraphy and floral ornament, is an unsigned copy of an original by Abu'l Hasan, who was also the leading court painter of emperor Jahangir (r. 1605–27), Shah Jahan's father. The original may have been copied numerous times for dissemination as a commemorative portrait to neighbouring Indian, Persian and European courts.

1625–1650
Mughal India
Opaque watercolour, ink and gold on paper
Height 15.5 cm, width 10.5 cm
Donated by Mr and Mrs Anthony N. Stuart, 1969,0317,0.2

2. Bowl decorated with an aphorism in foliated _kufic_

The Arabic inscription, attributed to Ali, the fourth caliph and first Shi'a imam, reads:

The noblest of riches is the abandonment of desire.

10th century
Nishapur, northeastern Iran
Earthenware covered in a white slip and painted in black and red slip under a transparent glaze
Diameter 21.5 cm, height 7 cm
Brooke Sewell Permanent Fund, 1967,1213.1

3. Set of four architectural tiles with geometric ornament

These tiles were manufactured using the _arista_ technique (corresponding to the Islamic _cuerda seca_, see p. 136). The moulded sunken patterns with raised edges prevent the coloured tin glazes from running into each other during the firing process.

16th century
Seville (found in Castilla-La Mancha, Toledo), Spain
Earthenware
Height 30 cm, width 30 cm
Donated by Don Guillermo Joaquin de Osma, 1896,1120.3

As already discussed earlier (p. 35), Arabic, as the language of the Qur'an, has retained an elevated position in Islamic contexts alongside the calligrapher's craft. Manuscripts of the holy scripture have been copied out and embellished by hand more than any other book in the Islamic world. The application of Qur'anic verses as well as other religious and literary texts and aphorisms on buildings, textiles, objects and coinage throughout history attests to a high degree of artistic experimentation. Appreciation for the written word and calligraphy in Islamic culture was also transferred to secular contexts and many objects of daily life feature visually exciting depictions of writing on them in Arabic, Persian and Ottoman Turkish, among other languages (**2**). Even seemingly illegible pseudo-script was still cherished for its design possibilities.

Geometric designs were already a feature of the art and material culture of Late Antiquity in the Byzantine and Sasanian regions, and they were inherited by the early Muslim empires. However, geometric ornament reached a pinnacle in the Islamic world as artists, architects and mathematicians worked together to elaborate on existing patterns and invent new designs and architectural structures that stressed the importance of unity, mathematical precision and order. Simple forms such as dots, circles, squares, triangles and straight lines formed the basis of the patterns and when combined, duplicated and interlaced, created complex arrangements that were infinitely expandable and, as some have argued, invited contemplations on the ordered geometry within natural phenomena (**3**). The mosaic tilework at the Alhambra in Granada (see p. 13) is among the most remarkable examples of geometric ornament.

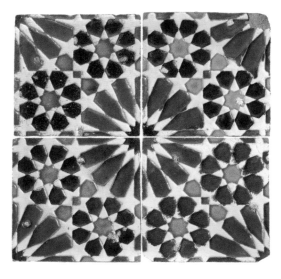

Vegetal and floral patterns, characterized by curving, twisting linear forms, such as stalks or stems as well as floral and leaf motifs, adorn a vast number of surfaces of buildings, manuscripts, objects and textiles throughout the Islamic world. Like geometric designs, vegetal patterns derived from existing traditions of Byzantine culture in the eastern Mediterranean and Sasanian Iraq and Iran (see pp. 24–25). Between the 10th and 12th centuries, a highly abstract and fully developed Islamic style emerged, featuring a leafy vine that expanded with geometric regularity and symmetry (4). Western art historians expounded on the origin and evolution of the motif, narrowly defining it as the ubiquitous 'arabesque', an essential feature of Islamic art that was driven by an anti-naturalistic Arab spirit, although empty of symbolic meaning. In their original contexts, floral and vegetal patterns had many nuanced names, forms and meanings, such as *tawriq* (to burst with leaves), *nabati* (vegetal), *khata'i* (lotus scrolls), *rumi/islimi* (foliated split palmettes) and *waq-waq* (vegetal scrolls with human and animal heads). In the 15th century, vegetal decoration underwent a further transformation with the introduction of Chinese-inspired (i.e. 'chinoiserie') motifs featuring peonies, lotus flowers, cloud bands and lobed trefoil shapes (5). From the 16th to 18th centuries, a more pronounced interest in naturalistic flowers and plants developed in Ottoman, Safavid and Mughal domains, in part bolstered by a thriving local garden culture and in part by the increased circulation of European herbal prints in the 17th century.

4. Cast brass tray inlaid with silver
The delicate, interlaced vegetal scrolls on this tray, inlaid in silver, is divided into four quadrants with symmetrically arranged ogival medallions; included is the signature of the late Mamluk master craftsman, Mahmud al-Kurdi. This type of metalwork was once thought to be the product of a Muslim workshop operating in Venice for European clientele, and was dubbed as 'Veneto-Saracenic' metalware.

1460–1500
Egypt or Syria
Brass and silver
Diameter 29 cm
Bequeathed by John Henderson, 1878,1230.705

5. Mosque lamp with chinoiserie ornament
This mosque lamp from Ottoman Turkey combines the blue-and-white aesthetic of Chinese porcelain and chinoiserie trefoils and flowers with Qur'anic inscriptions and geometrically interlaced bands and motifs. The dense floral patterning may be read as visual metaphors of the gardens of Paradise mentioned in the Qur'an (61:12). The Arabic inscriptions on this lamp include the names Allah, Muhammad and Ali, as well as a verse from the Qur'an (61:13):

Help from God and a speedy victory. So give glad tidings to the believers.

c. 1520
Iznik, Turkey
Stonepaste, painted in blue under a transparent glaze
Height 28.2 cm, diameter 18 cm
Bequeathed by Miss Edith Godman, G.4

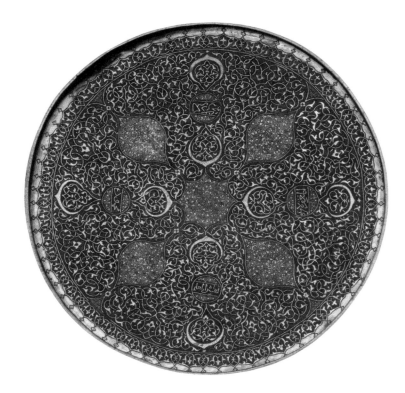

With the spread of Islam outward from the Arabian Peninsula in the 7th century, figural artistic traditions of the newly conquered lands profoundly influenced the development of Islamic art and its decorative vocabulary. Although the often-cited opposition in Islam to the depiction of human and animal forms mainly holds true for religious art and architecture, in the secular sphere such representations have flourished in nearly all Islamic cultures (**6**). Artistic expression within the context of the mosque largely remained aniconic (devoid of figures) in order to prevent mental distraction when praying to God and avoid the danger of image worship in keeping with the Qur'an and the *hadith* (the recorded sayings and actions of the Prophet).

Although the Qur'an clearly opposes the adoration or worship of idols (Qur'an 6:74), it does not reject representational art as such. It is sometimes argued that God's power as divine creator and giver of life must not be mimicked by humankind. In response, Muslim philosophers, such as the great 12th-century thinker Ibn Rushd (known in the West as Averroes, d. 1198), argued against the belief that God's pivotal role as creator invalidates human attempts at visually representing creation. Ibn Rushd, however, stressed that God is entirely unconstrained in his creation and is perfect, whereas human creativity has limitations.

The guidance that stems from the *hadith* provides evidence both in favour of and against the prohibition of figural depictions. It appears that during the Prophet's lifetime, the problem of figural representation was not a significant question requiring any official legislation. According to an account of the siege of Mecca in 630, the Prophet destroyed several hundred idols found in the holy Ka'ba, but left an image of the Virgin Mary with baby Jesus intact. This suggests that figural art as such did not pose a theological problem to him, although the worshipping of idols clearly did. According to another tradition, the Prophet asked his wife A'isha (d. 678) to remove a curtain in their home that had images of winged horses or birds on it because it distracted him during prayer. A'isha is said to have made cushions from the curtain, implying that this was permissible and less obtrusive. The notion that figural images can cause mental distraction during prayer seems to be a plausible basis for the long-standing practice of decorating mosques with calligraphic, geometric and vegetal designs while avoiding human and animal imagery.

In the medieval period, painted or drawn illustrations were often integral to literary and scientific manuscripts and acted as visual aids to the text. According to Ibn al-Muqaffa (d. 756), who translated and re-worked one of the most popular collections of Indo-Persian animal fables into Arabic, the *Kalila wa Dimna*, illustrated stories helped to engage and instruct youths, princes and philosophers in the wisdom of their ethical tales (**7**). (FS)

6. Vase in the form of a musician

This ceramic vase, depicting a royal drum (*daff*) player wearing a crown and richly adorned textiles, was produced in Iran in the early 13th century, by which time figural representation in the arts had reached new heights.

1201–1225
Iran, probably Kashan
Stonepaste painted under a turquoise glaze
Height 17.5 cm, width 9.5 cm
Donated by Henry Van den Bergh and The Art Fund (as NACF), 1928,0721.10

7. The gardener and the bear

This detached folio is from a manuscript of the *Anvar-i Suhayli* of al-Kashifi, the Persian translation and adaptation of Ibn al-Muqaffa's *Kalila wa Dimna* fables. In this tale, a gardener befriends a bear that later unwittingly kills him with a large stone as it tries to swat a fly off the sleeping man's face.

1550–1575
Iran
Opaque watercolour, ink and gold on paper
Height 18.8 cm, width 11.1 cm (full page)
Donated by Prof. R.A. Dara, 1933,0109,0.3

1 | 10 Iconoclasm

The resistance to the representation of living beings in some Islamic contexts stems from the belief that the creation of living forms is unique to God, and there are *hadith* recorded in which the Prophet is said to have declared: 'Those who make images will be punished on the Day of Resurrection and they will be called upon to breathe life into them, but they will not succeed in this task.' It is not clear how prevalent these ideas were during the earliest periods of Islam, both from the conflicting accounts already mentioned during the Prophet's lifetime (see p. 44) and because the *hadith* were compiled at least a century after his death. The 12th-century Persian scholar Ahmad-i Tusi wrote a treatise in favour of images, arguing that they could help trigger an emotional or intellectual response that allowed an individual to arrive at a lesson or truth (although he denounced the veneration of images).

Iconoclasm means 'the breaking of images', and examples in both religious and secular Islamic contexts are known, some of which occurred long after the objects themselves were made (**2, 3**). Acts of iconoclasm also occurred in Christian contexts in the 8th and 9th centuries, when Byzantine imperial legislation barred the production and use of figural images, and existing icons were destroyed or plastered over.

Regrettably, iconoclasm continues to this day: one of the most deplorable acts of recent times occurred in 2001 when the former Taliban government of Afghanistan dynamited and destroyed the Bamiyan Buddhas (**1**). (FS)

1. Rock-cut Buddha at Bamiyan
Before they were destroyed by the Taliban, the monumental statues at Bamiyan, carved into the side of a cliff, had stood for over 1,500 years; Muslims have celebrated these objects of wonder since medieval times. This hand-coloured lithograph of the smaller 35-metre-tall Buddha was redrawn in 1843 by Lowes Cato Dickinson as part of his 'Prison sketches' series (after Lieutenant Vincent Eyre). Ahmad-i Tusi remarked that the Buddhas were benevolent talismanic figures, with pigeons nesting in their noses, that smiled when the sun rose.

1843
London, United Kingdom
Height 10.1 cm, width 16.1 cm
Donated by Miss M.W. MacEwen, 1970,0527.2.29

2. Large lustre tile

Although the decoration on this tile, formed of a Qur'anic inscription intermingled with birds and vegetal motifs, was clearly inoffensive when it was produced in AD 1307/8 (AH 707) for the tomb of Abd al-Samad at Natanz in Iran, someone had strong reactions to it later, at an unspecified date, and carefully chipped off the head of each bird. The text reads *wala shukur* ('and no thanks') (Qur'an 76:9).

c. 1308
Kashan, Iran
Stonepaste, painted on an opaque white glaze
Height 36.2 cm, width 35.2 cm
Bequeathed by Miss Edith Godman, G.195

3. Portrait of Sarkhan Beg the chamberlain

Single-page idealized portraits were intended for inclusion in albums, with many produced in the royal workshops (*kitabkhana*s) of the Safavids, Ottomans and Mughals. This elegant portrait of a royal servant, Sarkhan Beg, was defaced at a later date. It was painted by Mir Musavvir (active *c.* 1525–50), a leading court artist of Safavid ruler, Shah Tahmasp (r. 1524–76), who was lauded for his flawless technique. The face has been erased but, interestingly, the figure's *taj*, or red baton, around which Sarkhan Beg's turban is wrapped, is also rubbed out, raising questions about the motive of the iconoclast in this instance. Was this merely a misguided act of piety against figural depiction or was it also a politically motivated insult against the rule of this Shi'a dynasty, since the red *taj* was an overt symbol of Safavid power?

c. 1530
Tabriz, Iran
Single-page painting mounted on a detached album folio
Opaque watercolour, ink and gold on paper
Height 40.7 cm, width 28.5 cm
1930,1112,0.2

1 | 11 Reading the skies

We have adorned the lowest heaven with stars. (Qur'an 37:6)

The study of the skies – what we would today call astronomy and astrology – was an essential part of everyday life until very recently, both in the Islamic world and elsewhere. From the 8th century onwards, the science of understanding the skies was assimilated from older sources and improved upon. This work was carried out by scholars connected to centres of learning whether secular, such as the great Mongol observatory at Maragha in Iran (**3**), or religious, like the Great Mosque of Damascus. A major aspect of astronomy in the Islamic world related to finding the correct time and direction of prayer, with the *qibla* (the direction of Mecca) acting as a unifying factor for Muslims across the world (**2**). Astrolabes and other devices could be used for a variety of secular purposes including agriculture, tax-collecting and travelling, as well as for astronomy (**1**, **3**). Astrology, which is no longer considered a science, was widely accepted in Islamic and other cultures until very recently. Astrologers were consulted by everyone from caliphs and emperors to ordinary people as a means of making decisions in an uncertain world and astrological signs and symbols permeated Islamic art (**4**). (WG)

1. Astrolabe

Astrolables were used primarily either for locating astronomical objects, for navigation (since they can determine the user's latitude) or for surveying. Heavily inlaid with silver and copper, this example features striking figural imagery on its front and back. It is signed Abd al-Karim *al-Asturlabi* ('the Astrolabist'), and the titles of three possible royal patrons – al-Malik, al-Mu'izz, and Shihab al-Din – are engraved on the back. This elite patronage, along with its large size and extensive decoration, suggest that it was a presentation piece meant to be admired rather than used, emphasizing the significance of *ilm al-nujum* ('the knowledge of the stars') within the visual language of Islamic societies.

AD 1240/1 (AH 638)
Southeast Turkey, northern Iraq or Syria
Brass, silver and copper
Diameter 42.9 cm
1855,0709.1

2. *Qibla* indicator

A distinctive feature of Islamic science is the requirement to accurately determine the *qibla* in order to carry out prayers properly. Designed for the Muslim traveller within and adjacent to Iranian territories, the instrument gives readings for over 20 cities; it also has a compass as well as a sundial to tell the time.

17th–18th century
Iran
Brass
Height 2 cm, diameter 9 cm
1890,0315.4

3. Celestial globe

Celestial globes show the position of stars and constellations by mapping them onto a sphere that represents the earth, and their complexity means that they are rare compared to astrolabes or quadrants. This globe was probably made for the observatory at Maragha, founded by the Mongol Ilkhanid ruler Hülagü (r. 1256–65) and directed by the polymath Nasir al-Din Tusi until his death in 1274. It is dated AH 674 (AD 1275/6), which shows that it was made after the second Mongol invasion of the Middle East, and the signature of Muhammad ibn Hilal *al-Munajjim al-Mawsili* ('the Astrologer from

Mosul') suggests that he was uprooted by the new overlords from his home in northern Iraq.

AD 1275/6 (AH 674)
Maragha, Iran
Brass and silver
Diameter 29 cm (globe), height 50 cm (globe and stand)
1871,0301.1.a-b

4. Coin showing the sun in Leo

The Mughal ruler Jahangir (r. 1605–27) took a particular interest in the design of coins; it is therefore not surprising that he claimed the design of zodiac coins such as this one as his own idea. As he explained in his memoirs, '…it entered my mind that in place of the month they should substitute the figure of the constellation which belonged to that month…. The figure of the constellation was to be on one face, as if the sun were emerging from it. This usage is my own, and has never been practised until now.' These coins also feature the sun (a symbol of royalty in India, Iran and elsewhere) on the reverse.

1621/2 (AH 1031, regnal year 17)
Agra, Mughal India
Gold
Diameter 2 cm
Bequeathed by Richard Payne Knight, RPK,p206.6.Zod

1 | 12 Chess

Although the precise origins of chess are lost to history, textual and linguistic evidence suggests that the game may have been invented in India in around AD 500. Its Arabic name – *shatranj* – derives from the Sanskrit *chaturanga* ('four limbs'), which references the four elements of an Indian army of the early centuries of the Christian era (**2**, **3**). Over a relatively brief period, chess spread westwards into pre-Islamic Iran and, following the collapse of the Sasanian Empire, it was adopted by the Arabs and was soon played across the Islamic world. The game became the topic of religious controversy, raising questions over what constituted a game of chance rather than one of skill but, despite this, there was a flowering of chess culture in the Abbasid court during the 9th and 10th centuries. Over time, and with the spread of the game into different cultures, the pieces themselves changed both in terms of name and form. For example, what is now referred to in English as the bishop was originally the *fil* or elephant (the name deriving from the Persian *pil*), representing the army's war elephants (**1**). (WG)

1. Chess piece (bishop)
This naturalistic depiction of an elephant with a *mahout* (elephant trainer or rider) on its back is an excellent example of a very early figural chess piece. The animal is clearly in the process of lifting itself from a sitting position, with the front legs straightened and leaning backward, and the back legs bent under its own weight and that of the rider.

c. AD 600–800
Sindh, Pakistan
Fired clay
Height 4 cm, width 2.3 cm
Given by Sir Marc Aurel Stein,
OA+.7838

2. Chess piece (rook)

The name of the modern rook is derived from the Sanskrit *ratha* (chariot) via the Persian *rukh*. This connection is shown very clearly by the example here, an early piece that still retains the form of horses pulling a chariot and its occupant. Over time, the motif was abstracted into a v-shaped piece, which in turn became a tower with two projections.

c. AD 600–800
Nishapur, Iran
Ivory
Height 5 cm, length 3.5 cm
1991,1012.1

3. Chess pieces

This group of four chess pieces, which comprises three kings and a knight (left), is part of a larger group of at least 13 in different collections, all of which can be attributed to the same workshop. Being solid ivory, pieces such as these would have been a marker of great wealth.

c. AD 1050–1200
Sicily
Ivory
Height 5.3 cm (largest piece)
1856,0612.4, 1862,0809.2,
1877,0802.8, 1881,0719.47

Timeline

570	Muhammad is born in Mecca, into the Quraysh tribe
610	Muhammad begins to receive the Qur'anic revelation through the Angel Gabriel
619	Death of Khadija, the Prophet's first wife and second Muslim after the Prophet
622	The emigration (*hijra*) to Medina and start of the Muslim lunar calendar
624	Battle of Badr, southwest of Medina, first major battle of the Prophet's career
625	Battle of Uhud, north of Medina, second major battle between Muslims and Meccans
628	Battle of Khaybar, northwest of Medina, between Muslim and Jewish tribes
630	The Muslims conquer Mecca
632	Death of the Prophet Muhammad
632	Death of Fatima, daughter of the Prophet and wife of Ali
632–34	Caliphate of Abu Bakr
634–44	Caliphate of Umar
644–56	Caliphate of Uthman
650–56	Codification of the Qur'an
656–61	Caliphate of Ali
657	Battle of Siffin, near Raqqa, Syria, between Ali and Mu'awiya (first Umayyad caliph)
680	Battle of Karbala and martyrdom of Husayn, grandson of the Prophet
691	Completion of the Dome of the Rock in Jerusalem by Umayyad caliph Abd al-Malik
740	Death of Zayd ibn Ali ibn al-Husayn, progenitor of Zaydi Shi'ism
756	Death of Imam Ja'far al-Sadiq, founder of the Twelver Shi'a Ja'fari school of law
756	Major split in Shi'ism between the Ithna Ashari (Twelver) and Isma'ili branches
767	Death of Imam Abu Hanifa, founder of the Sunni Hanafi school of law
768	Death of Ibn Ishaq, biographer of the Prophet
796	Death of Imam Malik ibn Anas, founder of the Sunni Maliki school of law
820	Death of Imam al-Shafi'i, founder of the Sunni Shafi'i school of law
833	Death of Ibn Hisham, biographer of the Prophet
855	Death of Imam Ahmad ibn Hanbal, founder of the Sunni Hanbali school of law
1094	Major split in Shi'ism between Nizari and Musta'li Isma'ili branches

2 Belief and practice

Islam begins with the divine revelation – the Qur'an. Muslims believe that the Arabic verses of the Qur'an were gradually revealed to the Prophet Muhammad through the conduit of the Archangel Gabriel, over a period of 20 years beginning in around AD 610. Muhammad's mission as the chosen and 'seal' of God's prophets was to deliver the divine message to mankind. The Qur'an is seen as confirming and completing – but not supplanting – previous Abrahamic scripture sent from God: 'We revealed to you as we revealed to Noah and the prophets after him, and as we revealed to Abraham and Ishmael and Isaac and Jacob and the tribes and Jesus and Job and Jonah and Aaron and Solomon and as we granted David the Psalms' (Qur'an 4:163). Therefore, Jews and Christians (and at times Zoroastrians, Qur'an 22:17) are considered to be 'People of the Book' (*ahl al-kitab* in Arabic) and the prophets of the Old and New Testaments are also prophets of Islam.

During Muhammad's lifetime, several of his closest companions prepared personal copies of the Qur'anic revelations, but these exhibited various differences. Attempts were made to standardize the text after the Prophet's death and the task was finally completed under the caliph Uthman (r. 644–56), who also ordered the destruction of all variant readings. The Qur'an is divided into 114 *sura*s (chapters) of unequal length, each comprising a number of *ayat* (verses). The *sura*s are not arranged in the order in which they were revealed to the Prophet, but generally by length, with the shorter ones appearing towards the end. Some would argue that the more succinct hymn-like verses encapsulate the essence or tenets of the faith. Virtually all the *sura*s begin with a pious formula known as the *basmala*: 'In the name of God, the Merciful, the Compassionate'. Muslims often evoke the *basmala* before commencing day-to-day activities, such as eating a meal, as well as on important occasions, from embarking on a long journey to delivering a speech.

The contents of the Qur'an are varied and include spiritual principles and divine decrees, rules for social and personal behaviour, stipulations for prayers and worship, descriptions of heaven and hell, and stories about past prophets and other parables. The verbal recitation, study and physical copying

1. Shaykh Lutfallah Mosque, Isfahan

The Iranian ruler Shah Abbas (r. 1587–1629) commissioned the jewel-like Mosque of Shaykh Lutfallah in Isfahan as a private place of worship for the Safavid royal family as part of his extensive building program in his new capital. Carefully selected Qur'anic inscriptions were designed in majestic *thuluth* script by the ruler's leading court calligrapher, Ali Riza Abbasi, for the exterior and interior spaces of the mosque. The image shows details of the *qibla* wall and part of the magnificent dome, which are covered with blue, yellow, turquoise and white tiles with intricate vine scrolls, cartouches and geometric designs. Numerous complete Qur'anic *sura*s are inscribed inside the prayer chamber alongside pious Shi'a texts and prayers in white lettering on a blue ground.

1603–19
Isfahan, Iran
Brick and glazed stonepaste mosaic tile decoration

2. Early Qur'an page

This detached Qur'an page is inscribed in angular *kufic* script with elongated horizontal strokes (which is why early *kufic* Qur'ans were written in wide, landscape formats). The verses (4:157–61) inscribed on this page from *Surat al-Nisa*, the chapter of 'Women', underscore the importance of Mary and Jesus in Islam.

9th–10th centuries
Probably Iraq
Ink on parchment
Height 15.6 cm, width 23.4 cm
2001,0605,0.1

3. Nassar Mansour (Jordanian, b. 1967), *Kun II* ('Be')

This modern calligraphic work features the Arabic word *kun* ('be') in black ink with the dot of the letter '*nun*' applied in gold leaf. It is inspired by a phrase from a Qur'anic verse (2:117) that asserts God's omnipotence as the divine creator: 'He is the Originator of the heavens and the earth, and when He decrees something, He says only, "Be," and it is.'

2006
Jordan/UK
Ink and gold on paper
Height 70 cm, width 40 cm
Donated by Nassar Mansour,
2006,0304,0.1

of the Qur'an has profoundly affected Muslim faith and practice for almost a millennium and a half. Muslims experience the divine through the oral cantillation of the Qur'an and many also express their faith and devotion through visual artistic means, by producing exquisite illuminated copies of the holy scripture (**2**) and calligraphy (**3**) or by inscribing the Word of God on architectural surfaces (**1**). Certain verses of the scripture are also memorized for the purposes of well-being and safety in both the physical and spiritual realms. One such verse is commonly referred to as the 'throne verse' (*ayat al-kursi*, Qur'an 2:255); it is recommended for its great talismanic power against the 'evil eye' and is often inscribed on personal amulets (**4**).

Once Muhammad accepted his prophetic mission and embraced Islam as the first Muslim, he began to preach the monotheistic message of the Qur'an to the people of Mecca, who were mainly polytheists, believing in several different deities. At first, Muhammad was accused of being a sorcerer or possessed by a malevolent spirit (*jinn*). Over time, however, the Muslims grew in number, arousing the attention and hostility of the Meccan authorities. With their lives in grave danger, Muhammad and the early Muslim community (*umma*) emigrated in 622 to the northern city of Yathrib or Medina (short for *Madinat al-Nabi*, the City of the Prophet), as it was later renamed. It took the Muslims eight years to conquer Mecca and finally gain the support of the

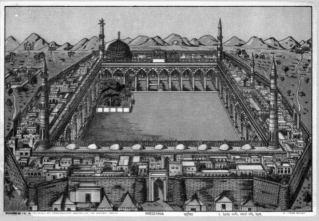

remaining Meccan elite. The emigration, or *hijra*, marks
the beginning of the Muslim calendar and Medina remains
one of the three holiest cities of Islam alongside Mecca and
Jerusalem. The first purpose-built mosque (*masjid*) at Medina
was the courtyard of the Prophet's house, which became
both a religious and political centre for the new community
(**5**). Architectural forms of mosques differ from region to
region, but most consist of a covered prayer hall preceded
by a colonnaded courtyard, and have one or more minarets,
towers from which the call to prayer (*adhan*) is made. All
have facilities for ritual ablutions and are oriented so that the
faithful pray facing towards Mecca (the direction known as
the *qibla*), indicated by an ornate prayer niche (*mihrab*) inside
the mosque.

Elements of the Islamic creed took more definite shape
during the Prophet's time at Medina, as the longer *sura*s of
the Qur'an detailing ritual practices and observances were
revealed to him there. Among these were the five basic duties
and observances that are obligatory for all Muslims. Known
as the 'pillars (*arkan*) of Islam', they are: the Profession of Faith
in Allah and His Messenger (*shahada*); ritual prayer (*salat*) (**6**);
charity or alms-giving (*zakat*) (**7**); observing the annual fast
(*sawm*); and pilgrimage to Mecca (*hajj*) (see p. 66). In addition
to the Qur'an and its multiple interpretations (*tafsir*), Muslims
also look to the *hadith*, that is the recorded sayings and actions
(*sunna*) attributed to the Prophet for guidance in the practice
of their faith. Over time, multiple schools of law (*madhhab*s)
and philosophical and mystical thought developed, leading to

**4. Amulet inscribed with the
shahada (centre) and the
'throne verse' (sides)**
*God, there is no god except Him,
the Living, the Eternal Sustainer.
Slumber seizes Him not, neither
sleep; to Him belongs all that
is in the heavens and the
earth. Who is there that shall
intercede with Him except by
His permission? He knows what
lies before them and what is
after them; and they encompass
nothing of His knowledge except
such as He wills. His throne
embraces the heavens and the
earth; and the preserving of them
wearies Him not. For He is the
High, the Tremendous.*
(Qur'an 2:255)

17th century
Iran
Chalcedony
Height 5.8 cm, width 4.6 cm
Bequeathed by Sir Hans Sloane,
SL.9

5. Print of mosque at Medina
The characteristic green dome in
this print immediately identifies
it as the Prophet's Mosque in
Medina. Although visiting Medina
is not an official rite as part of the
hajj, most pilgrims will go there
before or after visiting Mecca.

Early 20th century
Printed by Hemchandra Bhargava
Mumbai and Delhi, India
Height 35.7 cm, width 25 cm
1990,0707,0.33

6. Black coral prayer beads

Strings of prayer beads are usually comprised of 11, 33 or 99 beads, corresponding with the 99 Beautiful Names of God (*al-asma al-husna*) derived from the Qur'an. The black coral beads in this example are inlaid with silver pins.

c. 1880s–90s
Istanbul, Turkey or San'a, Yemen
Black coral, silver, ivory or bone and silk
Length 71 cm
2016,6028.2

7. Fragmentary water filter

Pierced filters such as this one were attached to water jars. Most were decorated with geometric designs but some bear figural motifs or pithy aphorisms in Arabic. This one reads 'Be generous and you will be rewarded', a notion rooted in the Bible (Proverbs 11:25) and the Qur'an (57:18), which strongly relates to the Islamic pillar of *zakat* (charity).

10th–12th century
Fustat, Egypt
Unglazed earthenware
Diameter 6.2 cm
1921,0301.13

different interpretations of the fundamental elements of Islamic faith.

During the Prophet's lifetime, Islam began spreading beyond the Arabian Peninsula. By the 8th century, Muslim communities were thriving in lands as distant as Spain and China and many of the diverse peoples of the ancient world gradually adhered to different branches of Islam. The material culture produced across these lands often blends vernacular forms and local artistic traditions with visual and aesthetic elements associated with Islam, as well as the Arabic language and script. While Arabic maintained its central religious role, in later centuries the Arabic alphabet, slightly modified to fit other languages such as Persian, Turkish, Urdu, Malay, Hausa and Swahili, continued to constitute a prime element of Islamic material culture. This chapter explores the diversity of Muslim faith and practice through objects as well as the commonalities shared among the People of the Book. (FS)

2 | 1 The Prophet and his successors

The earliest biographies (*sira*) of the Prophet (**3**) were composed a century after his death, and the first illustrated biographies, from the Mongol Ilkhanid world, date to around the 14th century. The Ottoman Turkish example illustrated opposite is much later, from the 16th century (**2**). They include accounts of the military expeditions of Muhammad and his companions in Arabia, with descriptions of the battles of Badr (624), Uhud (625) and Khaybar (628). *Sira* literature also includes the speeches of the Prophet, among them his sermon at the Farewell Pilgrimage (*hajj*) in 632, the year he died.

The Prophet's demise not only ended the line of prophethood and the period of Qur'anic revelations, it also brought to the fore the challenge to appoint a suitable successor. Muhammad had no sons and it was understood that one of his closest companions should be appointed to the role. Proximity to the Prophet became a defining feature in the race to succession, although how this proximity was defined was not unanimously agreed. For some, it meant privileging genealogical closeness and thus Ali, the Prophet's first cousin and son-in-law, was the right choice. Others championed Abu Bakr, Muhammad's father-in-law and chief advisor. Abu Bakr (r. 632–34) prevailed and took the title of *khalifat rasul Allah* (caliph/successor of God's Messenger). He was succeeded by Muhammad's companions Umar (r. 634–44) and Uthman (r. 644–56), and then by Ali (r. 656–61). Collectively these four are known as the 'Rightly Guided' (*Rashidun*) caliphs (**1**). The Muslim empire expanded across the Arabian Peninsula, Syria, Palestine, Egypt, Iraq, the Jazira and parts of Sasanian Iran during their caliphates. (FS)

1. Tile panel with the names of the four 'Rightly Guided' caliphs

The image on this tile panel represents the interior of a mosque with hanging lamps, cypress trees and a pot of carnations. The crescent-shaped finials above the domed arches and minarets refer to the period of Ottoman rule in Syria and Palestine at this time. The tiles are inscribed with Allah, Muhammad, and the names of the 'Rightly Guided' caliphs, Abu Bakr, Umar, Uthman and Ali (who may also be symbolized by the four upright cypresses). These six names are also found inscribed on the inner domes of some Ottoman mosques.

c. 18th century (bottom central tile is a later replacement)
Damascus, Syria (found in Palestine)
Stonepaste, painted in turquoise, blue and purple under a transparent glaze
Height 23 cm, width 23 cm (each tile)
OA+.14389, OA+.14399–OA+.14404

2. The battle of Badr, from Mustafa Darir's *Siyer-i Nebi* ('Life of the Prophet')

This Ottoman painting from an illustrated manuscript of the fourth volume of the *Siyer-i Nebi*, an epic history of the life of the Prophet composed in Turkish, depicts a moment during the pivotal battle of Badr when Ataba, a Meccan adversary of the Muslims, is slayed by Ali using his legendary bifurcated sword (*Dhu'l faqar*). The Prophet, seated on a throne and shown veiled and engulfed by a flaming halo (top right), blesses the heroes Ali and Hamza (behind Ali).

c. 1594
Ottoman Turkey
Gold, opaque watercolour and ink on paper
Height 37.1 cm, width 26.5 cm (page); height 29.5 cm, width 19.8 cm (image)
1985,0513,0.1

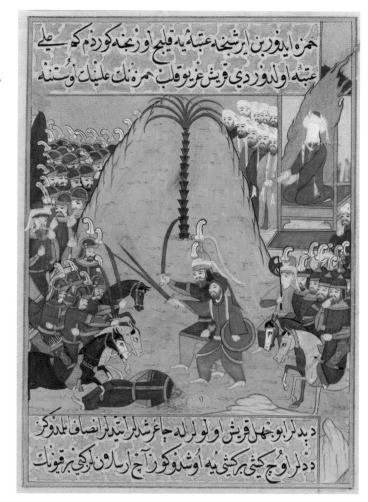

3. Gold amulet with a description of the Prophet Muhammad

Illustrations of the Prophet made and used by Muslims for historical manuscripts and for private, devotional purposes can be traced back to at least the 13th century. This amulet (or *maskeh*) bears a *hilya*, a verbal depiction of the Prophet's physical and moral qualities, as well as the *basmala*. Muhammad is described as handsome, fragrant, perfect in stature, round of face and beard, with bluish-black eyes, a large forehead, small ears, long hands and soft fingertips. Such devotional amulets were sewn onto clothing, possibly for protection against miscarriages.

1800–1890s
Ottoman Turkey
Gold
Diameter 3.1 cm
1849,1121.359

2 | 2 Shi'ism

Sunnis and Shi'a, followers of the two main branches of Islam, share a number of core beliefs and practices, including the belief in the Qur'an and a reverence for the Prophet and his family (*ahl al-bayt*, 'People of the [Prophet's] House'). However, the Shi'a model of authority assigns temporal and spiritual leadership exclusively to imams ('leaders') descended from the Prophet, through the progeny of the imam-caliph Ali and his wife Fatima, the Prophet's daughter (**1**). The term Shi'a derives from 'Shi'at Ali' or 'partisans/ supporters of Ali', and the Shi'a maintain that although the Prophet publicly designated Ali as his successor, he was sidelined until his appointment as caliph in 656. In contrast, the Sunni model relies on community consensus to select a leader, regardless of the individual's blood ties to the Prophet (although the post-*Rashidun* Sunni caliphates – the Umayyads, Abbasids and Ottomans – departed from this model, becoming dynastic in nature).

Muslims of all persuasions have traditionally accepted that one of the greatest calamities of early Islamic history was the brutal death of Ali's son Husayn and his family at the battle of Karbala, Iraq, by the armies of the Umayyad caliph Yazid in 680 (**3**). The martyrdom of Husayn and his family during the first ten days of the month of Muharram is commemorated through street processions, communal gatherings and theatrical performances (**2**).

Over time, succession disputes among the Shi'a led to the formation of distinct branches, including the Zaydis, Ithna Asharis ('Twelvers', or followers of the Twelve Imams) and Isma'ilis. A third branch of Islam, the Ibadis, developed in the 7th century, today based mainly in Oman, Zanzibar, Libya and Algeria; their religious beliefs and practices resemble those of the Sunnis. (FS)

1. Popular devotional poster of three Shi'a heroes
The captioned portraits from right to left are Ali ('There is no hero but Ali and no sword but *Dhu'l faqar*'); Hazrat Abbas ('Abu'l-Fazl, the standard-bearer of Karbala' and half brother of Husayn); and Husayn ('Husayn ibn Ali, the master of martyrs, peace be upon him'). The near identical, imagined portraits of these quintessential Shi'a heroes originated from a prototypical image of Ali that was made into an Imperial Order by Nasir al-Din Shah Qajar in 1856, and later widely circulated across Iran. Devotional images such as this poster continue to be reproduced in the modern era.

c. 2005
Tehran, Iran
Colour print on paper
Height 25.2 cm, width 35 cm
Funded by Shelia Canby,
2005,0511,0.7

2. Processional standard in the shape of a hand

Muharram standards (*alam*) in the shape of hands are symbols of Abu'l-Fazl Abbas, the half-brother of Husayn and standard-bearer at the battle of Karbala, whose hands were severed by Yazid's army while fetching water from the Euphrates for the Imam's family. This *alam* is engraved with the names of the Twelve Imams and an image of a Shi'a shrine (possibly Ali's at Najaf, Iraq, or Imam Reza's at Mashhad, Iran). This is flanked by two representations of the winged horse Buraq, which the Prophet Muhammad is said to have ridden on his miraculous 'night journey' (*mi'raj*) from Mecca to Jerusalem and to the heavens and back. Fish emblems, also engraved on the *alam*, are a symbol of the Shi'a Nawabs of Awadh (1722–1856), based at Lucknow.

1750s–1850s
Awadh, northern India
Brass
Height 41 cm, width 25.5 cm
OA+.7432

3. Prayer mat and prayer-stone

A circular prayer-stone (*muhr* or *turba*) made of compressed earth from Karbala, the sacred site in Iraq where Husayn and his family members were martyred in 680, sits on an embroidered sunburst motif at the top of this silk prayer mat (*sajjada*). Some Shi'a Muslims prostrate their foreheads upon a *muhr* during ritual prayers as a mark of respect and allegiance.

1790–1850 (mat); 1900–17 (stone)
Iran (mat); Karbala, Iraq (stone)
Silk, wool, cotton and silver-wrapped thread (mat)
Height 49 cm, width 34.5 cm (mat); height 0.8 cm, diameter 3 cm (stone)
2014,6013.8 (mat); Donated by R. Fleming Crooks, 1917,0414.11 (stone)

2 | 3 People of the Book

The Arabic term *ahl al-kitab* ('People of the Book' or 'Possessors of Scripture') is a Qur'anic phrase that refers primarily to Jews and Christians but sometimes also extends to Zoroastrians and other religious groups that received divine revelations which were recorded as scripture. The Psalms (*al-zabur*), the Torah (*al-tawrat*) and the Gospel (*al-injil*) form part of this recognized corpus of sacred texts recording the revealed Divine Word. The Qur'an is seen to build upon, complete and reaffirm these earlier revelations, rather than replace them.

The revered prophets in Judaism and Christianity are also recognized as God's messengers in Islam. They include among others, Noah (Nuh), Abraham (Ibrahim) (**1**), Job (Ayyub), Joseph (Yusuf), Moses (Musa), Solomon (Sulayman) (**2**) and Jesus (Isa) (**3**), all of whom played a part, at different times in history, in transmitting God's message to humanity. While there are vigorous doctrinal debates among the three faiths, they all share certain aspects of belief and practice, including the concept of one, all-powerful creator and the ritual practices of prayer, fasting, charity and pilgrimage. Judaism, Christianity and Islam are collectively referred to as Abrahamic faiths, because of their shared acknowledgment of Abraham as the spiritual progenitor of monotheism.

The *ahl al-kitab* were accorded special legal status and protection as religious minorities under Islamic rule in return for recognition of Islam as the predominant religion and compliance with Muslim political authority, with all the fiscal and legal implications that this entailed. Within such a framework, Christians and Jews were able to practise their faiths and pursue their crafts and trades freely, often rising to prominent positions in all aspects of political, social, economic and artistic life. (ZKH/FS)

1. Flask depicting Abraham's sacrifice

Abraham's unwavering faith in God and his willingness to sacrifice his own son in obedience to God's command is held in great reverence by the three monotheistic religions. While Jews and Christians believe that Abraham's sacrifice was of Isaac, son of Sarah, Muslims believe it was of his other son, Isma'il, born to Hagar. This flask depicts the pivotal moment when the Angel Gabriel intercedes to stop Abraham from performing the ultimate sacrifice, and presents him with a ram instead (detail). Made in Safavid Iran for an Armenian bishop, the flask is believed to have held consecrated holy oil (*mayrun*).

1700–1800
Iran
Pewter
Height 24.1 cm, width 12.8 cm, depth 6 cm
1956,0329.1

2. Solomon enthroned and surrounded by his court

In this painting produced in India, Solomon (Sulayman) is portrayed as a bejewelled and turbaned Indian ruler surrounded by members of his court, including his vizier Asaf, and by birds, animals, angels, fantastic beasts, *jinn* (spirits) and *div*s (demons). Solomon's wisdom, discerning counsel and justice were legendary and, according to tradition, he was granted vast esoteric knowledge by God, as well as the ability to understand the speech of birds and animals and to command natural phenomena, spirits and demons.

1750–1800
Deccan, India
Gold, opaque watercolour and ink on paper
Height 44 cm, width 25 cm (page)
1974,0617,0.17.2

3. Dish depicting Mary and the Christ Child

This Ottoman Iznik dish depicts Mary (Maryam in Arabic) holding the Christ Child tenderly on her lap. While Jesus (Isa) is recognized in Islam as a prophet and a 'mercy from God' (Qur'an 19:21), Mary is the most prominent female figure in the Qur'an and the only one identified by name (*sura* 19 is named after her). The annunciation and virgin birth are acknowledged in Islam and Mary is celebrated as an example of chastity, obedience and faith.

c. 1650
Iznik, Turkey
Stonepaste, painted in blue, green, red and black under a transparent glaze
Diameter 25.9 cm, height 5.5 cm
Donated by Sir Augustus Wollaston Franks, 1890,0716.12

2 | 4 Jerusalem: shared sacred space

Few places in the world evoke such emotion as Jerusalem, the city regarded as holy by the three Abrahamic faiths: Judaism, Christianity and Islam. For all, Jerusalem stands at the gates of Heaven and is home to several sacred sites.

For Jews, Jerusalem has always been central in traditional thought as the home of the dynasty founded by David, and the site of the First and Second Temple (1), to which prayer and meditation should be directed. For Christians, it is the site of Christ's passion, crucifixion, burial and resurrection (2). For Muslims, it defined the first *qibla* (direction of prayer) before the Prophet changed that to Mecca. It is also the site of the *mi'raj*, the Prophet's miraculous 'night journey' from Mecca to the 'farthest' mosque (al-Aqsa) (Qur'an 17:1), where he led prayers. Then, mounted on his winged steed Buraq, the Prophet rose to Heaven. This spot is marked by the Dome of the Rock (3), completed in 691 at the order of the Umayyad caliph Abd al-Malik (r. 685–705). These sacred associations have for centuries seen pilgrims of all three faiths flocking to Jerusalem, seeking to reaffirm their faith.

Over the centuries, the city has at times been privy to relatively harmonious coexistence and tolerance, cultural diversity and lucrative trade borne of pilgrimage, while at others it has been witness to tension and strife. Its unique place in history has led to repeated conflict as the struggle for control of its holy sites was attempted. Yet this complex city has always inspired profound emotion and spirituality as well as art of remarkable and inherent beauty. (ZKH)

1. *Challah* cover with a view of Jerusalem
Cloths such as this were used to cover special loaves of bread, *challah*, prepared for the Sabbath and other Jewish holidays. In the centre of this particular piece, the Western Wall, the Kotel, is represented surrounded by other Jewish holy sites in Jerusalem. Due to its association with the Temple Mount, the Western Wall is the holiest place for prayer and where Jews publicly mourn the destruction of the Temple. The Hebrew text on both sides of the central image includes traditional blessings (*kiddush*) for the Sabbath and other festivals, while the text below is a key to identify the buildings depicted. The smaller depictions around the central image illustrate named revered sites in the Holy Land and in Jerusalem including the cave of Machpelah (the cave of the Patriarchs) in Hebron, the tomb of Rachel in Bethlehem, the tombs of the kings of the house of David, the tomb of Prophet Zechariah and the tomb of Prophet Samuel as well as the cities of Jericho and Shechem (Nablus).

19th century
Possibly Jerusalem
Printed silk
Length 46.5 cm, width 44.5 cm
Donated by Hyman Montagu,
1893,0519.8

2. Inlaid model of the Church of the Holy Sepulchre

This richly decorated model, inlaid with ivory and mother-of-pearl, and comprising articulated parts, was produced for pilgrims visiting the Holy Land. The Church of the Holy Sepulchre, built on the site of Christ's burial and resurrection, is shared by Christians of various denominations, each community having a separate chapel within the building. Models such as these were usually made of olive wood due to this material's association with the cross of the crucifixion.

19th century
Palestine
Olive wood, ivory and mother-of-pearl
Length 47 cm, width 41 cm, height 26.5 cm
Donated by the Trustees of the Wellcome Institute for the History of Medicine, 1983,0107.1

3. Mosque lamp

The Dome of the Rock, originally completed in 691, was repaired, refurbished and re-endowed under the Ottoman sultan Süleyman the Magnificent (r. 1520–66). This lamp, associated with the Dome of the Rock, is inscribed with a *hadith* (saying) of the Prophet Muhammad in which the believer in the mosque is compared to a fish in water and a non-believer in the mosque to a bird in a cage. The lamp is signed on the base by the potter Musli and dedicated to Eşrefzade, a renowned Sufi mystic of Iznik, revered as a local saint.

Dated AD 1549 (AH 956)
Iznik, Turkey
Stonepaste, painted in blue, green and black under a transparent glaze
Height 38 cm; diameter 22.9 cm
Donated by Charles Drury Edward Fortnum, 1887,0516.1

2 | 5 Mecca, Medina and the *hajj*

Proclaim the pilgrimage to mankind. They will come to you on foot and on every kind of swift mount, emerging from every deep recess. (Qur'an 22:27)

Mecca, where the Prophet Muhammad was born in about AD 570, was a focus of pilgrimage long before the coming of Islam. It is the site of a sacred cube-shaped structure known as the Ka'ba (**2**), which the Qur'an states was originally built by the Prophet Ibrahim (Abraham) and his son Isma'il (Ishmael).

Believers can go to Mecca at any time in a pilgrimage known as *umra*. *Hajj* is different: one of the Five Pillars of Islam, it takes place at a set time of year, beginning on the eighth day of Dhu'l-Hijja, the last month of the Muslim calendar, and over a five-day period. If they are able, Muslims must go at least once in their lives (**1**). In both *umra* and *hajj,* pilgrims dress in plain white garments, known as *ihram*, and follow a series of specific rituals, which include drinking from the sacred Well of Zamzam (**3**). For *umra* these take place in Mecca, but during *hajj* they take place outside the city (pilgrims visit, for example, the sacred mount of Arafat where the Prophet Muhammad gave his last sermon just before his death in 632). The *hajj,* which brings Muslims to the heart of Islam, is both an intense personal experience and a public affirmation of belief, and pilgrims, or *hajjis*, have been making this spiritual journey since the 7th century. They come from the furthest reaches of the world where Muslims reside, from Africa to China, a journey that, before the days of modern travel, could be long and dangerous. Although Medina, sacred to Muslims as the burial place of the Prophet Muhammad, is not part of the rituals, pilgrims will generally visit the city before or after their *hajj* (**4**). (VP)

**1. Ayman Yossri
(Saudi Arabian, b. 1966),
*We were people***
Contemporary Saudi Arabian artist Ayman Yossri here captures a scene from a 1992 film (with Arabic subtitles) about the Afro-American Muslim activist Malcolm X, who went on *hajj* in 1964, the year before he was assassinated. He was particularly struck by the spirit of unity that bound all races and peoples while on *hajj*. Rendered into a still photograph, Yossri has manipulated the image by applying light and shade. The words read: 'We were people of different colours and races who believe in one god and one humanity.'

2011
Photograph, black and white lambada print on resin-coated paper (Edition 1/3)
Height 87 cm, width 155 cm
Funded by CaMMEA,
2013,6006.2

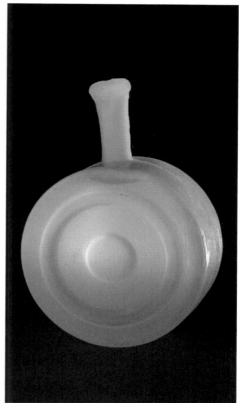

2. Mecca tile

This tile depicts the sanctuary at Mecca known as the *Masjid al-Haram*, or sacred mosque. At the centre is the Ka'ba, on the left side of which is the black stone that pilgrims try to touch as they circumambulate the Ka'ba. Around it are structures that mark the four schools of Islamic law: Maliki, Shafi'i, Hanafi and Hanbali. Possibly made to commemorate a pilgrimage to Mecca, this tile bears the name of its owner, Şihabettin (Shihab al-Din) Efendi.

Mid-17th century
Iznik or Kütahya, Turkey
Stonepaste, painted under a transparent glaze
Height 23.3 cm, width 17 cm
2009,6039.1

3. Zamzam water flask

Drinking from the Well of Zamzam forms part of the rituals of *hajj* and containers of Zamzam water are a popular souvenir. This small flask, still containing water, was acquired in Mali in 2010.

Late 20th–early 21st century
Plastic
Diameter 7 cm
Modern Museum Fund,
2011,6044.1

4. Adel al-Quraishi (Saudi Arabian, b. 1968), Portrait of Ahmed Ali Yassin

In a series called 'the Guardians' (in Arabic *aqawat*), al-Quraishi photographed the last seven eunuchs who kept the keys of the burial chamber of the Prophet within the sanctuary of the *Masjid al-Nabawi* at Medina. In a tradition going back to the Ottoman era, the Guardians came from East Africa. The photographs are a unique record of the end of this tradition.

2013
Height 117.2 cm, width 97.5 cm
Donated by H.R.H. Prince Faisal bin Salman Al Saud, 2014,6048.3

2 | 6 Sufism

There is no clearly defined way to practise Sufism, which is generally described as Islamic mysticism. Its foundations lie in orthodox Islam, the belief in one God and in Muhammad as His messenger. Ultimately, Sufis (often also referred to as dervishes) seek enlightenment in attaining oneness with God, a mystical union known as *tawhid*. The *tariqa*, or path, to enlightenment is led by the Sufi's inner light, which grows brighter as the believer distances him- or herself from the material aspects of the world (**1, 2**). With the help of prayer and *dhikr* – where God's names and other sacred phrases are remembered and meditated upon through constant repetition – the Sufi believer hopes ultimately to achieve *tawhid* and become surrounded by God's light.

While some believe Sufism originated with the Prophet Muhammad, others suggest it began in 8th-century Syria and Iraq and spread eastwards to northeastern Iran and Afghanistan. From the beginning, Sufism acknowledged, drew from and adapted the traditions of other faiths and cultures into its own evolution. Its initially ascetic and reclusive nature developed into a more social and communal one in the 9th and 10th centuries, when Sufism became institutionalized with the formation of different orders led by masters known as *pirs* or *shaykhs* and it appeared in contemporary mystical literature (**3**). Although it reached its height in the 12th and 13th centuries in the Arab, Iranian and Indian lands, the practice of Sufism has continued to the present day and may be found in cultures all over the world (**4**). (LA/FS)

1. Dervish with horn and begging bowl

Sufis appeared in Persian manuscripts and single-page compositions from the late 15th century, suggesting they did not always wander in seclusion. In this painting, the dervish is identified by characteristic Sufi attributes, such as a coarse woollen robe and sheepskin cover (the word Sufi is thought to derive from *suf*, the Arabic word for 'wool'), his domed cap (identifying his brotherhood), an alms bowl held in one hand, and the ibex horn he blows with the other.

Early 17th century
Isfahan or Qazvin, Iran
Single-page painting mounted on a detached album folio; ink, opaque watercolour and gold on paper
Height 23.5 cm, width 15.2 cm (page); height 11 cm, width 6.4 cm (image)
1930,0607,0.15

2. Begging bowl

Begging bowls (*kashkul*) represent a Sufi's renouncement of worldly goods and aspirations. Symbolically, they also signify the emptiness of his soul or ego (*nafs*), abandoned along his mystical path. The shells from the coco de mer palm from which this bowl (depicting a Sufi holding a similar bowl) and others were made are native to islands of the Indian Ocean, and may have been washed up on Iranian shores. Their lengthy sea voyage became a metaphor for the Sufi's mystical journey. This bowl is also inscribed with the names of the Prophet Muhammad, his daughter Fatima and the Twelve Imams, and is signed by the artist, Darvish Ghulam Husayn.

Dated 1878 (AH 1295)
Iran
Coco de mer and metal
Length 35 cm
OA+.2610

3. Dervish's felt hat

The Sufi reverence for Imam Ali as a spiritual master and guide is attested from the devotional epithets embroidered in Arabic on the horizontal band around this dervish's hat:

*O Ali the favourite [of God]!
O vanquisher of enemies! O
guardian of the friends [of God]!
O manifestation of marvels!*

The poetic verses embroidered in Persian within four arched cartouches describe the qualities of a true dervish:

*He is called a dervish (*qalandar*)
Who receives a royal crown and
    presents it to others
Not he who placed a flowery
    crown on his head
and became a dervish*

1890s–1940s
Mashhad area, Iran
Wool and silk
Height 23 cm, diameter 19 cm
2017,6002.1

4. Calligraphy by Hassan Massoudy (Iraqi, b. 1944)

'I follow the religion of Love: whatever way Love's camels take, that is my religion and my faith.' So wrote the Andalusian Sufi mystic Ibn Arabi (1165–1240) in the *Tarjuman al-Ashwaq* ('The Interpreter of Desires'), a collection of mystical odes on divine love written in the guise of passionate poems to a young girl. Here the words appear in an angular Arabic script in red, with the exception of *hubb* ('love'), which dominates the composition in a deep blue.

2003
Iraq/France
Coloured pigments on paper
Height 75 cm, width 55 cm
Brooke Sewell Permanent Fund,
2005,0715,0.2

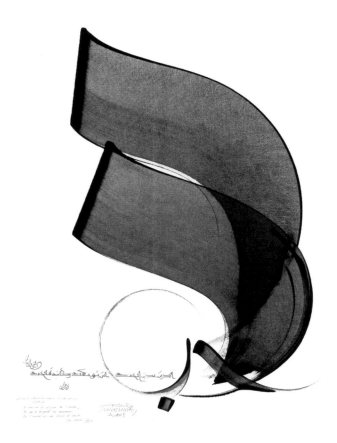

2 | 7 Healing and protection

To prevent misfortune and guard against the evil eye, Muslims call upon God, invoke the names of revered figures, utter protective verses from the Qur'an or, for example, place a blue bead on a child's clothing. A range of objects were made for the purposes of protection, and these generally have sacred texts inscribed upon them. For safety in battle, a protective talismanic shirt could be worn (**1**), to cure sickness a person might drink from a magic bowl (**5**), drink water used to wipe clean a writing board with Qur'anic verses, or have an amulet made (**2–5**). The texts inscribed on many of these objects vary from particular verses from the Qur'an, such as *ayat al-kursi*, the 'throne verse' (Qur'an 2:255), to more esoteric signs, symbols and magic squares. (FS/VP)

1. Talismanic tunic

The tradition of talismanic tunics worn to protect a warrior in battle dates back to at least the 15th century in South Asia, Iran and the Ottoman Empire. Skilled calligraphers covered entire garments with prayers, Qur'anic inscriptions, the 99 Beautiful Names of God, magic squares and amuletic motifs. This West African tunic (*rigan yaki* in Hausa) also has numerous leather pouches housing paper amulets sewn on the inside for added effectiveness. Such tunics were also worn for protection against disease, during childbirth, when travelling or to obtain political favour.

1900–1930s
Northern Nigeria (?)
Cotton, ink and leather
Height 91 cm, width 88 cm
Donated by Captain Alfred Walter
Francis Fuller, Af1940,23.1

2. Gold amulet

With a hole at the top so that it could be sewn onto clothing, this amulet is engraved on both sides with the names of the Seven Sleepers of Ephesus. These seven legendary youths were fleeing religious persecution under the Roman emperor Decius (r. 201–51) when, with their dog, they happened to fall asleep in a cave; they slept for several hundred years, only waking when Christians were no longer being persecuted. Their story is told in the Qur'an (18:9–25) and they are figures of reverence, their names often appearing on amulets. Around the sides of the amulet are the words:

He has provided safety to the one who came [the Prophet Muhammad] and has been kind in what he sent down [the Qur'an].

18th–19th century
Ottoman Turkey
Gold
Height 7.1 cm, width 6.4 cm
Bequeathed by Edward Gilbertson, 1994,0915.888

3. Brass amulet

Inscribed on both sides in reverse, the power of this amulet is activated when it has been stamped onto something, probably paper. It was made for the purposes of healing, and six passages from the Qur'an containing the word for healing (*shafaya*) are inscribed on it, along with a 3 x 3 magic square in the centre known as *buduh*, believed to aid with the pains of childbirth. In addition, there are verses written in individual rather than joined up letters; text written in this way is regarded as particularly efficacious.

19th century
Probably India
Brass
Diameter 7 cm
Donated by Rev. Thomas Calvert, 1893,0215.1

4. 'Hand of Fatima' pendant

The belief in the protective power of the hand dates back millennia. In the Middle East and North Africa they are referred to as *khamsa*s ('five') and used by Jews, Christians and Muslims to ward off the 'evil eye' or the 'eye of envy'. Among Muslim women, the *khamsa* came to be associated with Fatima, the Prophet's daughter.

c. 1890s
Morocco
Silver, glass and enamel
Height 13 cm, width 8 cm
2014,6009.1

5. Magic bowl

A 14th-century treatise asserts that 'protection against delusions and melancholia could be gained by drinking…from a bowl on which Qur'anic verses and a particular magic square had been written.' Based on metal bowls commonly used since the 12th century, this Chinese example was either made for export to Iran or for local use. In addition to *ayat al-kursi*, the 'throne verse', is the phrase 'there is no hero except for Ali, and no sword except for *Dhu'l faqar*'. Inside the bowl is a 4 x 4 magic square.

18th–19th century
China
Porcelain
Diameter 20.5 cm
Donated by Sir Augustus Wollaston Franks, Franks.619.a

2 | 8 Divination

Geomancy is a popular divinatory science practised across the Islamic world, from West Africa to Southeast Asia. In Arabic it is known as *ilm al-raml*, literally the science of the sand. This was an ancient practice of obscure origins whereby a tableau was created by the placing of grains of sand in clusters of dots with up to 16 combinations. The initial four clusters, cast randomly and known as mothers (*umahat*), determine the position of a further 12 clusters. The ensuing set of patterns enable the interpretation of specific questions, often concerning daily life, that are put to the geomancer by the client: the health of a child, the infidelity of a spouse, or the success of a business dealing, for example.

The principles of *ilm al-raml* were transferred onto a unique 13th-century geomantic instrument (**1**). The front consists of a series of dials and arcs, and to use the device, the first step was to move each of the four slides on the right to an open position, thus randomly revealing clusters of silver dots. The purpose of the slides is explained in the inscription above the arcs: 'We have placed these arcs in order to generate the figures (or clusters of dots), and so those that appear next to the separating line at the point of visibility are to be considered, and from them you generate the mothers.' The next step would be to turn the sixteen dials so that they each contain the correct clusters of dots. These dials are placed to the left of the arcs, in two groups of four at the top, two groups of three below, and one on either side of the base of the large dial. They are known as 'houses' (*buyut*) and the attributes of each are named above the dials in *kufic* script, for example House I, 'the house of the soul and life', House II, 'the house of property and wages', and so on. To interpret the tableau – that is the arrangement of all the clusters of dots – the geomancer would have used the large central dial and the three smaller ones to the right. The large one, as explained in the inscription above it, gives a prognosis, good or bad, associating it with a particular season, a lunar mansion or compass direction. 'We have established this circle so that you might learn from it the correspondences of the forms of the figures with the lunar mansions, rising and setting. Thereupon the power to interpret might belong to it (the circle), but God knows best.'

Geomancers in the Muslim world believed that they were practising a sacred art linked to the Prophet Idris (the Biblical Enoch) through the intermediary of the Archangel Gabriel. Manuals existed to aid the geomancers in their interpretations, but there are none to accompany this particular instrument. Elaborately constructed, it is signed on the front below the arcs by Muhammad ibn Kutlukh al-Mawsili, who came from a family of prolific metalworkers originating in Mosul, Iraq (see p. 120). It was probably made in Damascus, as suggested by an incense burner known to have been made there and also signed by this craftsman. Another later inscription on the back relates to a subsequent owner, Muhammad al-Muhtasib al-Najjari (or al-Bukhari). (VP)

1. Geomantic instrument
I am the possessor of eloquence and the silent speaker and through my speech [arise] desires and fears. The judicious one hides his secret thoughts, but I disclose them, just as if hearts were created as my parts.

Inscribed on its front left corner, these verses highlight the mystery of this remarkable object. The instrument is made up of four elements: a front plate (top) with a series of dials and arcs, with texts explaining the purpose of the instrument, with further poetry on a frame, a back plate (below) with bands of benedictory inscriptions, and an openwork projection with a hook for suspension.

Dated AD 1241/2 (AH 639)
Syria, probably Damascus
Brass alloy inlaid with silver and gold
Height 26.8 cm, width 33.6 cm
1888,0526.1

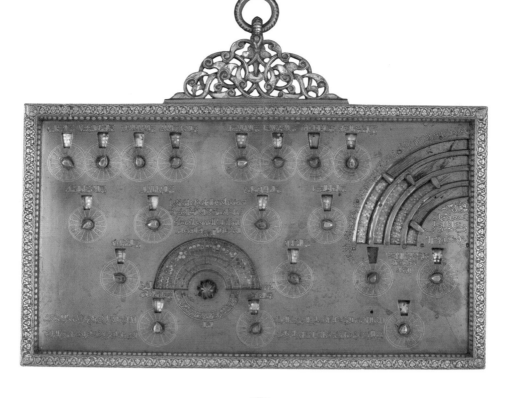

Timeline

632–61	Rightly Guided caliphs
634	Battle of Ajnadayn, Palestine (against the Byzantines)
636	Battle of Qadisiyya, Iraq (against the Sasanians)
661–750	Umayyad caliphs rule from Damascus
711	Muslim armies invade Spain
732	Muslim armies are defeated by Charles Martel at the battle of Poitiers
751	Muslim armies reach Tashkent; Tang Chinese army defeated at the battle of Talas
750–1258	Abbasid caliphs rule from Baghdad
836	Founding of Samarra in Iraq
756–1031	Spanish Umayyads rule from Cordoba
819–1005	Samanid rule in Khurasan and Transoxiana
861–1003	Saffarid dynasty
909–1171	Fatimids rule from North Africa and Egypt
945–1055	Buyid dynasty rule in western Iran and Iraq
969	Founding of Cairo in Egypt
977–1186	Ghaznavids in Khurasan, Afghanistan and northern India
992–1212	Qarakhanid dynasty
1095–99	First Crusade and the capture of Jerusalem
c. 1040–1194	Great Saljuqs rule in Iran and Iraq
1081–1308	Saljuqs of Rum ruling Anatolia
1127–1234	Saljuq Atabegs rule over Mosul and Aleppo
1144	Imad al-Din Zangi retakes Edessa from the Crusaders
c. 1148–1206	Ghurid dynasty
1171–1250	Ayyubid rule in Syria and Egypt
1187	Salah al-Din (Saladin) defeats the Crusaders at the battle of Hattin and retakes Jerusalem
1227	Death of Chinggis Khan
1232–1492	Nasrid rule in Granada
1233–59	Badr al-Din Lu'lu rule in Mosul
1258–1353	Ilkhanid rule in Iran and Iraq
1250–1517	Mamluk rule in Syria and Egypt
1260	Mamluks defeat the Mongols at the battle of Ayn Jalut
1281–1924	Ottomans in Anatolia, Balkans and Arab lands
1370–1506	Timurid rule in Transoxiana and Iran
1400	Sack of Damascus by Timur
1453	Mehmed II conquers Constantinople

3 Interconnected worlds
750–1500

Following the Muslim conquest of Arabia in the 7th century, the territories of Islam expanded rapidly into the former lands of the Sasanian and Byzantine empires and new dynastic polities vied for power. The first Islamic dynasty, the Umayyads (661–750), ruled from its capital at Damascus, followed by the Abbasids, who governed from Baghdad (750–1258) and for a short period from the palace-city of Samarra (836–892). Under the Umayyad caliph Abd al-Malik (r. 685–705), the Dome of the Rock in Jerusalem was completed in 691.

The Abbasid rise to power marked a regional and cultural shift eastwards, with Baghdad situated at the heart of a caliphate that would endure until the Mongol invasion in 1258. The vast archaeological remains at the city of Samarra, comprising mosques, palaces and bathhouses decorated with painted and carved stucco, stand testament to the grandeur of their ambition. Global commerce also played a significant role in this period, forming the foundation of the empire's wealth within an era of international trade, travel and exploration. Contact with Tang China (618–907) brought coveted Chinese porcelain wares to the Middle East; Chinese craftsmen were even said to have reached Baghdad in the 8th century. Siraf, a southern Iranian city on the Persian Gulf coast, served as one of the major ports, its rich finds demonstrating the vast networks that existed at this period.

1. The Offa *dinar*

This coin shows the influence of the Islamic world in Britain as early as the 8th century AD. There are no other examples of coins of this type and its significance lies in the fact that the words 'OFFA REX' have been stamped between part of the Profession of Faith (*shahada*): *Muhammad rasul Allah* ('Muhammad is the messenger of God'). The coin, dated AH 157 (AD 773/4), is a garbled imitation of one struck by the Abbasid caliph al-Mansur (r. 754–75). The fact that the *shahada* is upside down suggests that the maker of the die was not aware of the significance of the Arabic text. The circumstances of its manufacture are unclear; gold was rare in Britain at this time and the coin may have been a presentation piece or used in commerce. Offa was king of Mercia (r. 757–96) and a contemporary of the well-known rulers Harun al-Rashid (r. 786–809) and Charlemagne (r. 742–814), who are known to have exchanged diplomatic gifts.

AD 773–96
Mercia, Britain
Diameter 2 cm, weight 4.276 g
1913,1213.1

For more than a century, the Abbasids solely controlled an immense region that stretched from North Africa to Central Asia; by the 900s, however, this vast empire had begun to break up. To the west, in Spain, an extension of the Umayyad dynasty had established a new kingdom (756–1031), initiating a chapter of Muslim rule that would continue through to the fall of the Nasrid dynasty (1232–1492) in Granada. Other independent dynasties included the Tulunids (868–905) and Fatimids (909–1171), the latter having founded the city of Cairo in 969. In Iran and Central Asia, the 800s saw the rise of the Samanid dynasty (819–1005), who turned Bukhara into a cultural hub that prompted a resurgence of Persian language and literature, including the production of the Iranian national epic, the *Shahnama* ('Book of Kings'), in the year 1000. Succeeding dynasties included the powerful Iranian Buyids (934–1055) and rulers of Turkic descent, such the Ghaznavids (977–1186), based in Ghazni, Afghanistan, and the Saljuqs (1040–1194), who ruled over Iran, Iraq and much of Syria. During this time of great artistic patronage, monumental *madrasas* (religious colleges) sprang up in the main centres. A great ceramics industry was also established in Iran, particularly in Kashan, although fine ceramic tiles and other wares were to be found across Iran and Central Asia.

This period also marked the revival of Sunni Islam in the face of the existential threat of the Christian Crusaders who had conquered Jerusalem in 1099 and established a series of kingdoms across Syria and Palestine, remaining there until they were finally ejected in 1291. The complex politics of this period belie the artistic interactions between Christian and Muslim patrons and artisans, which are evidenced in the iconography and techniques of the material culture.

Despite their independence, many of these ruling entities continued to pledge their spiritual allegiance to the caliphs in Baghdad as vicegerents of God on earth. All this changed, however, in the 1200s, when Chinggis (or Genghis) Khan (r. 1206–27), the great leader of the Mongols, set out from northeast Asia on a series of campaigns across Central Asia, eventually crossing the Oxus River into Iran. After his death, his grandson Hülagü, the first Mongol ruler of the Ilkhanid dynasty of Iran (r. 1256–65), pushed these campaigns further west into Baghdad, sacking the Abbasid capital and ending the caliphate in 1258. Despite its violence and destruction, this encounter opened up the Middle East to the arts of China, introducing a new vocabulary that was to pervade the arts across the entire region. The Mongol advance was finally halted in 1260 by the Mamluk sultan Qutuz (r. 1259–60) at the battle of Ayn Jalut in Palestine. Contemporaries of the Ilkhanids, the Mamluks of Egypt and Syria were slave-soldiers who in 1250 had taken over from the Ayyubids, the dynasty founded by Salah al-Din (Saladin). Under their rule, Damascus and Cairo witnessed an upsurge of building activity and a flowering of the arts, including enamelled glass and metalwork. Eventual disarray in the Mamluk domain became the backdrop for the invasion of Syria and the sack of Damascus in 1400 by the fearless Turkic leader Timur (or Tamerlane; r. 1336–1405), who, following in the footsteps of Chinggis Khan, conquered Iran and Central Asia in the 1370s. The architectural remnants of the magnificent blue-tiled Timurid buildings in Samarqand and elsewhere attest to the legacy of Timur's megalomaniacal vision.

Throughout the period covered in this chapter, global trade not only underpinned the economies of the region but, along with pilgrimage, diplomacy and the movement (both voluntary and imposed) of artisans, became the mechanism through which ideas, techniques and artistic styles

2. Oliphant
According to the *Chanson de Roland*, an epic poem written in the age of Charlemagne (742–814), the hero Roland blew on an oliphant appealing for help before his death in the battle of Roncevaux against the Arab forces in 778. According to the epic poem, his oliphant entered the church treasury of St Seurin in Bordeaux and hung over the church altar. Combining Mediterranean with Islamic designs, ivory horns such as this one, made from a complete elephant's tusk, are generally associated with the Fatimid era or Norman Sicily. Many have been found in Europe, preserved in church treasuries and kept as relics, in memory of the martyrdom of Roland and embodying the myth of his tragic demise. Hooks on the metal bands would have held the carrying straps.

11th–12th century
Egypt or Sicily
Ivory and silver
Length 46.5 cm, diameter 8 cm (mouth)
OA+.1302

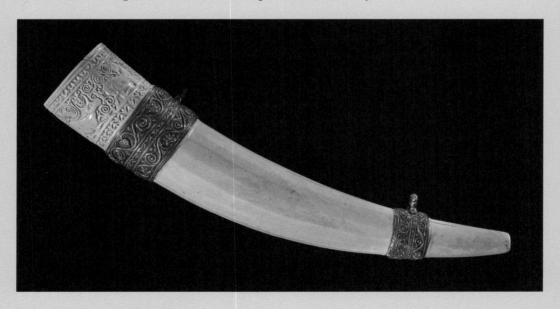

3. Star and cross tiles

These tiles, some of which are dated AD 1266–67 (AH 664–65), are believed to belong to a group from the interior of the Imamzada Ja'far, a Shi'a shrine in Damghan, Iran. *Shahnama* verses in Persian *naskh* script suggest they may have originally been intended for a royal residence.

Iran, probably Kashan
Stonepaste, moulded and painted in blue, turquoise and lustre over an opaque white glaze
Stars: height and width 20.7 cm (max), thickness 1.2 cm (max)
Bequeathed by Miss Edith Godman, G.230, 231, 232.1–2

travelled and evolved. An exchange of commodities took place across land and sea routes in three major arenas: the Indian Ocean, where the chief commodities traded were Chinese porcelain and spices; Africa, for slaves, gold and raw materials such as ivory and rock crystal; and to the east (in about the 900s), the Viking trade, which brought silver struck in Iran and Central Asia to northern Europe. Cities such as Baghdad, Cairo, Damascus, Tabriz, Nishapur, Isfahan, Samarqand and Herat became major centres of learning and artistic patronage. Bringing together artisans and patrons from across the world, the objects, monuments and visual culture produced and disseminated from these centres reflect the extraordinary diversity of the peoples inhabiting these lands. (LA/VP)

3 | 1 Samarra: a palatial city

Al-Mu'tasim brought from every town those who did all sorts of work or had one of the skills of development, cultivation, date palms, plants, water engineering, water measurement….He brought from Egypt people who make papyrus…from Basra people who make glass, pottery and mats…from al-Kufa people who make pottery…and paints….Al-Mu'tasim built…palaces and placed in every orchard a palace in which there were majlises, *basins and* maydans. (Ya'qubi in *Kitab al-Buldan*)

Samarra, from the Arabic *Surra man ra'a* ('Happy is he who sees it'), situated on the banks of the Tigris, north of Baghdad, was built on lands previously inhabited by the Sasanians and was the vision of the Abbasid caliph al-Mu'tasim (r. 836–42). The site is some 57 sq. km in size, and although only the caliphal capital between 836 and 892, it became 'a paradigm of majestic power and extravagant taste'. Samarra's buildings included two congregational mosques with tall spiralling minarets inspired by the ancient Babylonian ziggurats (1). The main palace and seat of government was the Dar al-Khilafa, prominently positioned above the floodplain of the River Tigris; there were palatial houses, wide avenues, hunting grounds, military compounds, polo grounds and race courses. The architecture was largely of mud-brick, with interior walls rendered with carved and painted stucco. Although fragmentary, the extent of the physical remains of the buildings has provided an understanding of the aesthetic principles underlying the choices of design: there are abstracted arabesque patterns in the carved stucco and woodwork (3), and painted faces, Turkic in origin, adorned houses and palaces (2), but not mosques. In addition, there are rich finds of pottery, made in Iraq, some probably on the site itself, sherds of imported Chinese porcelain, and stone objects relating to daily life. (RWH/VP)

1. Postcard
Aerial view taken by the Royal Air Force showing the Great Mosque at Samarra, built by the caliph al-Mutawakkil (r. 847–61). Its iconic spiral minaret is known as the Malwiyya. There is a similar, almost contemporary minaret to the north of the site belonging to a smaller mosque known as Abu Dulaf (not visible in this image). In the background is the modern walled town, with the al-Askari shrine where the Shi'a imams Ali al-Nadi (d. 868) and Hasan al-Askari (d. 874) and members of their families are buried. The town walls are built with despoliated bricks and other building materials from the site. As Abu Tammam (d. 845) wrote of Samarra during the reign of al-Mu'tasim (r. 796–842):

The gardens will be forgotten; but what his deeds have forged will ever, despite the passage of the nights, be remembered.

c. 1935–36
Printed by A&K Naman
Height 8.8 cm, width 13.3 cm
EPH-ME.5417

2. Painted stucco

The decoration of private houses in Samarra and the Dar al-Khilafa palace included friezes of polychrome designs featuring animal, human and mythical monsters. This face in semi-profile probably portrays a *ghulam* or servant, part of a paradisiacal scene. The excavators of the site only found one figural frieze *in situ*, in a private house, positioned above a carved stucco dado.

c. 9th century
Iraq (excavated at Samarra)
Height 11 cm, width 10 cm (max)
Acquired from the 1911–13 excavations of German Scholars Ernst Herzfeld and Friedrich Sarre, OA+.10621

3. Carved teak door panel

This teak door leaf has three inset, geometric, slant-carved panels in the so-called 'bevelled style' (which was also used on most other media, such as stucco, marble and glass). Contemporary 9th-century sources relate that the palaces of Samarra were despoliated when the court returned to Baghdad in 892. Precious materials such as teak, imported from southern Asia specially for the grand buildings of the city, would have had a substantial recycling value. This example was found not on the site itself but in nearby Tikrit.

9th century
Iraq
Height 157.5 cm, width 31.1 cm
The Art Fund (as NACF), 1944,0513.1

3 | 2 Siraf: a port city

Siraf was a major port city during the early Islamic period. Previously occupied by the Sasanians, it lay at the centre of a maritime exchange network that reached most parts of the Indian Ocean world during the 8th to 10th centuries. The remains of this once-thriving cosmopolitan centre lie on a barren, isolated stretch of the Persian Gulf coast in southern Iran, and are confined to a narrow strip of land between the Zagros Mountains and the sea. Extensive excavations took place between 1966 and 1973 under the direction of David Whitehouse, on behalf of the British Institute of Persian Studies (**1**). This work produced vast quantities of finds, including over three million pieces of pottery (**4**). The assemblage provides clear evidence of the city's far-reaching connections together with clues to the multi-ethnic constitution of its population, the complex array of manufacturing activities that helped to balance trade imports, and the strong cultural imprint of the central Abbasid state (**2–5**). (SP/LA)

1. Excavation of the Great Mosque foundation platform at Siraf
Coin-dating evidence indicates that the mosque, overlying an earlier fort, was constructed shortly after AD 803/4. The building measured 57 m by 44 m and sat on a foundation platform standing over 2 m high. Outside was an ablution facility and shops that extend on into the adjacent city bazaar.

c. 1970–71
British Museum Siraf Archive

2. Grave cover
This carved and crested grave cover is of a type associated with the Gulf region. Its inscription consists of two bands of elaborate *kufic* script and, unusually, contains a dedication to two individuals: Abu Ali, whose memorial this is and who died in the month of Muharram AH 381 (AD 991), and Abd al-Rahim ibn Muhammad, his father, who may have ordered the grave cover and who pledges his accountability for any sins his son may have committed.

Dated AD 991 (AH 381)
Siraf, Iran
Limestone
Height 53 cm, width 143.5 cm
Donated by Benjamin Traill Ffinch, 1891,0718.1

3. Clay *bulla*

This *bulla* was used to seal and witness an important document, perhaps a legal contract. On the back (left) are crossed lines and pierced holes where strings secured the document. On the front (right) are the stamp impressions of several different individuals. The object was found during the excavation of the Great Mosque.

c. 9th–10th century
Siraf, Iran
Height 3.5 cm, width 3.4 cm, thickness 1.2 cm
2007,6001.10680

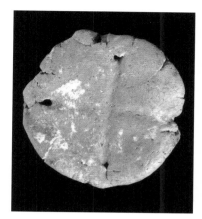

4. Complete Indian cooking pot

Examples of similar vessels to this one have been found as broken fragments from many of the contemporary coastal settlements in the Persian Gulf and East Africa. Such vessels appear to have been part of the everyday household equipment of South Asian emigrants involved in Indian Ocean trade, although they may have also been used by the wider community.

c. 7th–9th century
South Asia
Earthenware, unglazed
Height 21 cm, diameter 17 cm
2007,6001.9858

5. Incense burner

This burner was found in one of the elaborate, multi-storey courtyard houses in the rich merchants quarter at Siraf. The main source of the aromatics that would have been burnt in it was South Arabia. The possession and use of incense such as frankincense or myrrh would have been an important status marker.

c. 9th–10th century
Siraf, Iran
Carved soft-stone (chlorite)
Height 7 cm, length (max) 19.9 cm
2007,6001.10362

3 | 3 Pottery and the China trade

I made up my mind to go to sea and so I went off to buy a variety of trade goods....I boarded a ship and sailed down river from Basra with a number of other merchants. We then put out to sea and sailed for a number of days and nights, passing island after island and going from sea to sea and from one land to another. Whenever we passed land, we bought, sold, bartered and we sailed like this until we reached an island that which looked like the meadows of Paradise.

These are the words of Sinbad the sailor in the *Arabian Nights* as he sets off on his travels. The prize in trading terms was Chinese porcelain, shipped in great ocean-going dhows; the Abbasid caliph Harun al-Rashid (r. 786–809) was said to have quantities of it at his court and it has been found at sites all over the Middle East (**1**). The potters of Iraq could not replicate this early porcelain; the earthenware pottery they made was covered with a creamy white glaze containing tin, onto which copper green or cobalt pigments were applied. The shapes too, from small bowls to storage jars, were inspired by the Chinese imports (**2**). The port city of Basra mentioned by Sinbad is likely to have been one of the manufacturing centres (**3**). The trade, however, was not all one way: quantities of Islamic 'trade goods' have been found at sites in South and Southeast Asia and even in China (**4**).

One of the most significant finds of recent years is a shipwreck that sank in the mid-9th century in the South China Sea off the coast of Belitung island near Sumatra. This Arab dhow full of cargo – some 60,000 objects including quantities of Chinese porcelain have been recovered – was on its way back to the Middle East from China. (VP)

1. Chinese bowl
White porcelain has been found in quantity at sites across the Middle East, either in the form of complete vessels such as this one from Nishapur in Iran, or as sherds from the sites of Samarra and Siraf (see pp. 80–83), testifying to the magnitude of the trade.

Five Dynasties period,
10th century
Found in Nishapur, Iran
Porcelain
Height 6 cm, depth 17.8 cm
1970,1103.3

2. Storage jar

In shape, this jar, now without its lid, echoes a Chinese type exported to the Middle East containing exotic spices such as star anise, as part of the China trade. The potters in Iraq copied the shape and decorated it in green and cobalt blue.

9th–10th century
Iraq
Earthenware, painted in green and blue on an opaque white glaze
Height 24 cm, diameter 28.3 cm
1930,0310.1

3. Condiment dish

The decoration on this object is a survival in Egypt of late Roman moulded relief ware. The Arabic *kufic* inscription states: 'the work of Abu Nasr of Basra in Egypt, praise be [to] God'. Basra was an important urban centre, and it is likely that a range of objects were made there, including fine pottery. Artisans in the medieval period frequently moved across the region in search of new centres of patronage; in Egypt, Abu Nasr is likely to have worked at the Fustat potteries in Old Cairo.

9th century
Egypt
Earthenware, relief moulded and painted under a transparent glaze
Height 2 cm, width 15.5 cm
Donated by Sir Augustus
Wollaston Franks, 1889,0706.75

4. Bird-shaped cup

Lustre pottery was a luxury ware much in demand both in the Middle East and elsewhere and was exported as part of the Indian Ocean trade. Examples have been found from as far as the site of Mantai in Sri Lanka. This cup was found at Brahminabad in Sindh, Pakistan, conquered by the Muslims in the 8th century.

9th century
Iraq
Earthenware, painted in lustre on an opaque white glaze
Height 3.5 cm, length 13.5 cm
Donated by Augustus Fortunatus
Bellasis, 1857,1118.295

3 | 4 The Vikings and Islam

Connections between Europe and the Islamic Middle East occurred with great frequency and from a very early period, occasioned more often by trade than military confrontation. Muslim eyewitnesses of the 9th and 10th centuries write of a lively trade in furs and slaves carried out between the *Rus* (Vikings) and the wealthy cities of the Middle East and Central Asia. Viking traders travelled south down the River Volga and across the Caspian Sea, then overland to Baghdad or Rayy (near modern Tehran). The behaviour of these rough yet impressive northerners was of great interest to the 10th-century Arab chronicler Ibn Fadlan, who wrote that:

I saw the Rus, who had come for trade, and camped by the River Itil. I have never seen bodies more perfect than theirs. They were like palm trees. They are fair and ruddy…the filthiest of God's creatures.

The effects of this meeting of cultures can be seen in the material culture of the period. Objects of Middle Eastern workmanship, such as jewellery with Arabic inscriptions (**1**), were clearly valued as luxury items. However, the most obvious effect was to concentrate silver *dirhams*, particularly from Samanid Central Asia, in northern Europe, where they would mainly have been melted down for reuse. The Viking hoards that have been uncovered from the period (with 50,000 *dirhams* found on the Swedish island of Gotland alone) represent only a tiny proportion of what was accrued (**2**). (WG)

1. The Ballycottin cross brooch

Found in a bog close to the town of Ballycottin near Cork, a major Viking centre of 8th- to 9th-century Ireland, this brooch is of a type popular in northwest Europe during the Carolingian period (*c.* 714–911). What makes it of particular interest is the seal which is set in it, bearing the Arabic inscription *tubna lillah* ('we have repented to God'), which is commonly found on Islamic seals of this period. Although the brooch's maker, and probably also the wearer, may not have been able to read the inscription – the seal would have been sideways when the brooch was worn – it would have been valuable as a piece of exotica from far to the east, and doubly so when combined with a brooch from elsewhere in the Viking cultural sphere. Finger rings with Islamic seals have been found in Russia and Sweden, perhaps brought back as part of the trade with Muslim merchants along the River Volga in modern Russia. The exceptionally close fit of the brooch to the seal suggests that it was made specifically to hold it.

c. 700–900
Middle East or Central Asia (seal), northwest Europe (brooch)
Black glass, gilt copper alloy
Height 4.4 cm, width 4.5 cm
Donated by Philip T. Gardner, 1875,1211.1

2. Samanid coin from the Vale of York Hoard

Tightly packed into a silver cup and buried in around AD 927, the Vale of York Hoard, found near Harrogate in England, contained coins and other items of silver and gold that were probably obtained through a mixture of trade and plunder, giving an idea of the global connections of the Vikings. Among the coins were a group of 13 minted in Central Asia under the Samanid dynasty. Rather than the product of raiding (although this also occurred), these coins probably entered Viking possession via the river systems of what is today Russia, along what Neil MacGregor, former director of the British Museum, has described as a trade route that 'stretched from Scunthorpe to Samarqand'. It has been estimated that up to 100 million *dirham*s (just under 300 tonnes of silver) entered the Viking heartlands from the Islamic world between AD 800 and 1000, with the number of coins dwindling from the 940s onward.

c. 875–925
Central Asia, possibly Samarqand or Shash
Silver
Diameter *c.* 2.8 cm
Acquired through the Treasure Act with contribution from The Art Fund, National Heritage Memorial Fund, British Museum Friends, York Museums Trust, and Wolfson Foundation, 2009,4133.689

1. Tile

This tile may belong to a larger group from the interior or exterior decoration of a Ghurid (*c.* 1148–1206) palace. Italian excavations at Ghazni in Afghanistan revealed a number of similar tiles, small in format, with moulded relief decoration depicting felines, birds and flowers under a monochrome glaze in green, yellow or brown, many of them in fragmentary condition.

Late 12th–early 13th century
Ghazni, Afghanistan
Earthenware, relief moulded under a brown glaze
Height and width 10.6 cm, thickness 1.2 cm
Donated by E. Roesdahl, 2003,1205.1

2. Turquoise-glazed bowl

This glazed, moulded bowl represents a monochrome variety of the numerous types of decoration found on stonepaste-bodied ceramics from 12th- to 13th-century Iran. Its panels contain alternating sphinxes and horsemen holding a wreath, the horsemen being a Sasanian motif found on rock reliefs in western Iran.

c. 1150–1200
Iran
Stonepaste, moulded with turquoise glaze
Height 14 cm, diameter 18 cm
Bequeathed by Oscar Charles Raphael, 1945,1017.265

Iran and Central Asia: Kashan to Samarqand

The story of Islamic visual culture in Iran and Central Asia is one of inheritance, adaptation and, most importantly, continual experimentation and innovation. It is also the story of the formation and development of Persianate culture in the broadest sense, where Persian language and artistic and literary traditions inspired or played a prominent role both in and beyond Iran, including at courts and within societies that were not ethnically Iranian. Key to the continuous growth of this visual culture was its prolific dissemination throughout and beyond the Persianate sphere, and this – as in many parts of the Islamic world – occurred through trade, diplomacy and the constant movement (voluntary or forced) of artists and craftsmen from one cultural centre to another. The mobility of artisans, in particular, cannot be underestimated, as with them moved not only styles but also skills and technologies.

From the 9th through to the mid-13th centuries, the Iranian world was ruled by several autonomous regional authorities operating under the nominal power of the Abbasid caliphate. Baghdad, the Abbasid capital, remained a key centre where ancient Greco-Roman, Byzantine, Persian, Indian and East Asian traditions converged with Arab and Islamic ones, but new centres of cultural patronage also emerged in Iran and Central Asia under indigenous dynasties such as the Saffarids (861–1003) and the Samanids (819–1005). The latter were a Persian dynasty exercising independent control of the eastern provinces of Khurasan and Transoxiana. Under their rule, pre-Islamic Persianate culture underwent a revival driven significantly by the convergence of Persian literature with Islamic socio-political thought and the concept of *adab*, which comprises both Islamic belles-lettres literature and an ethos of personal cultivation and learning in Islamic society,

particularly witnessed in social gatherings involving feasting and entertainment. Within this context, the production of fine ceramics including elegant Samanid epigraphic wares (see pp. 41, 90) flourished in centres such as Nishapur and Samarqand.

Towards the end of the 10th century, Turkic nomadic peoples from the Central Asian steppe infiltrated the Iranian sphere, quickly forming dynasties that wove themselves into Iran's history and added a Turkic dimension to the complexity of the local visual culture. These included the Ghaznavids (977–1186, once slave-guards for the Samanids), the Ghurids (*c.* 1148–1206) (**1**), the Qarakhanids (992–1212), the Great Saljuqs (1040–1194), and their successors. Under the Ghaznavids, whose empire extended into parts of North India, important advances were made in the metalwork industry, such as the development of inlay; this flourished in the city of Herat, which would continue to play a leading role in cultural innovation for a few centuries to come (see pp. 94–97). The Ghaznavids were eventually defeated by the Saljuqs, who at one point ruled from eastern Iran to Syria, and later splintered off to form a separate state in Anatolia (the Rum Saljuqs). During this period, Kashan features as an important centre of ceramic production, where the introduction of stonepaste (**2**), the eastward movement of lustre technology, and exposure to other visual traditions inspired a diversity of decorative techniques including *mina'i* or *haft rangi* and lustre wares (pp. 102–5). Both the Ghaznavids and Saljuqs embraced Persian language and traditions; in fact, it was at the court of the Ghaznavid ruler Sultan Mahmud in 1010 that the Persian poet Abu'l Qasim Firdawsi presented the completed manuscript of the *Shahnama* ('Book of Kings'), the Persian national epic, which would later inspire the names of several Saljuq rulers. (LA)

3 | 5 Early ceramic traditions

Some of the finest ceramics from the 10th and 11th centuries were produced in Iran and Central Asia. Nishapur and Samarqand (in Iran and Uzbekistan, respectively), as two of the main cultural and political hubs in this region, were also the two chief centres of high-quality ceramic production. Among the significant technological and artistic advances in pottery at this time, two groups stand out for their remarkable qualities as well as their apparent contrast to each other.

'Samanid epigraphic wares' (**1**), so called for their association with the Iranian Samanid dynasty (819–1005) of Khurasan and Transoxiana, are praised as the most sophisticated of 'slipwares', admired for their size, precision and elegant calligraphic decoration. Arabic proverbs or good wishes composed radially or across an object in a bold *kufic* script evoke a rhythm recalling the finest calligraphy found in manuscripts or on architecture and suggest the diverse skillset of their makers. Both the blessings and aphorisms (which generally prescribe generosity, virtuous conduct or knowledge) insinuate the function of these vessels within the context of a society that valued and promoted moral conduct in literature and through social gatherings.

'Nishapur polychrome wares' (**2**) feature an early form of polychrome glaze technology that probably was in use in the broader Khurasan region at this time. These wares are striking for their colourful black, yellow, green and red slips, but they are considered more 'popular' than refined in style. They feature figural decoration against a motif-filled background, with depictions of stylized animals as well as people standing or sitting while holding cups or fruit, playing music, and appearing as hunters or warriors. Previously connected to astrological iconography, ancient Iranian visual traditions, as well as to Iranian and Central Asian folklore and local concepts of chivalrous conduct (*javanmardi*) as possible sources of inspiration, this ambiguous imagery has more recently been alternatively considered within the context of feasting culture in ancient Indo-Iranian cultic traditions such as Nawruz (new year) or Mihragan (autumn equinox). Images of fruits and wine evoked this culture, as did hunting, which would have culminated in a celebratory feast. (LA)

1. Samanid epigraphic bowl

This 'slipware' bowl is an exemplar of the underglazing technique of slip painting, where diluted clay solutions coloured with different mineral pigments were applied over a white slip-covered earthenware surface. The 'black-and-white' contrast as well as the shape of the vessel reveal an inspiration in metalwork with niello on silver decoration. The proverb on the bowl reads:

He who speaks, his speech is silver, but silence is a ruby. With good health and prosperity.

10th–11th century
Iran, probably Nishapur
Earthenware; white slip with brownish-black slip decoration under a transparent glaze
Height 12 cm, diameter 34.6 cm
1958,1218.1

2. Nishapur bowl depicting a figure, birds and flowers

Depicting a standing male figure holding a cup and flanked by a bird and rosettes, this bowl might have a connection to the feasts of Nawruz or Mihragan, where wine would have been consumed. Nishapur polychrome wares favour figural imagery that would have carried meaning among diverse communities, many of which would have celebrated such feasts regardless of their religion.

10th century
Iran, probably Nishapur
Earthenware, painted in black and red slip, and yellow and green under a transparent glaze
Height 8 cm, diameter 18 cm
1959,0413.2

3 | 6 Early Iranian glass

Glassmakers in the early Islamic world, like their counterparts in the pottery and metalwork industries, initially followed the pre-existing traditions and decorative vocabularies used by the Romans and Sasanians. Unlike ceramics and metalwork, however, where a culture of courtly patronage can sometimes be deduced from inscribed objects naming their patrons and carrying clear connections to some of the great Islamic dynasties, glass production in the early Iranian world appears mostly to have developed independently of a major court. As a result, attributions to a specific place of production remain a challenge and it would be premature to assign such works to a particular dynasty. Regardless, cut glass stands out as one of the great technologies of the region between the 9th and 11th centuries, suggesting that glassmakers were also held in high regard.

Cut-glass designs such as palmettes or animals, as seen on the objects illustrated here, could be engraved through the wheel-cutting of cold glass, where the surface of the object would be removed to bring out the desired design in relief. In the case of the long-necked bottle depicting animals (**3**), the surface removal would have involved an extra outer layer of coloured glass to achieve the dramatic cameo effect. One of the most common shapes produced in the Iranian world between the 9th and 11th centuries was the conical beaker with flared rim and splayed foot. The two beakers illustrated below display the close relationship in form, technique and decorative language between rock crystal, a transparent colourless quartz that was admired and worked in Iran as it was in Fatimid Egypt (see pp. 106–7), and glass (**1**, **2**). (LA)

1. Conical rock-crystal beaker
The decoration on this rock-crystal beaker features stylized alternating whole and half palmettes.

9th–10th century
Iran
Rock-crystal; relief-cut with raised outlines
Height 8.2 cm, diameter 6.5 cm
Funded by P.T. Brooke Sewell, Esq., 1954,1013.1

2. Conical glass beaker
This beaker, with an inverted conical shape and low splayed foot, is one of many similarly shaped vessels produced in the Iranian world. Its relief-cut decoration includes three birds, a common motif on cut glass, appearing between two horizontal bands.

Late 9th–early 10th century
Iran
Glass; relief-cut with raised outlines
Height 10 cm, diameter 8.5 cm
Brooke Sewell Permanent Fund, 1964,1012.1

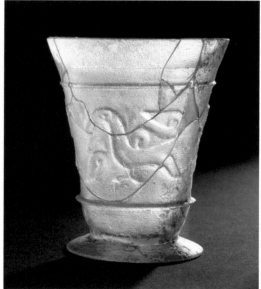

3. Long-necked glass bottle

The most striking feature on this long, cylindrical-necked bottle with a globular body and flat rim is its overlay or 'cameo' decoration. Two green 'pads' of glass, applied during the hot-working phase when the glass was first blown, were later (after undergoing a controlled, gradual cooling) cut back on the wheel to produce the two animal silhouettes in profile. One of these has a split palmette tail and may be identified as a hare by its long ear.

9th–10th century
Western Asia, possibly Iran
Translucent green over colourless glass; blown, applied and cut
Height 15.2 cm, diameter 8.5 cm (max), rim diameter 2.2 cm
Brooke Sewell Permanent Fund, 1967,1211.1

3 | 7 Herat and the inlaid metalworking industry

In the 12th century, Herat, which historically enjoyed status as a major cultural hub, emerged as one of the earliest centres for the production of metalwork inlaid with copper, silver and gold. Transforming ordinary base metal into a glittering surface, the inlay technique carried great appeal and elevated otherwise plain objects to a position comparable to gold or silver. A shortage of silver, a rising middle class and an evolution in metalwork engraving techniques have all been suggested as catalysts for the development of Islamic inlay, which eventually spread to other manufacturing centres.

Although inlay had been used in Iran and the Middle East prior to the Islamic period, the close contact between Khurasan and northern India under dynasties such as the Ghaznavids (977–1186) and Ghurids (c. 1148–1206) meant that Iranian metalworkers were likely exposed to the technologies of Indian craftsmen, who were using copper and silver inlays in Kashmir and northeast India in the 11th and 12th centuries. By the end of the 12th century, silver had replaced copper in the embellishment of fine metal wares, and the inlay technique elevated brass as a luxury item worthy of competition with silver and gold and surpassing fine ceramics (1–4).

1. Inlaid brass ewer
This belongs to a group of similarly shaped ewers attributed to Herat in the late 12th and early 13th centuries, one of which is inscribed with a poem praising the object's beauty and alluding to its function (for washing). Its decoration consists of a masterfully orchestrated and rendered composition of figural, celestial and calligraphic imagery: repoussé lions and parakeets appear on the neck and shoulder; the planets, each with the sign of the zodiac representing its day or night house, appear on the widest register; and benedictory Arabic inscriptions in *kufic* and *naskh* are animated with human heads, emphasized in silver. The detail illustrates the brilliant effect of inlay on base metal, with silver and copper glittering upon the fluted sheet brass.

1180–1200
Herat, Afghanistan
Sheet brass; with repoussé decoration and inlaid with copper and silver
Height 40 cm, diameter 20 cm (max)
1848,0805.2

The status of Herat as a major centre for inlaid metalwork is suggested by its mention in the inscriptions on two important objects, one of which is a ewer resembling the one illustrated in this section (**1**). Yet the appearance of cities such as Merv, Nishapur and Tus in metalworkers' names suggests the probability of multiple centres of production. The inlaid metalworking industry in Herat flourished until the Mongol conquests of Khurasan, after which it appears to have transferred westwards to centres in western Iran, Anatolia, Syria and Egypt, through the movement of both objects and craftsmen. (LA)

2. Pilgrim flask with ibex-shaped handles

This bottle appears to incorporate a hybrid variety of Khurasani/Islamic and Indian/ Buddhist characteristics, inspiring different interpretations about its origins and function. Its convex shape, inscription and overall inlay decoration appear more aligned with Islamic or Khurasani objects, while the ibex-shaped handles and long neck have been compared to Indian inlay techniques and to Buddhist ritual 'long-necked bottles' (*kundika*s). Its provenance in the Punjab suggests it was made in Indian provinces under Ghurid rule. The bottle testifies to the transmission of techniques and styles through the mobility of craftsmen: production centres were natural palimpsests of different cultural traditions.

c. 1200
Khurasan (Iran or Afghanistan) or the Punjab
Cast copper alloy, engraved and inlaid with silver
Height 32 cm, width 22 cm, depth 6 cm
Donated by Sir Augustus Wollaston Franks, 1883,1019.7

3. Lidded bowl known as the 'Vaso Vescovali'

This intricately decorated lidded bowl stands out among inlaid metal wares for its craftsmanship and complex astrological imagery. The body contains 12 roundels representing the signs of the zodiac as well as the personification of each sign's 'planet lord'. The detail illustrated here shows a figure riding a ram: this is Mars in his night house Aries. The lid (originally not matched with the bowl) complements the bowl's iconography with eight roundels depicting personifications of the planets, each with six arms to carry symbolic attributes. Objects decorated with such themes were believed to carry talismanic powers to protect their owners against illness and misfortune.

c. 1200
Khurasan (Iran or Afghanistan)
High-tin bronze, engraved and inlaid with silver
Height 21.5 cm, diameter 18.5 cm
1950,0725.1

4. Lidded container

This container, which resembles two others in similar shape and form attributed to Khurasan, features astrological imagery depicting the 12 signs of the zodiac and their 'planet lords'. In contrast to the extensive figural imagery of the Vaso Vescovali (above), the images here were adapted to exclude figures in their fully recognizable forms. Bands of benedictory inscriptions in *naskh* and *kufic* script complete the decorative programme.

Late 12th–early 13th century
Khurasan (Iran or Afghanistan)
Brass, engraved and inlaid with copper
Height 16.7 cm, diameter 23.5 cm
Brooke Sewell Permanent Fund, 1967,0724.1

3 | 8 The Nihavand hoard

A hoard discovered at Nihavand in the Iranian province of Hamadan is believed to have included a group of about 40 objects made of precious metals, many of which suggest a nomadic connection (1–2). Associated with this find are horse trappings, weapon parts, buckle fragments (one of which bears an inscription that identifies a Saljuq Turkish official, Abu Shuja Inju-Takin), an amulet inscribed with Qur'anic verses, and an inscribed gold wine bowl (2). With the exception of the bowl, all objects are silver and decorated with gilding or niello (black inlay).

The small size and minimal weight of these objects, as well as their material and function, support the nomadic lifestyle of those in the military elite, who would inevitably spend long stretches of time in transit while on campaign. The amulet and gold bowl suggest other elements of their nomadic life: the practice of faith and the desire and need for protection, as well as the enjoyment of courtly activities such as feasting and literary and musical entertainment, which pre-date the Islamic period in Iran. The Arabic inscription on the bowl, which makes a poetic allusion to its function as a vessel for drinking wine, comprises verses by the 10th-century poet Ibn al-Tammar al-Wasiti. The poem also appears in one of the anthologies of Al-Tha'alibi (961–1038), the celebrated writer from Nishapur, which later became a Saljuq capital. (LA)

1. Objects from the Nihavand hoard

11th century
Possibly Hamadan (Nihavand), Iran
Silver decorated with gilding or niello, gold engraved and inscribed (bowl)
Lengths approx. 1.5–5.8 cm
1938,1112.1, 1939,0313.1, 1939,0313.2, 1939,0313.3, 1939,0313.6, 1939,0313.7, 1939,0313.8

2. Inscribed wine bowl from the Nihavand hoard, with duck motif

The floriated *kufic* Arabic inscription below the outer rim of this gold vessel derives from the work of the 10th-century poet Ibn al-Tammar al-Wasiti and reveals the cup's purpose for holding wine:

Wine is a sun in a garment of red Chinese silk / It flows; its sources is the flask // Drink, then, in the garden of time, since our day / Is a day of delight which has brought dew.

The duck motif and engraved roundels suggest transmission from both earlier Sasanian silver and contemporary textiles with similar designs.

11th century
Possibly Hamadan (Nihavand), Iran
Gold, engraved and inscribed
Diameter 7.6 cm
The Art Fund, 1938,1112.1

3 | 9 Iranian mirrors

Surviving in great quantities and in many common styles from the early Islamic period, Iranian mirrors form part of the larger story of metalworking in Khurasan. Most examples were cast in bronze with relief decoration and a central knob through which a cord could be threaded to suspend the object. Given that relief casting first appeared in Iran in AD 1100 and that Khurasan is known to have had a robust bronze industry in the 12th and 13th centuries, most surviving mirrors have been attributed to this period, although the 10th-century Persian historian and geographer Ibn al-Faqih also wrote of a mirror industry existing in this region during his time. Earlier examples, some of which were handled mirrors, survive in fewer numbers.

Most Islamic mirrors suggest a clear inspiration from contemporary and earlier Chinese mirrors, the latter which may have reached the Islamic world via Central Asia. Chinese and Islamic mirrors alike were polished on one side for reflection and decorated on the other with a pierced central knob. Their most common decorative repertoire features a pair of addorsed sphinxes framed within a band of benedictory inscriptions (2), but they may also include astrological or hunting iconography.

In both Iran and China, mirrors held protective agency. Chinese bronze mirrors, believed to possess a symbolic power to avert disaster, were buried to provide protection in the afterlife. In Iran, mirrors were invested with a talismanic role in daily life. They could also carry associations with magic and cosmology. The engraving of mirror faces with 'magical' inscriptions and imagery as an added layer of protection became common in Iran around the 13th century (1), alongside an interest in healing magic and the use of magic medicinal bowls (see pp. 70–71). (LA)

1. Mirror with four running sphinxes

The back of this mirror depicts four winged sphinxes in relief around a central pierced knob, framed by an unclear *kufic* inscription. An additional inscriptional band on the mirror face was added later, as tool marks indicate it was chased onto the polished surface rather than part of the initial casting. It includes the names of the Seven Sleepers of Ephesus, each introduced with the *basmala* and appearing with magic squares, the 'seven signs', letters and numbers. Interpretations of the Qur'anic account of the legend of the Seven Sleepers, Christian men who fell asleep for several hundred years while fleeing from Roman persecution, emphasize the talismanic value of reciting their names (see p. 71).

12–13th century
Iran, probably Khurasan
High tin bronze, cast in relief and inscribed through chasing
Diameter 19 cm, thickness 1 cm
Donated by Brenda Zara Seligman, 1963,0718.1

2. Mirror with a pair of addorsed sphinxes

One of the most common motifs on Iranian mirrors is that of a pair of addorsed sphinxes surrounded by an inscriptional band of Arabic blessings on the rim. The iconography of the sphinx on such mirrors has been linked to Saljuq courtly imagery but also with the extraordinary and mystical qualities associated with mirrors as objects of reflection. The large number of surviving examples of similar decoration and size supports the theory that the mirrors were relief cast, possibly in sand moulds.

12th century
Iran
Bronze, cast in relief
Diameter 10.5 cm, thickness 1.3 cm
1866,1229.76

3 | 10 Luxury stonepaste ceramics

In the 12th century, some revolutionary technological innovations changed the course of ceramic production and decoration in Iran, inspiring a dynamic range of decorative techniques and styles across an extraordinary variety of fine objects and tilework. First among these was the introduction of stonepaste, originally developed in medieval Egypt and which replaced earthenware as the main ceramic body. Described in a treatise dated 1301 by Abu'l Qasim of Kashan, who belonged to a famous family of potters, stonepaste was composed of 10 parts quartz to one or two parts each of clay and powder-glaze. The end product was a pale, whitish, hard fabric that offered a thin, elegant profile, low weight and resonant sound when tapped. The rise of finely potted vessels at this time coincided with the use of already present techniques such as lustre (**1, 5**), pierced bodies (**3**) and a new kind of decoration, *haft rangi* or *mina'i* ('enamelled') ware (**2, 4**), which allowed for a hitherto unheard of ceramic design palette. Kashan is recognized as the major centre of ceramic production at this time due to Abu'l Qasim's treatise and because some works were signed by Kashan potters (the *nisba* in their names indicating place of origin), but it would not be surprising to find evidence of contemporary centres of production given the widespread dissemination of lustre decoration throughout Iran and Central Asia.

1. Lustre-painted bottle

The decoration on this fragmentary bottle consists of a series of bands of varying widths featuring depictions of seated and haloed human figures, prowling animals (in two bands), floral and vegetal motifs, and inscriptions. Representing the so-called 'miniature' painting style associated with contemporary manuscript illustration, this is one of the earliest known examples of Persian lustreware. Persian verses inscribed around the centre of the bottle read:

O Heavenly sphere, why do you set affliction before me? / O fortune, why do you scatter salt on my wounds? / O Enemy of mine, how often will you strike at me? / I am stuck by my own fate and fortune. / May joy, exultation and cheerfulness be with you. / May prosperity, happiness and triumph be your companions.

Dated June/July AD 1179
(Muharram AH 575)
Iran, probably Kashan
Stonepaste, painted in lustre over an opaque white glaze
Height 15 cm, diameter 13 cm, foot diameter 6 cm
1920,0326.1

2. 'Muharram' bowl

This bowl, attributed to the potter Abu Zayd, depicts an enthroned royal figure, attendants and a seated visitor. The scene has been identified as illustrating two elements of a continuous narrative of the *ta'ziya* ceremony, a Shi'a ritual commemorating the death of the Prophet's grandson Husayn at the battle of Karbala (see pp. 224–25) and which takes place during the first 10 days in the month of Muharram. If true, the enthronement scene represents the ceremony itself, during which a reciter narrates the story as others perform independent roles. The figure at left, separated in time and space by a tree, appears in the ruler's own robe, symbolizing the robe of honour bestowed upon prominent reciters or other distinguished guests by their rulers. The Persian inscription below the figures and on the exterior rim includes verses from different poems. X-ray and ultraviolet light examinations confirm that the bowl was restored using elements of different contemporary ceramic vessels and overpainting, but also suggest the date (shown in detail below) is original and untouched.

Dated Muharram AH 583 / March/April AD 1187
Iran, probably Kashan
Stonepaste, *haft rangi* or *mina'i*; in-glaze turquoise and blue over an opaque white glaze and overglaze red and black
Height 9.5 cm, diameter 21 cm, base diameter 8.8 cm
Bequeathed by Oscar Charles Raphael, 1945,1017.261

Appearing in the late 12th century, *haft rangi* (literally, 'seven-coloured', but implying multicoloured) wares were produced in two firings with several colours painted either under or over the glaze, depending on their required firing temperature. Their decoration emphasizes figural imagery, including scenes from the princely cycle such as hunting, feasting and entertainment, or fantastical creatures such as sphinxes and harpies, but there are also examples with abstract decoration, as seen on the surface of the cheetah-handled vessel illustrated here (**4**). Lustre-painted wares formed the other fine ceramic type in this period (**5**), also appearing in the late 12th century as suggested by the earliest dated wares, including a bottle dated Muharram AH 575 (June/July AD 1179) (**1**).

Two celebrated masters of this period were Abu Zayd and Abu Tahir, both of whom came from families of potters. They are known to have worked in the *haft rangi* and lustre techniques, but Abu Zayd is the only potter known to have worked on both objects and tiles. His signature appears on several surviving examples of these techniques, some of them inscribed with dates of production, which supports the idea that there was a close association between workshops producing these styles. Most interestingly, the fact that he appears to have composed some of the poetry appearing on his vessels shows how closely involved ceramic artists could be in the literary culture of this era. His and other artists' signatures on works invested these objects with a value beyond their demonstration of technical prowess, one that made them worthy of collecting. (LA)

This page, left
3. House model
This object, which depicts figures seated around a tray of items within a courtyard house representing medieval vernacular architecture, belongs to a larger group of house models previously identified variously as cups, inkwells, toys, mosque models, hanging decorations or Buddhist offerings, or connected to Chinese traditions of house models made for tombs. More recently, they have been considered within the wider medieval socio-cultural context of feasting, music and celebration on the occasions of Nawruz (the Persian new year) or weddings, where they would be offered as gifts. The central tray may hold fruit or possibly the *haftsin*, the seven symbolic items displayed at Nawruz.

12th–13th century
Iran
Stonepaste, moulded, modelled and painted in a greenish-turquoise glaze
Height 6 cm, length 15 cm, width 10 cm
Donated by G.P. Devey, 1886,0803.1

Opposite, right

4. Cheetah-handled vessel
While its handles take the form
of cheetahs and its spouts that
of deer heads, the main overall
decoration of this *haft rangi*
vessel represents a simpler,
non-figural repertoire of stylized
vegetal motifs in green, blue
and red.

c. 1200–25
Iran
Stonepaste, in-glaze turquoise
and blue over an opaque white
glaze and overglaze in red
Height 6.5 cm, diameter 22 cm
Donated by Harvey Hadden,
1930,0719.65

5. Jar with kneeling figures
This cylindrical fluted jar's large-
scale depiction of eight kneeling
figures and abstract motifs
painted in reserve characterize
the 'monumental style' of Persian
lustreware, which is believed
to recall painting on lustre
objects produced in 11th-
and 12th-century Syria (p. 111).
The exterior lustre-painted
decoration is offset by a blue
glaze covering the vessel's
interior, including a lustre-painted
but illegible (possibly pseudo-)
inscription on the inner neck.
The figures' round 'moon faces'
invoke descriptions of such
faces in Persian poetry as ideals
of beauty.

c. 1170–1200
Iran, probably Kashan
Stonepaste, painted in lustre over
an opaque white glaze
Height 30.5 cm, diameter 12.8 cm
Bequeathed by Miss Edith
Godman, G.234

3 | 11 The Fatimids

Cairo, the capital city of Egypt and one of the most important centres of religious, cultural and political life in the Arab Muslim world, was founded in 969 as a palace-city by the Fatimid dynasty (909–1171) just north of the city of Fustat (Old Cairo). The Fatimids, who had been ruling from their seat in North Africa since 909, were a Shi'a Isma'ili dynasty who claimed descent from Ali, the fourth Muslim caliph, and from his wife Fatima, the Prophet's daughter, whom they were named after. As both caliphs and Shi'a imams, they posed a religious and ideological challenge to the two main Sunni caliphates – the Abbasids of Baghdad (750–1258) and the Umayyads of Spain (756–1031). The Fatimid caliphs and their courtiers built impressive city gates, palaces, libraries and mosques, including the mosque of al-Azhar ('the radiant'), which is considered the oldest extant educational-religious institution in Egypt (**1**).

Fatimid Cairo became the centre of a flourishing commercial network linking the Mediterranean basin to the Indian Ocean and beyond as a result of the stability of the dynasty's administrative and financial apparatus, a powerful army and navy, and an influx of African gold (**2**). The rulers actively engaged in diplomatic and commercial relations with the Byzantines of Constantinople and the Normans of Sicily. At the height of their power, the Fatimids controlled nearly all of North Africa, Sicily and Egypt, parts of Syria, Palestine and the Yemen and, for extended periods, Mecca and Medina.

Among the artistic hallmarks of this period are rock-crystal objects including large and small vessels, lamps and chess pieces. This material was extolled not only for its crystalline beauty, described by the medieval Iranian polymath al-Biruni (d. 1048) as an amalgam of air and water, but also for the healing and protective powers that were ascribed to it. Many extant pieces of Islamic rock crystal found their way into medieval church treasuries and were re-purposed as containers for holy relics. A perfume bottle inscribed in

1. Mosque of al-Azhar
Completed in 971 as al-Qahira's (i.e. Cairo's) first mosque, the name al-Azhar ('the radiant/ brilliant') is derived from the epithet of the Prophet's daughter, *Fatima al-Zahra* ('Fatima the radiant'). In this early 20th-century postcard, men sit in small discussion groups in the interior courtyard of the mosque. The image echoes an account by the Egyptian historian al-Maqrizi (d. 1442) describing the sessions of learning at al-Azhar in the late 10th century: 'Each Friday [the salaried jurists] assembled in the mosque and formed circles after the [midday] prayer until the time of the afternoon prayer.' Separate public lectures on Isma'ili law were held at al-Azhar for women, including the caliph's wives and noblewomen of the palaces. Salah al-Din (d. 1193), the last of the dynasty's military viziers, swiftly abolished the sessions at al-Azhar and removed all Isma'ili jurists from office. He ended 262 years of Fatimid rule and re-established Sunnism as Egypt's state religion in 1171. He founded his own Ayyubid dynasty in 1174, which governed areas including Egypt, Syria and the Yemen until the end of the 15th century.

1900–1920
Printed in Cairo, Egypt, by the Cairo Postcard Trust
Height 9 cm, width 14 cm
EPH-ME.2465

CAIRO - Interior of the Al Azhar Mosque

2. Gold pendant with birds

Both the crescent-shaped design of this gold filigree pendant and the enamelled bird motifs derive from earlier Byzantine models.

11th century
Palestine or Egypt
Gold, inset with cloisonné enamel
Height 9 cm, width 14 cm
1981,0707.2

3. Rock-crystal reliquary

Three centuries after this perfume or cosmetic bottle was made it was re-purposed as a church reliquary with silver mounts.

10th–11th century (bottle);
14th century (mounts)
Egypt (bottle); Europe (mounts)
Rock crystal with nielloed silver mounts
Height 9 cm, diameter 12 mm
Bequeathed by Sir Augustus Wollaston Franks, AF.3129

4. Marble architectural inscription

Badr al-Jamali's titles on this inscription include: 'Sword of Islam, Helper of the Imam [al-Mustansir], Protector of the judges of the Muslims, and Guide of the missionaries of the believers.'

Dated AD 1084 (AH 477)
Cairo, Egypt
Marble
Height 42 cm, width 107 cm, depth 10 cm
OA+.355

Arabic with 'blessings to the owner' (*baraka li-sahibi*) was later made into a reliquary with silver-gilt mounts inscribed in Latin with 'the hair of the Blessed Mary' (*Capillus Beate Marie*) (**3**).

The Fatimid dynasty's rule also suffered periods of misery and famine, military rebellions, internal schisms, political intrigue, the menace of crusading armies, and the intervention of foreign powers – all of which progressively weakened the dynasty and eventually led to its end. The reign of Imam al-Mustansir (r. 1036–1094) was marred by famine, economic crisis and rioting due to the low rising of the Nile for seven consecutive years (1065–1072). As a result, the caliph's Turkish guards looted the Fatimid treasuries and dispersed their contents on the open market. Al-Mustansir summoned the powerful Armenian military vizier, Badr al-Jamali (d. 1094), from Syria to restore peace and stability in Egypt. But al-Jamali set up his own dictatorial regime, marking a turning point in Fatimid history. A fragmentary inscription bearing his titles attests to the power he wielded (**4**). His son, the vizier al-Afdal, did away with the established line of caliphal succession to further usurp Fatimid authority, and this subsequently resulted in a major schism within Isma'ilism. (FS)

3 | 12 Daily life in medieval Egypt

Our knowledge of the lives of ordinary citizens of Fatimid Egypt relies significantly on the Geniza documents, dating from the 10th to 13th centuries. These fragmentary manuscripts were discovered in the 19th century hidden in a synagogue in Cairo. Mainly written in Arabic in Hebrew script (i.e. Judaeo-Arabic), the cache included religious, commercial and legal documents, bridal trousseau lists, literary texts, drawings, paper amulets and personal letters exchanged by seafaring merchants. A vivid picture is painted of a multi-religious and socially and economically diverse population that included a sizable middle class who generally prospered from the influx of people, products and ideas through commerce and maritime trade.

As the Isma'ili Shi'a caliphs did not adopt a policy of forced conversion, they governed lands that were predominantly Sunni Muslim with significant Christian and Jewish populations. The dynasty's economic prosperity and the favourable position granted to Jewish, Christian and Muslim elites at court bolstered intense intellectual, literary and artistic activity through the patronage of scholars, scientists, poets, architects and artisans. In parallel to this courtly milieu, affluent, urban middle classes of all religious creeds were able to purchase valuable textiles, jewellery, rock crystal and ivory objects, inlaid furniture, manuscripts, and metal, glass and ceramic vessels from the markets of Cairo and Fustat (Old Cairo), the empire's industrial capital. In contrast to the private caliphal ceremonies held in Abbasid Baghdad, the Fatimids took part in elaborate public ceremonies and processions on feast days, parading courtiers and soldiers alongside horses, elephants and giraffes, allowing citizens direct access to courtly ritual and material culture. (FS)

1. Doll with painted details
Many carved bone dolls have been excavated in Egypt, indicating that they were common objects, used for play. This one includes incised and painted facial and anatomical details including almond-shaped eyes, a small mouth and nose, breasts and navel. The curvilinear and heart-shaped painted motifs, identified as tattoos or henna patterns, were considered amuletic against the 'evil eye'. This particular doll once had movable arms, hair and earrings.

980s–1180s
Egypt
Bone and organic pigment
Height 15.5 cm, width 4 cm, depth 2 cm
1979,1017.203

2. Lustre-painted jar

Lustre-painted ceramics gleamed like silver and gold, and were the most expensive type of pottery produced in Fatimid Egypt – appreciated by the elite and middle classes alike. The technique was labour- and resource-intensive and its decorative repertoire of lively figural scenes reflecting contemporary culture reached new heights in this period. This jar, painted with vegetal motifs, would have been a luxury object for use and display in the home.

11th century
Egypt
Earthenware, painted in lustre on an opaque white glaze
Height 23 cm, diameter 14 cm
1970,1105.1

3. Brightly painted ceramic bowl

The runny, lead glazes on this bowl, in hues of aubergine, aquamarine, light green, ochre and white, are painted in a radial design around two overlapping triangles and fixed under a transparent glaze. Among the Geniza documents is a letter addressed from someone in Alexandria who placed an order for 50 ceramic bowls and 10 platters with colourful decorations from Cairo. This gives the impression

that tableware for special occasions was commissioned as matching dinner services.

11th–12th century
Egypt
Earthenware, painted in slip under a transparent glaze
Height 6.5 cm, diameter 23 cm
Donated by Oscar Charles Raphael, 1932,0615.1

4. Water jar stand

Carved from a single block of marble and decorated in relief with lions, fantastical beasts and Arabic blessings, this stand (*kilga*) was used to support a clay or marble jar of water. The Qur'an repeatedly instructs Muslims to provide water to the thirsty, and this *kilga* may have been commissioned by an individual as an act of piety in order to provide refreshment to passers-by in a public setting.

12th century
Egypt
Marble
Height 40 cm, length 57 cm, width 40 cm
Donated by Prof. J.M. Rogers, 1988,1107.1

3 | 13 Fatimid textiles: *tiraz* production

With the arrival of the Arabs and new rulership, textile production in Egypt became a caliphal and royal monopoly, controlled in state workshops or *tiraz*. Derived from the Persian word *tarazidan* ('to embroider'), the workshops were of two types. The private *tiraz al-khassa* was for the exclusive use of the caliph, where his clothes, palace furnishings and honorific garments presented as diplomatic gifts (*khilat*) were produced. The public *tiraz al-amma* produced textiles for local use, trade and export. Workshops were mainly based in centres with an established textile tradition, such as Alexandria or Akhmim in Upper Egypt. The presence of male Egyptian weavers who were Copts (from the Arabic *qibti*, the name given to Egypt's majority Christian population) and constituted the majority of employees in the textile industry until the 10th century, explains the new mix of techniques and iconographies that occurred between the 7th and 12th centuries.

Textiles produced in these workshops were also named *tiraz*, distinguished by their original and characteristic embroidered decoration. They can be identified by the bands of *kufic* script that they bear, which often included the name of the caliph, place of production and verses from the Qur'an or pious phrases. Often combined with geometric, vegetal and animal motifs inherited from classical imagery, these Arabic inscriptions were found on utilitarian textiles, such as saddle cloths; furnishings including cushions, hangings and curtains; and garments, applied onto tunic sleeves and headgear. (AM)

1. *Tiraz* fragment
Initially, Egyptian *tiraz* were embroidered in blue silk on a white linen ground. From the 10th century, however, they were mainly produced in multicoloured wool and/or silk tapestry, as in this example. At the same time, the development of a more cursive Arabic script led to a decline in the use of the angular *kufic* and to the adoption of a loose, cursive style, as seen here alongside stylized classical scrolls and quadrupeds.

c. 11th–12th century
Akhmim, Egypt
Linen and silk
Height 29.5 cm, width 32.5 cm
1893,0514.188

2. Lustre-painted sherd

In addition to the traditional T-shaped woven tunic, men, women and children during the Fatimid period began wearing Eastern-style tunics made of several pieces of fabric cut and sewn together. Such outfits are distinguished by their large sleeves bearing *tiraz* bands and a ground fabric decorated with spiral scrolls and interlaced motifs similar to those appearing on the shoulders and torso of the figure on the left side of this sherd.

Mid-12th century
Egypt or Syria
Stonepaste, painted in lustre over an opaque white glaze
Height 13.3 cm, width 6.3 cm
Brooke Sewell Bequest,
1986,0415.1

3. Page from an illustrated manuscript of the *Maqamat* of al-Hariri

The well-known, illustrated *Maqamat* ('Assemblies') of al-Hariri (d. 1122) offers visual evidence of *tiraz* bands as a common feature on textiles throughout the medieval Islamic world. In this painting, by Yahya ibn Mahmud al-Wasiti, the main protagonist Abu Zayd and his son are before a judge. The men depicted wear garments of varied colours marking different status, but they all bear *tiraz* bands on the sleeves and headgear. Similar inscribed bands appear on the curtain and cushion cover.

Dated AD 1236/7 (AH 634)
Iraq
Ink, opaque watercolour and gold on paper
Bibliothèque Nationale de France, Ms Arabe 5847, folio 114v

1. The Chertsey tiles

These tiles are part of a series representing Salah al-Din in combat with Richard I (the Lionheart, r. 1189–99); the Third Crusade (1189–1192), in which they both fought (although they never actually met), has been personified as a duel between them. The tiles formed part of the floor at the Benedictine abbey of Chertsey in Surrey. Richard was both feared and respected by contemporary Muslims. Ibn al-Athir, writing in about 1191, describes him as 'the man of his age as regards courage, shrewdness, endurance and forbearance and because of him the Muslims were sorely tempted by unprecedented disaster.' The very practice of making tiles for flooring seems to have been imported into western Europe from the Crusader arena, spreading from France to England and elsewhere in the late 12th and 13th centuries.

c. 1250
Chertsey, England
Earthenware floor tiles, lead-glazed with inlaid slip decoration
Donated by Dr H. Manwaring Shurlock, 1885,1113.9065–9070

2. Kashan *haft rangi* and Raqqa ware bowls

At the ceramic workshops of both Iran (making Kashan ware, above) and northern Syria (making Raqqa ware, below), one of the styles adopted was the decoration of vessels with courtly figural scenes likely to have been inspired by manuscript illustration. While Kashan wares were decorated in the overglaze and underglaze technique known as *haft rangi* (see pp. 102–5), in Syria the same scenes were painted under the glaze only.

c. 1175–25
Probably Kashan, Iran
Stonepaste, opaque white glaze with in-glaze and overglaze painting
Height 4.9 cm, diameter 12.8 cm
Donated through The Art Fund (as NACF), 1912,1207.4

c. 1200–25
Syria
Stonepaste, painted in black, blue and red under a transparent glaze
Height 12 cm, diameter 21 cm
1922,0516.1

The Ayyubids
and the Crusades

The objects highlighted in the following sections were made within the geographical region of Syria, Palestine and the Jazira, literally 'the island' between the rivers Tigris and Euphrates. The 12th and 13th centuries in this region were politically complex: the replacement of the Isma'ili Shi'a dynasty of the Fatimids by Salah al-Din (1), founder of the Ayyubid dynasty, in 1171 gave way to the rule of the Mamluks in 1250 (which lasted until 1517). The First Crusade with its capture of Jerusalem in 1099 came suddenly and with dramatic effect to a region riven by internal conflict and an absence of strong rulers. By 1110, conquerors and settlers from northern and western Europe had established four states in the Middle East: Jerusalem, Edessa (today's Urfa, Turkey), Antioch (Antakya, Turkey) and Tripoli (in northern Lebanon). While there was conflict on a political level, with Muslims killed or expelled from their lands, and some territories through which they could not travel, at a more practical level there was close interaction between the Crusaders, their Christian and Muslim subjects and their Muslim neighbours.

The artistic legacy of this period offers fascinating insights. There are depictions, for example, of shared pursuits centred on horsemanship and hunting. Pottery from the Crusader-controlled port of Antioch (known as St Symeon ware) is found in Fustat (Old Cairo), and Christian imagery appears on metalwork made in Damascus and in representations of warrior-knights on enamelled glass. A fragmentary gilded glass vessel (see p. 115) may carry the name Imad al-Din Zangi, the ruler who took Edessa from the Franks in 1194; the designs painted upon it, including an eagle, reflect shared iconographies of the Mediterranean. The Byzantine legacy is also evident on the cut-glass Hedwig beaker (see p. 114).

Metalwork, ceramics and glass made in Syria and the Jazira demonstrate both continuity and innovation. The major metalworking centre of the period was undoubtedly Mosul, where the Blacas ewer (see p. 120) was made and which became renowned under its ruler Badr al-Din Lu'lu (r. 1233–59). Eight objects survive that were made for him or members of his court. The Andalusian traveller Ibn Sa'id, who visited Mosul in 1250, wrote 'there are many crafts in the city, especially inlaid brass vessels exported to rulers.' Both the style of inlaid metalwork and the objects themselves travelled across the region: the appellation 'Mawsuli' is known to have been used by no less than 27 craftsmen on 35 metal objects made in Mosul, Damascus and Cairo.

In northern Syria, pottery was made in a series of centres including Aleppo, Balis-Meskene and Raqqa. The latter, once a capital of the Abbasid caliphs, gives its name to Syrian wares made from stonepaste, a man-made fabric manufactured from ground quartz mixed with clay and originally developed in Fatimid Egypt. Stonepaste wares were produced at potteries across the region including at Kashan, in Iran, a major centre of ceramic production (see p. 102). The Syrian fabric tends to be a little coarser than its Iranian cousin, but there are interesting stylistic interactions between the Iranian and Syrian productions (2).

Syrian glassmakers, also centred in northern Syria, were highly proficient in the ancient practice of marvered (or trailed) glass, among other techniques. In Crusader lands, the glass industry was in the hands of Jewish craftsmen. Glass was produced for local consumption, but also traded far and wide, following both commercial and pilgrimage routes. (VP/WG)

3 | 14 Glass: Mediterranean iconographies

Glass has a long history in the eastern Mediterranean region, and by the time of the Arab conquests it had already been produced in the Middle East for over 2,000 years. During the era of the Crusades, glassmakers operating along what is now the coast of Syria, Lebanon and Israel/Palestine produced huge amounts of both raw and finished glass, whether for local consumption or export both eastwards and westwards. The wide-ranging cultural connections of the period, in which war did little to stop trade in glass as well as many other goods, ensured a degree of common culture around the Mediterranean.

Where this glass arrived in Europe, its clarity and beauty ensured that it became a rare luxury, associated with saints and nobles (**1**). In northern Syria around the same time, the technique of lustre painting on glass was replaced by gold painting, in which the finely ground metal was applied to the surface of the glass and fired, leaving a thin layer fused to the body of the vessel (**2**). The details of the decoration (such as leaves, feathers or folds of clothing) would then be scratched out using a needle. (WG)

1. Hedwig beaker
The Hedwig beakers, of which 14 complete examples are known, are a long-standing puzzle in the field of Islamic art, having been attributed to everywhere from pre-Islamic Iran to modern Europe. They gained their name through an association with St Hedwig (*c.* 1174–1243), a saintly noblewoman of Silesia (southwestern Poland) who was said to have changed water into wine within one of them. These glass vessels are decorated either with a combination of lions, griffins and eagles or vegetal ornaments. However, the British Museum beaker is unique in featuring all of these elements. All the beakers were found in Europe, but most scholars believe that the mixture of Islamic and Christian iconography found on them shows that they may have been produced in Sicily or the Levant. Chemical analyses have ascertained that the raw materials were produced in the eastern Mediterranean, although glass was widely recycled and thus the beakers could have been fashioned elsewhere. The Hedwig beakers are an example of the shared artistic culture of the medieval Mediterranean, and the designs on them can be linked to Byzantine, Norman and Fatimid artistic styles.

c. 1150–1220
Eastern Mediterranean or Sicily
Cut glass
Height 14 cm, diameter 10.8 cm
Funded by P.T. Brooke Sewell, Esq., 1959,0414.1

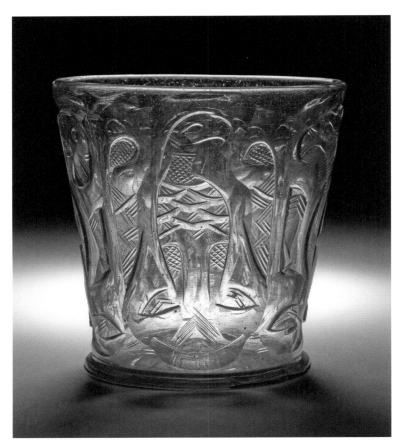

2. Gilded glass flask

Although it is now in a fragmentary state, it is still possible to appreciate the beauty of this gilded glass flask. The surviving inscription bears a dedication to Imad al-Din, which has been interpreted by some scholars to suggest that the vessel was made for Imad al-Din Zangi, the *atabeg* (regent) of Mosul and northern Syria between 1127 and 1146 and founder of the Zangid dynasty. The elegant dancer in her long-sleeved dress resembles those found on near-contemporary works from as far apart as Sicily and the Caucasus, and in combination with the lush pomegranate trees evokes the pleasures of both this world and the next. The eagles on the lower part of the flask strongly resemble their counterpart on the Hedwig beaker, illustrated opposite, and as such can be seen as emblematic of a cross-cultural Mediterranean symbolism of royalty and power appreciated equally by Norman kings, Byzantine emperors and Saljuq sultans.

Mid-12th century
Syria
Gilded glass
Height 12.8 cm, width 16.1 cm
1906,0719.1

3 | 15 Cultural exchanges

Among the Franks there are some who have become acclimatized and frequent the company of Muslims. They are much better than those recently arrived from their lands, but they are the exception and should not be considered representative.

This was the verdict of the aristocratic Syrian scholar, warrior, bureaucrat and hunter *par excellence* Usama ibn Munqidh (1095–1188) on the European warriors who irrupted into the eastern Mediterranean in the late 11th century. Such ambivalence was exhibited both by Crusaders and Muslims, as religious and political differences barely disguised similar interests, especially among the warrior elites. Muslim and Christian noblemen of Crusader Syria enjoyed many of the same pursuits, including the horse-centred pastimes of hunting, polo and, of course, fighting. The movement of objects between the two sides was common. Pictorial evidence on drawings from the rubbish heaps of Fustat (Old Cairo), shows that European-style shields were adopted by the Muslim soldiery (**1**). Meanwhile, ceramics from northwest Syria were widely traded across the 13th-century Mediterranean, and imitated in both Christian and Muslim contexts (**2**, **3**). (WG)

1. Drawing of a battle

This fragment of paper shows a remarkably detailed scene in which Muslims and Crusaders fight below the walls of a fortified city. In the lower part, a bearded horseman charges out of the city, and may have killed the man lying on the ground, whose horse continues running towards the walls. Two archers shoot from the ramparts, while two foot soldiers with spears face a warrior with a large sword and round shield at the top right. The detail of this Norman-style shield, and the kite-shaped ones carried by the other men as well as other elements of arms and armour, is specific enough to suggest that this painting was made in the 13th century, a period in which Crusaders led by King Louis IX of France (r. 1214–70) attempted a direct assault on Egypt itself.

13th century
Egypt
Opaque watercolour on paper
Height 21 cm, width 31.4 cm
1938,0312,0.1

2. Sgraffito bowl

The sgraffito technique used in the manufacture of this bowl, with coloured slip scratched through to reveal a darker body beneath, relates to the 12th- to 13th-century ceramics of Iran as well as works from the Byzantine Empire, the Crusader kingdoms of Syria and Cyprus, and parts of Italy. Irrespective of its exact place of manufacture, the bowl demonstrates the interconnectedness of medieval Syria and the wider world in the age of the Crusades.

13th century
Northern Syria
Earthenware, white slip with incised decoration in brown and green in a transparent glaze
Diameter 26.3 cm
1931,0716.1

3. Dish

Port St Symeon (modern Samandağ, historic al-Mina) was a maritime outlet of the great Crusader city of Antioch. This St Symeon ware bowl has a mix of Frankish, Islamic and Byzantine influences. The models for these ceramics originally came from the eastern Islamic world, but the overall decorative scheme generally represented local Crusader tastes and the cultural pluralism of the region. This vessel was probably produced at Port St Symeon itself, as studies have shown that some of the finest and most complicated designs were produced by potters there, although there were multiple production centres both within and without Antioch. The description of ceramics of this type as 'Crusader' is complicated by the fact that production continued in the region after the Mamluk conquest of Antioch in 1268.

13th or early 14th century
Hatay Province, Turkey
Earthenware, white slip with incised decoration in brown and green in a transparent glaze
Diameter 19 cm
1937,0317.5

3 | 16 Arts of medieval Syria

The arts flourished in medieval Syria under the patronage of the Ayyubids and early Mamluk rulers. The practice of inlaid metalwork, made in Damascus, is represented here by an incense burner with Christian scenes (**2**), and demonstrates that objects were made for a variety of patrons both Christian and Muslim. In northern Syria, contemporary with the production of pottery at Kashan and elsewhere in Iran (see pp. 102–5), ceramics were made in production centres along the Euphrates, including Raqqa (**3**, **4**), and Syrian workshops are also associated with the production of fine glass (**1**). (VP)

1. The Durighiello bottle
The marvered glass technique, in which glass of contrasting colours is trailed or combed to create wavy patterns, has its roots in the Late Roman period. It reached its apogee in the Syrian workshops between the 12th and 14th centuries. This bottle, of Syrian origin and recognized as one of the finest of its type, is said to have been found at Adana in present-day Turkey, an active commercial centre in medieval times. It is named after its former owner, Joseph-Ange Durighiello.

13th century
Syria
Glass, free blown and marvered
Height 20 cm, diameter 11 cm (max)
Donated by Charles Fairfax Murray and William Locket Agnew, 1913,0522.39

2. Inlaid incense burner
The shape of this incense
burner developed from a type
popular in the Byzantine period.
It is richly inlaid with silver, a
legacy of the styles developed
in the workshops of Mosul in
the early 13th century. On the
lid and around the body stand
ecclesiastical figures who hold
censers and other objects
associated with Christian church
ritual. Although uninscribed, it is
likely to have been made for a
Christian patron.

c. 1250–1300
Syria, probably Damascus
Cast brass, pierced at the top,
inlaid with silver
Height 20.5 cm, width 13 cm
Bequeathed by John Henderson,
1878,1230.679

3. Raqqa ware dish
This dish, painted in abstract
leaf forms, shows traces of
iridescence, caused by the
destruction of the surface
of the glaze during its burial
in the ground.

Late 12th–early 13th century
Raqqa, Syria
Stonepaste, painted in black
under a turquoise glaze
Height 6.8 cm, diameter 25.4 cm
1926,0423.1

**4. *Laqabi*-style Raqqa
ware dish**
Featuring a human-headed bird,
the harpy, this dish is decorated
in a style known as *laqabi*, with
designs carved into the surface
and then painted in different
colours. The term *laqabi*, meaning
'water-stained' in Persian, was
coined by dealers in the 1930s.

This style of ware was also made
at Kashan.

Late 12th–early 13th century
Raqqa, Syria
Stonepaste, incised and painted
in blue and brown under a
transparent glaze
Height 6 cm, diameter 42 cm
1923,0217.1

The Blacas ewer and metalworking in Mosul

Mosul in present-day Iraq was a significant centre for the production of fine inlaid metalwork in the 13th century. Metalworkers achieved the highest standards in the inlaying of silver and other metals, a technique originally developed a century earlier in Herat (see p. 94). Many objects bear the *nisba* 'al-Mawsili' (of Mosul), and on a visit in 1250 the traveller Ibn Sa'id mentions the reputation of the city as a metalworking hub. While a number of objects state unequivocally in their inscriptions that they were made in Mosul, or were connected to the ruler, the Kurdish general Badr al-Din Lu'lu (r. 1233–59), other objects are known to have been made in Damascus or elsewhere, such as a geomantic instrument (p. 72) and a celestial globe (p. 49), both craftsmen in those cases using the *nisba* 'al-Mawsili'. Detailed study has revealed a network of metalworkers connected to each other through an apprentice system, making objects in the Mosul style for close to a hundred years. (VP)

1. The Blacas ewer
This ewer, named after its former owner Pierre Louis Jean duc de Blacas (d. 1866), is inlaid with the date and place where it was made – Mosul in AH 629 (AD 1232) – and the name of its maker Shuja ibn Man'a al-Mawsili. Although the name of this craftsman does not appear on any other surviving object, he is known to have come from an important Mosul family. Made of brass, the Blacas ewer is a prime example of the virtuosity of the inlay technique, with fine wires of silver worked into intricate grooved lines and small pieces of silver and copper set into recesses cut into the brass.

Dated April AD 1232 (Rajab AH 629)
Mosul, Iraq
Brass, inlaid, spout and foot missing and with replacement handle
Height 30.4 cm
1866,1229.61

2. Inlaid brass box

This brass box was made for the Kurdish general Badr al-Din Lu'lu (r. 1233–59), a ruler not only of great political acumen but a dedicated patron of the arts. It is one of five surviving metal objects known to have been commissioned by him. The inscription around the rim gives his full name and titles: 'Glory to our lord Atabeg al-Malik al-Rahim the wise, the just, the God-aided, the triumphant, the victorious, the warrior for the Faith, warden of Islam, Badr al-Dunya wa'l-Din Lu'lu, sword blade of the Amir of the Faithful.' The decoration of inlaid silver wire shows similarities to that of the Blacas ewer and is enhanced by a black paste in the background. The hinge and catch are later additions.

1233–59
Mosul, Iraq
Brass, inlaid
Height 9.8 cm, diameter 11 cm
Bequeathed by John Henderson, 1878,1230.674

3. Detail of the Blacas ewer

The vignettes on the Blacas ewer, one of which is shown here, feature scenes of courtly life: enthroned rulers, musicians and huntsmen. The scene featured here is of a woman carried in a *howda* on a camel, accompanied by servants. Details including faces, garments and animals, in a style indebted to miniature painting, were skilfully drawn onto the thin inlays with a fine, blunt tool.

1866,1229.61

3 | 18 Out of the fire: the story of lustre

That which has been evenly fired reflects like red gold and shines like the light of the sun. (Abu'l Qasim al-Kashani)

In 1301, the potter Abu'l Qasim al-Kashani wrote a treatise on the production of pottery at his workshop in Kashan. He came from a family of potters working across several generations who signed their works and, in addition to describing how to make stonepaste (see p. 102), he also described in detail the process for making lustre. This technique, intended to replicate the look of precious metal, or possibly marble or precious stones, was one of the most significant contributions by Islamic potters to world ceramics.

The technique involves mixing silver and copper oxides with a little vinegar, which is then painted onto the surface of vessels or tiles that have been fired once already. These are then fired again in a reduction kiln, where low oxygen levels cause the metallic compounds to break down and create a thin metallic film on top of the glaze. Only once the objects come out of the kiln and are cleaned are the bright metallic colours revealed, as evocatively described by Abu'l Qasim. Perfected on pottery in 9th-century Iraq (**2**), through the migration of craftsmen seeking new patrons, lustre painting was practised between the 10th and 14th centuries in Egypt, Syria and Iran. From Egypt, it was transferred to Muslim Spain (see p. 134) and from there to Italy (**3**).

The complex method of achieving the lustre effect was always regarded as mysterious, and the exact process kept secret. The celebrated Italian potter Piccolpasso, in his treatise on pottery of 1558, wrote: 'many make them [the kilns] on the floors of houses which are locked and kept under close guard, for they look on the manner of making the kiln as an important secret and say that in this consists the whole art.' The technique was re-invented by the great British potter William de Morgan in the 19th century (**4**) and its best-known contemporary practitioner is Alan Caiger-Smith. (VP)

1. Egyptian glass bowl
The lustre effect achieved by Iraqi potters is related to a technique developed on glass in Egypt in the 6th and 7th centuries. On glass, though, the metallic pigment behaved differently, creating a dark stain. This bowl was found in Atfih, ancient Aphroditopolis in Egypt.

c. 11th century
Egypt
Mould-blown glass
Height 8.5 cm, diameter 10.9 cm
1902,0517.2

2. Lustre-painted bowl

The potters of Iraq made lustre in a number of colours, including brilliant ruby. Finds of lustre pottery have been made at the caliphal city of Samarra, and the question of where in Iraq these wares were made continues to be debated. Bowls such as this one imitate the form of imported Chinese pottery (see p. 84), but they departed from the Chinese prototypes by using the white tin-glazed surface as a palette for a range of colourful motifs.

c. 9th century
Iraq
Earthenware, painted in lustre on an opaque white glaze
Height 7 cm, diameter 20 cm
Donated by Sir Alan and Lady Nora Barlow, 1956,0728.2

3. Lustre-painted dish

Hispano-Moresque lustreware, which started to be made in centres such as Manises and Granada in Spain in the mid-14th century, achieved great commercial success. Such was its popularity in Italy that from the mid-15th century Italian potters had mastered the technique themselves, with Deruta and Gubbio key centres of production. Designs were often derived from Renaissance painting, as in this example.

1500–1520
Deruta, Italy
Earthenware, painted in lustre on an opaque white glaze
Height 7.9 cm, diameter 41.5 cm
Bequeathed by John Henderson, 1878,1230.376

4. Arts and Crafts lustre tile

William de Morgan (d. 1917) began to work with lustre during the 1870s. He was familiar with and inspired by Islamic pottery, and his designs often featured birds and animals.

c. 1888–1905
London
Earthenware, painted in lustre on an opaque white glaze
Height and width 15.3 cm
1980,0307.173.d

هذا رسم المحمل الشريف النبوي المصري الذي إنشأ الملك القاهري بمدينة القاهرة حفظها

1. Procession of the *mahmal*

The tent-like *mahmal* at the centre of the annual *hajj* procession represented the authority of the ruler. Begun by the Mamluk sultan Baybars (r. 1260–77), the tradition of the *mahmal* continued unchanged until 1926.

1880–89
Stencil-printed lithograph by Camille Burkhardt, Wissenberg
Height 42 cm, width 59 cm
2012,7020.86

2. Sir William Gell (d. 1836), *Court of the Lions, Alhambra*

November 1808
Pencil on paper from a sketchbook
Height 46.6 cm, width 24.2 cm
Bequeathed by the Hon. Richard Keppel Craven, 1853,0307.669

3. Owen Jones (d. 1874), Interior of the *madrasa* and Friday mosque of Sultan Hasan

c. 1832–74
Pencil on paper
Height 28.4 cm, width 19.8 cm
1939,0627.7

Mamluks and Nasrids

Two contemporary ruling dynasties in different parts of the Muslim world were to have a profound impact on patronage and the arts: the Mamluks, who ruled Egypt and Syria (1250–1517), and the Nasrids of Granada (1232–1492).

The Mamluks were a military aristocracy made up of young slaves (*mamluk* means 'property') who had been bought on the steppe north of the Black Sea and transported to Egypt and Syria initially by the Ayyubid sultans. Falling into two groups, the Bahri Mamluks (1250–1382) were named after the barracks on the island of Rawda in the Nile (*bahr* meaning 'of the river'), and were ethnically primarily Qipchaqs from the territories of present-day Ukraine. The Burji Mamluks (1382–1517) gained their name from the citadel (*burj*) where they were quartered, and were mainly Circassians from the Caucasus. Ruling from their capital Cairo, in which they built magnificent architecture (**3**; and p. 10), the Mamluks established a formidable empire, their overlordship extending to the Hijaz in present-day Saudi Arabia, where they oversaw the holy cities of Mecca and Medina. They also instituted the tradition of the *mahmal*, the ceremonial palanquin that headed the yearly caravan from Cairo to Mecca for the *hajj* pilgrimage (**1**).

A distinctive feature of Mamluk arts is the regular presence of heraldic emblems, a reflection of the complex and hierarchical structure of the Mamluk state. Medieval chroniclers note the use of emblems in the preceeding Ayyubid period including the fleur-de-lys and a double-headed eagle, which were to inform the style of the emblems used by the Mamluks. Heraldic emblems were also used in Europe and, while the traditional view has been that the Muslim rulers adopted the practice from the West, it is far more likely, as demonstrated by recent scholarship, that heraldry developed in Western Europe following the Second Crusade (1145–49), in response to what the Crusaders saw in the Middle East. Emblems such as those mentioned above, along with others including insignia on the banners of the Saljuqs of Rum, who the Crusader armies first encountered when they arrived in the region, would have been clearly visible on a range of objects. In addition, there are words used to describe French heraldry such as *guelles*, which is derived from the Turkic and Persian word *gul* meaning 'flower' or 'rose'.

In the Islamic world, it was under the Mamluks that the system of heraldic emblems (known as *rang* from the Persian for 'colour') was fully developed. While some emblems were directly associated with particular people – the sultan Baybars (r. 1260–77) used a representation of a lion, for example – others denoted a particular position at court. Thus, a cup symbol indicated the role of cup-bearer (*saqi*), a penbox the secretary (*dawadar*), and a napkin the master of the robes (*jamdar*), while the sword signified the role of sword-bearer (*silah-dar*) (see pp. 127, 131–32).

The Nasrids were the last Muslims to rule Spain. In 1232, Muhammad I established a sultanate in the province of Granada, turning its citadel the 'Red (*al-hamra*) Fortress' into a remarkable palace, the Alhambra, that still survives today (**2**). Surrounded by Christian Spain, the Nasrids not only managed to maintain their power but also created an unparalleled centre of culture to which flocked scholars and poets from all over the Muslim world. Ibn Khaldun (1332–1406), whose study of world history, the *Muqaddima*, is still widely read, served as ambassador to the Nasrids.

After two centuries of rule, the union of Aragon and Castile was to seal the fate of the Nasrids and, in 1492, the last of the sultans, Muhammad XII (Abu Abdallah, known in the west as Boabdil), fled to exile to Morocco, as did the majority of his Muslim and Jewish subjects. (VP/WG)

3 | 19 Enamelled glass

Enamelling on glass is one of the major achievements of the glassmakers of Syria and Egypt during the 13th and 14th centuries (**1, 2**). Made under the patronage of the Ayyubid and Mamluk sultans, these objects were highly prized and made not only for local patrons but also widely exported to Europe, influencing the manufacture of glass in Italy. Vessels were shaped by the glassmaker before the enamelled colours or gilding was applied. The colours were made from opaque coloured glass or gold reduced to a powder and mixed with an oily medium such as gum arabic. Among the most complex items to make were the mosque lamps that were used to light the interiors of the mosques and shrines of Cairo and Damascus (**2**). (VP)

1. Enamelled glass flask
A complex combination of iconographies forms the decoration of this glass flask. The sides are flanked by men with halos on horseback. These are unmistakably Christian warrior saints, their garments and headdress in Crusader style, particularly the kettle-helmet of one of the figures. Below them, however, are roundels that include a seated female harpist flanked by a beaker of red wine and a platter of fruit. Intricate vegetal ornament is another feature, with human and animal heads emerging out of the ends of the scrolls (see p. 25).

c. 1275–1300
Syria or Egypt
Gilded and enamelled glass
Height 22.5 cm, diameter
21.3 cm (max)
Bequeathed by Felix Slade,
1869,0120.3

2. Pair of mosque lamps

These lamps bear the name of an amir, Sayf al-Din Tuquzdamur. He was governor of Hama in Syria and Amir of the Assembly (*amir al-majlis*) for the Mamluk sultan al-Nasir Muhammad ibn Qalawun (r. 1293–1341). The inscription at the mouth of the lamp is the 'Light verse' from the Qur'an (24:35):

God is the light of the heavens and the earth; the likeness of His light is as a niche wherein is a lamp (the lamp in a glass, the glass as it were a glittering star).

Two symbols, a cup and an eagle, are enclosed within a pointed, European-style shield: the cup indicates Tuquzdamur's position of cup-bearer (*saqi*), while the eagle is his personal emblem. The lamps would have been suspended with chains inside a mosque or shrine (see ill. 3 on p. 124); a narrow tube inside the base contained oil and a floating wick.

c. 1330–45
Egypt or Syria
Gilded and enamelled glass
Height 33 cm, diameter 25 cm (max)
Bequeathed by Felix Slade, 1869,0624.1–2

3 | 20 Mamluk metalwork

The tradition of metal inlay, which had its origins in 12th-century Herat (see pp. 94–97), and continued in Mosul (pp. 120–21), flourished in Syria and Egypt during the 13th and 14th centuries (**1–5**), as well as in Iran during the Ilkhanid era (pp. 142–43). Designs from the late 13th century include Chinese lotuses (**2**) and flying cranes, a sign of the influence of the Mongols on all the arts of this period. Metal vessels in a variety of shapes were made for the local market but were also much in demand in Europe, with pieces made specially for Italian patrons (**5**). (VP)

1. Incense burner

This spherical incense burner was made for an important Mamluk amir, Badr al-Din Baysari, who served two Mamluk sultans during the mid-13th century. His emblem, a double-headed eagle, along with the inscription bearing his name and titles, are prominently placed around the object. Coal and incense would have been placed in a container held by gimbals, the smoke from which poured out from the perforated surface.

c. 1270
Cairo
Brass inlaid with silver
Diameter 18.4 cm
Bequeathed by John Henderson, 1878,1230.682

2. Basin

This magnificent basin was made for one of the most significant patrons of the period, the Mamluk sultan al-Nasir Muhammad ibn Qalawun (r. 1293–1341, with interruptions). Known to have commissioned a large number of objects, he is also associated with an extensive building programme in Cairo and elsewhere. The imposing Arabic inscription on the basin, which gives his name and titles, lies against a background of Chinese lotuses. The basin also bears his epigraphic emblem 'Glory to our lord the sultan Nasir al-Din'. This style of emblem was initiated by him and used by subsequent sultans.

c. 1330
Cairo or Damascus
Brass, inlaid with silver and gold
Height 22.7 cm, diameter 54 cm
1851,0104.1

3. Jug

The bold Arabic inscriptions on this jug, extolling the virtues of an unnamed sultan, are in a striking style of script in which the letters terminate in the shape of flames. Another feature of the decoration is the roundel at the base of the handle, filled with a dense design of flying cranes.

1250–1300
Damascus or Cairo
Brass inlaid with silver and gold
Height 28.5 cm
1887,0612.1

4. Lunch box

This box, now missing the metal shafts that would have held it together, consists of a series of separate containers. Bands of dense geometric ornament, typical of the later Mamluk period, are juxtaposed with a repeated inscription:

He who contemplates my beauty will find me a delight to the eye, I have a form which includes all the essence of good.

15th century
Damascus
Brass, engraved
Height 18.4 cm
1908,0328.2

5. Candlestick

This candlestick bears an Italian coat of arms possibly associated with the Venetian family Boldù; the emblem may have been added in Europe. Around the body are scenes of animal combat.

c. 1400
Damascus
Cast brass, inlaid with silver and gold
Height 12.4 cm
Bequeathed by John Henderson,
1878,1230.721

3 | 21 Mamluk pottery

An extensive ceramic industry in Egypt and Syria during the Mamluk period produced a wide range of vessels and tiles. The main centres of production were at Fustat (Old Cairo) and Damascus. From Fustat were recovered quantities of sherds of pottery that were made locally as well as blue-and-white porcelain and celadons imported from China. Both these imports were to have an impact on the local potters, and Mamluk wares often exhibit exuberant hybrid styles in which Chinese floral elements combine with local motifs (**1**). Very different in style are the utilitarian earthenware vessels made in Cairo, which are characterized by the use of emblems associated with the roles of functionaries (**3**). Blue-and-white tiles were used to decorate secular and religious buildings, and a group still *in situ* in the tomb of the Mamluk dignitary Ghars al-Din Khalil al-Tawrizi in Damascus, dateable to about 1420, is signed by a potter calling himself Ghaibi and with the same *nisba*, 'al-Tawrizi'. This points to a connection with Tabriz in Iran, and also provides a framework for the dating of similar tiles removed from their context (**2**). (VP)

1. Mamluk *albarello*

Jars such as this one were exported to Europe, filled with medicinal herbs and spices that were used by apothecaries. The shape took hold in Italy where it was made in majolica and called *albarello*. The designs on the jar skilfully combine Chinese and local elements: the lotus petals on the shoulder as well as the scrolls in blue derive directly from Chinese porcelain, complementing the black plants between, which are either papyrus flowers or water weeds.

c. 1430
Egypt or Syria
Stonepaste, painted in blue and black under a transparent glaze
Height 32 cm
1987,1119.1

2. Peacock tile

Tiles found in 15th-century buildings in Syria and Egypt exhibit the same hybrid style of decoration found on vessels. Here a peacock is surrounded by Chinese-style floral sprigs.

c. 1430
Egypt or Syria
Stonepaste, painted in blue and black under a transparent glaze
Height 26.1 cm
1905,1128.1

3. Sgraffito bowl

Associated with the potteries of Fustat (Old Cairo) under the Mamluks, this style of pottery is principally painted in greens and browns and with sgraffito (scratched) designs, and often includes inscriptions as well as emblems within the decorative scheme. The Arabic inscription here repeats the phrase 'the one favourable to God' (*al-muwaffaq billah*) while the lozenge shape represents the office of the master of the robes (*jamdar*).

14th–15th century
Egypt
Earthenware, white slip with incised decoration in brown and green under a transparent glaze
Height 12.5 cm, diameter 23.5 cm
Donated by M. Stora,
1908,0722.1

3 | 22 Mamluk textiles

Politics, the environment and the new Mamluk rulers' tastes had a direct impact on the production and trade of fibre and cloth, resulting in a notable change in direction for Egyptian textile history. Several poor Nile floods and excessive taxation on linen explain the decline of its growth and use in the textile industry from the 13th century onwards, in favour of silk and cotton. After 1250, *tiraz* production progressively decreased until 1341, when the private royal workshops officially closed. The courtly device most associated with the new regime then became the blazon (**1**).

Clothing habits and fashion also faced changes. Dress – in terms of both material and colour – became an important sign of social rank and faith. In keeping with their predecessors and former masters, the Ayyubids, the Mamluks took on yellow as their dynastic colour, while green was worn by the Prophet Muhammad's descendants and blue by Jews and Christians. First appearing under the Fatimids, shirts and tunics made of several pieces of fabric cut and sewn together were the most common item of clothing for men, women and children at this time. These boasted stripes of different hues and geometric designs, the fashion of the period (**2, 3**). Embroidery became the main technique used to produce the patterns characteristic of Mamluk iconography as it was ideally suited to create regular, symmetrical and well-balanced designs (**4**). When ordering garments as well as large-scale furnishing cloth, customers could choose patterns, fibres and stitches from samples of work at large bazaars in Egyptian textile production centres. (AM)

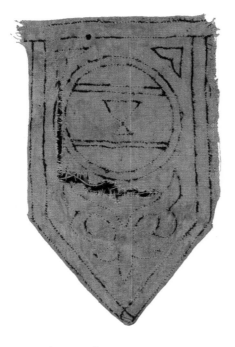

1. Textile pennant

This plain cotton pennant bears a black embroidered linen design of the blazon of a cup-bearer (*saqi*): a stemmed cup set within a circle surrounded by palmette motifs. The surface was flax-glazed to give a shiny and smooth appearance to the textile, a preparation characteristic of the most precious fabrics produced under the Fatimids and Mamluks in Egypt. Such banners were sewn as insignia onto the tents of Mamluk emirs, or military commanders.

c. 14th–15th century
Cairo or Fustat, Egypt
Linen, cotton and wax
Height 21 cm, width 10 cm
1979,0704.1

2. Sleeve end

This sleeve, decorated with multicoloured stripes, represents the new Mamluk fashion. Such patterns and fibres were particularly favoured at court, and are often found on honorific garments. The sleeve probably belonged to a young adult's tunic similar in style to the *gallabiyya*, still worn today in Egypt.

c. 14th–16th century
Egypt
Cotton and silk
Height 14.5 cm, width 22.5 cm
Donated by Maj. William Joseph Myers, 1901,0314.42

3. Detail of a carved frame (part of a book cover)

Carrying a ewer and a napkin, this servant wears an outfit representative of Mamluk fashion. His tunic is embellished with geometric and stylized vegetal motifs, probably embroidered or made of silk-woven patterns. His boots bear a blazon in the shape of a napkin, the insignia of his duties as master of the robes (*jamdar*) at court.

c. 1340–70
Cairo, Egypt
Elephant ivory (one of a pair)
Length 17.5 cm, width 3 cm
Donated by Sir Augustus Wollaston Franks, 1874,0302.7

4. Fragmentary panel

The geometric design on this fabric panel is characteristic of Mamluk textile production. Embroidered in dark blue cotton on a linen plain weave, the main pattern is of repeating zigzags with small flowers at points, while the border consists of lozenges and an angular interlaced pattern. Such panels were often found on bodies buried in Mamluk cemeteries and probably come from garments such as sashes or turbans, as their shape suggests.

c. 13th–14th century
Fustat, Egypt
Linen and cotton
Length 23 cm, width 12 cm
Donated by Maj. William Joseph Myers, 1901,0314.8

3 | 23 Nasrid Granada

Arabs and Berbers from North Africa brought Islam to al-Andalus (modern Spain and Portugal) in 711. Until the fall of the Nasrids in 1492, al-Andalus witnessed a flourishing of culture and civilization that influenced both the Islamic world and Europe. The Nasrid rulers were responsible from 1232 for the construction of the Alhambra in Granada, one of the best-known examples of Islamic architecture in the world (see p. 113). The palace buildings were adorned with both objects (**1**) and architectural elements (**2**) to demonstrate the power and wealth of the Nasrids, even as the dynasty fought to hold on in the face of attacks from the increasingly confident and aggressive Christian rulers to the north. However, the skill of Granadine craftsmen was such that it could be appreciated across the religious divide, even beyond Spain itself (**3**). (WG)

1. Spanish *albarello*

The *albarello*, associated with the storage of pharmaceutical products, is known from earlier Iraqi, Syrian and Egyptian examples. They were also widely produced by the potters of southern Spain, many of whom were Muslims living under Christian control, known as *mudejars* (from the Arabic *mudajjan*, meaning 'tamed'). The inscription in Arabic around this vessel's neck clearly links it to a Muslim cultural context, and it is believed to have been among the possessions of the Nasrid rulers of Granada.

14th century
Manises or Granada, Spain
Earthenware, painted in lustre and blue on an opaque white glaze
Height 29.5 cm, diameter 9.5 cm
Bequeathed by Miss Edith Godman, G.585

2. Alhambra tile

This tile was acquired from the Alhambra by a traveller there in 1791. Inside the central shield-shaped device is the motto of the Nasrid rulers – *wa la ghalib ila Allah* ('there is no victor but God'). This phrase can be found on a variety of objects made under Nasrid rule, ranging from architectural decorations to coins and arms.

Late 14th century
Malaga or Granada, Spain
Earthenware, painted over and incised in an opaque white glaze
Height 19 cm, width 19 cm
Donated by the Hon. Mrs Anne Seymour Damer, 1802,0508.1.a

3. Horse bridle

The only survival of its type from al-Andalus, this bridle is a luxury item that would have adorned the horse of a person of high rank. Enamelled arms and armour of similar design were produced in Granada, the last Muslim kingdom in the Iberian Peninsula, during the 15th century and are associated with the last ruler, Muhammad XII (Abu Abdallah, known as Boabdil in European sources; r. 1482–92). There is little doubt that this bridle and similar pieces were made in the royal workshops, although they were owned by both Muslim and Christian patrons. The designs relate very closely to those found on Granadine architecture of the period, including that of the Alhambra. A remarkably similar horse bridle appears in a painting by Vincenzo Catena, demonstrating the high value given to Islamic objects by Renaissance Europeans.

15th century
Granada, Spain
Copper-gilt and enamel on leather
Length 38 cm, width 21 cm
Donated by Sir Augustus Wollaston Franks, 1890,1004.1

1. Stone inscribed with the name of Jalal al-Din Khwarazmshah

This large stone is decorated with a foliated *mihrab* arch and columns and bears the name of Sultan Jalal al-Din Mangubirti Khwarazmshah (r. 1220–31), the last major ruler of Khwarazm and son of Ala al-Din Muhammad (r. 1200–20), the ruler credited with provoking Chinggis Khan's invasion of Khwarazm in 1219.

Dated AD 1230–31 (AH 628)
Nishapur, Iran
Stone, carved and engraved
Height 50 cm, width 29 cm,
thickness 32 cm, weight 35 kg
1990,0612.1

2. Ilkhanid manuscript page

In the illustration to this page from the *Shahnama* ('Book of Kings') of the poet Abu'l Qasim Firdawsi (d. 1020), the Iranian prince Isfandiyar has been battling the Turanians (Turks) with his father. Wounded by the Turanian Gurgsar, Isfandiyar still manages to lasso his opponent. The manuscript belongs to the

earliest group of *Shahnama*s attributed to the Ilkhanid period.

c. 1300
Possibly Baghdad, Iraq
Ink, opaque watercolour and gold on paper
Height 17 cm, width 13.4 cm
Bequeathed by Sir Bernard Eckstein, Bart, 1948,1211,0.22

3. Star tile

Probably from the Madrasa al-Ghiyathiyya, this tile is decorated in the *cuerda seca* ('dry-cord') technique, developed before the 14th century, where manganese is used to keep colours from running into each other during the firing process.

c. 1442–46
Madrasa al-Ghiyathiyya, Khargird, Iran
Stonepaste, painted in polychrome glazes with manganese and leaf gilding
Diameter 39.5 cm
Bequeathed by Miss Edith Godman, G.486

Iran and Central Asia: the Mongol legacy

The Mongol invasions of the 13th century changed the course of history in the pre-modern world. The clans of the Eurasian steppe swept west across Central Asia and the Middle East as well as the Caucasus and Russia. They also moved east into China, eventually building what would become the largest continuous land empire ever known. Their brutal campaigns, initiated as retribution for a thwarted mission sent by the Mongols to the Khwarazmian governor of Utrar (in modern Kazakhstan) in 1217 (**1**), were first led by the empire's founder and Great Khan, Chinggis (or Genghis; r. 1206–27). Chinggis's successors continued his campaigns after his death in 1227, leading in 1258 to the sack of Baghdad, seat of the Abbasid caliphate, and the execution of the last actively ruling caliph.

In spite of the unspeakable devastation they inflicted upon humanity during their conquests, the Mongols spared the lives of artisans, whose skills and expertise could be consolidated and exploited in new centres of Mongol authority. In addition, Mongol rulers increasingly found the need to adapt their nomadic lifestyle to that of the sedentary civilizations they conquered, the largest of these being China and Iran.

The close relationship between Iran and China during the Mongol period and the cultural transmission this enabled contributed to a sea change in the arts of the Ilkhanate, the name for Mongol Iran and Central Asia. A Chinese-inspired aesthetic appeared in Ilkhanid visual culture from its early days, including textiles, manuscript illustration and illumination, ceramics, metalwork and woodwork, and reaching a monumental scale in architectural decoration. Along with other Ilkhanid socio-political and cultural legacies, this idiom would continue long after the dynasty's demise, eventually becoming a standardized part of the Persianate visual repertoire and rising to great heights under

the leadership of another nomadic warlord of Turko-Mongolian origins. Timur (known in the West as Tamerlane, a corruption of Timur-i lang, or 'Timur the lame') was born in 1336 near Samarqand to the Barlas Turkic tribe, which had converted to Islam after the Mongol invasions. Forging a connection to Chinggis Khan through marriage to a Chinggisid princess, Timur founded the Timurid dynasty and mercilessly pursued the domains once gained by his Mongol predecessors. Like them, he spared the lives of skilled artists and craftsmen, relocating them to Samarqand and Herat.

Timur expanded his empire from Central Asia into Iran, Iraq, Syria, eastern Turkey, and parts of southern Russia and India, but died in 1405 while on campaign in China. His successors, particularly those who came after his son Shahrukh (r. 1405–47), lacked military prowess, leading to a fragmentary empire of principalities until the dynasty's eventual demise in 1507, as other neighbouring powers closed in. In the west, the Qaraqoyunlu ('Black Sheep') and then the Aqqoyunlu ('White Sheep') Turkmen took the city of Tabriz in northwest Iran, while to the east, the Uzbek Shaybanids gained power over the Timurids and became a challenge to Safavid rule. Capturing Herat, the Uzbeks forced the last Timurid prince, Babur, to flee his principalities of Ferghana and Kabul (he eventually became the founder of his own dynasty in India).

Persianate culture flourished under the Timurids, who established an extensive cultural programme combining Iranian, Islamic and their own Central Asian steppe traditions into architecture, the arts of the book and other portable arts. While the empire only lasted a hundred years, the sophistication achieved in the arts created a legacy that would inspire the work of later artists in Iran, Central Asia, India and the Ottoman lands under Safavid, Uzbek, Mughal and Ottoman rulers, respectively. (LA)

3 | 24 Ilkhanid lustre tiles

Lustre quality and production experienced a great decline in Iran during the 1220s, but picked up again in the 1260s. In the Ilkhanid period, both lustre and glazed tiles widely embellished the facades and interiors of religious and secular buildings (**1–3**), although only one example of secular architecture survives. Known as Takht-i Sulayman (Persian for 'Throne of Solomon'), this was a seasonal palace and Mongol camp built upon the ruins of a Sasanian site with a Zoroastrian fire temple between 1270 and 1275 by the Ilkhanid ruler Abaqa Khan (r. 1265–82). German excavations in 1959 and 1978 revealed several stonepaste tile fragments of different sizes and shapes and exhibiting a variety of decorative techniques. Among these, a group of lustre frieze tiles played a significant part of the interior decorative programme, with inscriptions and images of scenes from the *Shahnama* ('Book of Kings') (**1**). This visual and textual reference to the ancient kings of Iran, combined with the palace's location over an ancient Iranian site, may have been part of a dynastic strategy to weave the Ilkhanids into Iran's history.

In the religious sphere, the conversion of the Ilkhanids to Islam in 1295 led to the patronage of numerous mosques, while its tolerance and support of Shi'ism and Sufism became manifested visually in the building of several funerary complexes and shrines with elaborate decorative programmes also featuring lustre (**3**). That lustre production continued well into the Ilkhanid period is evidenced by a handful of tiles dating to the 1330s and naming Kashan as their place of production, each albeit with the inclusion of an ominous prayer inscribed in Arabic, asking for God to 'protect it from the accidents of time.' (LA)

This page, left
1. Frieze tile inscribed with verses from the *Shahnama*
This tile belongs to a larger group associated with Takht-i Sulayman, and was probably once part of an extended frieze situated above groups of smaller tiles. Some are dated in the AH 670s (AD 1270s) and many include verses from the *Shahnama*. The inscription here refers to a passage describing autumn from the book of Bahram Gur. Tile moulds and kiln finds at Takht-i Sulayman suggest that some of the tiles found there must have been produced on site.

c. 1270s
Iran, possibly Kashan or Takht-i Sulayman
Stonepaste, with moulded decoration, painted in blue, turquoise and lustre over an opaque white glaze
Height 29.7 cm, width 30.3 cm
Bequeathed by John Henderson, 1878,1230.573.2

Opposite, right

2. Star tile with seated figure and attendant

This eight-pointed tile, repaired in three small areas with other contemporary fragments, depicts a Mongol scene of epicurean pleasure, with a seated figure enjoying fruit from a bowl on a tripod as an attendant pours him wine. The inscription includes Persian verses by three different poets. The main verses come from Sana'i-yi Qaznavi (1080–1131) and Ibn Yamin Fariyumadi (1290–1374), while one of the 'fills' contains part of the *Shahnama* story of Giv going to Turan in search of Kay Khusraw.

Dated AD 1338/9 (AH 739)
Kashan, Iran
Stonepaste, moulded and painted in blue, turquoise and lustre over an opaque white glaze
Height 21.2 cm, width 21.6 cm, thickness 1.6 cm
OA+.1123

3. Tiles from a cenotaph in the form of a *mihrab*

Made in the shape of a *mihrab*, or prayer niche and missing its lowermost tile, this tile panel marked the tombstone of a *qadi*, or Islamic judge, named Jalal al-din Abd al-Malik. Its central inscriptions in Arabic describe the judge as a *malik al-ulama* ('king of learned men') and provide a genealogy of judges crossing seven generations. The celebrated *ayat al-kursi*, or 'throne verse' (Qur'an 2:255), adorns the outer frame.

1300–50
Iran, probably Kashan
Stonepaste, with moulded decoration, painted in lustre, blue and turquoise over an opaque white glaze
Height 131 cm
Bequeathed by Miss Edith Godman, G.499

3 | 25 An Ilkhanid aesthetic

As in the case of tiles, there was a continuing taste for portable lustre-painted objects in the Ilkhanid period. These often featured verses of poetry in Persian, the language of the court, testifying to the value of literature as a courtly art (1). Members of the Ilkhanid court would have been accustomed to living in and frequenting luxurious buildings and camps with lavishly decorated interiors, and they would have dressed in the finest robes and enjoyed access to functional objects of the highest quality.

One of the most distinctive elements of Ilkhanid visual culture is a Chinese- or East Asia-inspired idiom known as *khata'i* (Persian for 'of Cathay', a term referring specifically to north China but also referencing the abstract 'Far East'), which comprises Chinese motifs such as cloud bands, lotuses, peonies, phoenixes or dragons, and East Asian artistic techniques and forms. Two important developments in ceramic production that often featured *khata'i* are *lajvardina* and Sultanabad wares, the latter named after the region in Iran with which it was traditionally associated. The *lajvardina* technique is considered the successor to the *haft rangi* or *mina'i* under- and overglaze painting of the 12th and 13th centuries (see pp. 102–5). But the *lajvardina* ceramics of the Ilkhanid period depart from the earlier wares mainly through the use of an overall background of deep blue or turquoise glaze, extensive gold over-painting, and the preference for geometric, epigraphic and *khata'i* designs (2). Sultanabad wares require a single firing and comprise a heavier body, often covered with a grey slip on which Chinese motifs are painted in heavily outlined forms (3). They may also contain designs or illustrations in black under a turquoise glaze. (LA)

1. Bottle inscribed with Persian poetry

As with the appearance of text from the Iranian national epic on the tiles of the Ilkhanid palace of Takht-i Sulayman, verses of Persian poetry inscribed onto this bottle suggest a visual connection between the nomadic Mongols and the settled community they inhabited:

I am wandering in the desert separated from my love. I write these words on this flask that they may be a remembrance of me. In the year of the hijra 669. Trusting that she, of whom I dream ever more, may refresh herself by putting this pitcher to her lip, that she will know my writing and think of me and take on my love.

Dated AD 1270/1 (AH 669)
Iran, probably Kashan
Stonepaste, painted in lustre over an opaque white glaze
Height 12.3 cm, diameter 9 cm (rim), diameter 18 cm (max)
Bequeathed by Miss Edith Godman, G.242

2. *Lajvardina* bottle fragment

Despite the damage, this fragment of a bottle is one of the finest examples of the *lajvardina* decorative technique, unique to ceramics of the Ilkhanid period. *Lajvardina* refers to a rare type of deep-blue glaze reminiscent of *lajvard*, Persian for lapis lazuli. After an initial firing in this blue glaze, potters would paint elaborate decorative patterns with enamel-like colour and gold leaf onto the glazed surface before a second firing.

Late 13th–early 14th century
Iran
Lajvardina ware; stonepaste, painted in red and white with gold leaf on a cobalt blue glaze
Width 20 cm
Donated by Frederick Du Cane Godman, 1891,0625.84

3. Bowl with phoenixes in flight

Known as *simurgh*s in Persian, phoenixes flying in a circular motion in groups of two, three or four comprise one of the most common subjects on Sultanabad bowls. Shown among dense foliage with lotuses or peonies, their overall composition recalls Chinese lacquer wares and textiles with the same subject matter produced under the Yuan (1271–1368) or preceding Song (960–1279) dynasties.

14th century
Iran
Sultanabad ware; stonepaste, painted in grey-green slip, white slip and black under a transparent glaze
Height 9.5 cm, rim diameter 18.6 cm, base diameter 7.5 cm
Bequeathed by Miss Edith Godman, G.280

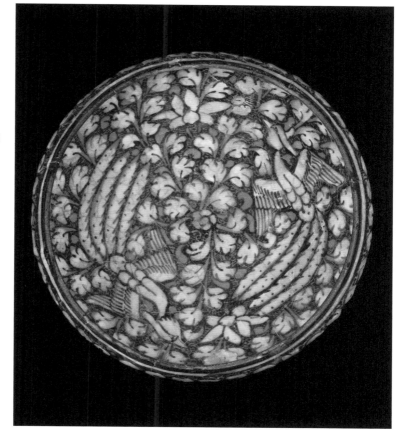

3 | 26 Local patronage under the Ilkhanids

In spite of the havoc wreaked by the Mongol invasions, metalwork production continued to thrive, whether in previously well-known centres such as Mosul, Shiraz or Herat, or through the movement of craftsmen from these areas to one of the Ilkhanid capitals, such as Tabriz in northwestern Iran (1). Similarly to ceramics, Ilkhanid metalwork incorporated and synthesized aspects of local settled traditions with a Chinese-inspired idiom coming from the Mongol connection to China. Alongside brilliant lustre-painted objects and interiors and *lajvardina* ceramic wares, members of the court and their guests would have seen and used bronze or brass objects skilfully inlaid in silver and/or gold, from storage jars and wash basins to serving trays, wine bottles and footed bowls (1–4). Inscriptions including blessings or dedications to the owner often appeared on these lavish and costly courtly objects (1, 3), which sometimes also carried dates and the signatures of their makers, and Persian poetry referring to the object's function increasingly began to accompany or even supplant the Arabic good wishes (4). (LA)

1. Tray inscribed with good wishes to the owner
The craftsmanship and iconography on this tray, such as the seated figures in lobed medallions holding crescent moons, recalls the style prevalent in Mosul before the Mongols conquered it in 1261. The tray, which in the centre depicts an enthroned ruler, might have been made by Mosul craftsmen moved by the Ilkhanids to Tabriz. The eastward transmission of the 'Mosul style' to Iran is supported by two inlaid brass vessels signed by a Mosul craftsman found in a hoard near Hamadan, one dated 1274.

Late 13th century
Northwestern Iran
Brass, inlaid with silver and gold
Height 5 cm, diameter 46.3 cm
Bequeathed by John Henderson, 1878,1230.706

2. Pen box

This magnificent pen box once held an inkwell and stored writing implements. An interlacing design terminating in animal heads adorns the exterior and complements roundels containing astrological and courtly figures, including musicians and dancers. Its exquisite craftsmanship reflects both western and eastern Iranian metalwork traditions and makes this object one of the finest examples of inlaid metalwork produced in Iran. The signature of the maker, Mahmud ibn Sunqur, and the date of manufacture, both hidden under the clasp, testify to the high status of calligraphers in the Islamic world.

Dated AD 1281/2 (AH 680)
Iran
Brass, inlaid with silver and gold
Height 3.1 cm, length 19.7 cm,
width 5.2 cm
1891,0623.5

3. Bowl

The southern province of Fars (and probably Shiraz, in particular) housed an important centre of metalwork production in the 14th and 15th centuries, when the region was ruled locally by the Injuid and then Muzaffarid dynasties. Fars metalwork features bold Arabic inscriptions exalting an unnamed ruler, with titles interspersed with courtly scenes reminiscent of ones in local illustrated manuscripts. This bowl's shape and inscription recall contemporary Mamluk bowls. The inscription reads:

Glory to our Lord, the most exalted, the most just, the most learned sultan, king that curbs nations, master of the sultans of the Arabs and the non-Arabs.

Mid-14th century
Shiraz, Iran
Brass, inlaid with silver
Height 11 cm, diameter 24 cm
Donated by Friends of the British Museum, 1901,0606.3

4. Footed bowl

This elaborately decorated inlaid footed cup belongs to a group of high-tin bronze inlaid stemmed cups from a local but still unidentified school of metalwork in 14th-century Iran. It synthesizes medieval metalworking traditions, such as good wishes inscribed in Arabic to an unnamed owner and the depiction of figures enjoying feasting and other courtly activities, with a Chinese-inspired floral background of lotus and peony blossoms. There is also a post-Mongol addition of Persian poetry (here under the rim) referencing the object's function, and with an esoteric layer of meaning:

O sweet beverage of our pleasures / O transparent Fount of Mirth / If Alexander had not seen you / O world-revealing bowl of Mani's / How could his mind have conceived / The notion of the Fount of Life.

1300–50
Iran
High-tin bronze, inlaid with silver and gold
Height 13 cm, diameter 14 cm
1891,0623.4

3 | 27 Timurid princely patronage

If you have doubts about our grandeur, look at our edifice. Abd al-Razzaq Samarqandi (1413–82)

Timur's wealth allowed him to initiate a major building programme that both expressed and reinforced his power. After his death in 1405, architectural patronage continued, albeit on a smaller scale. Based in Herat, Timur's son and successor Shahrukh focused on strengthening or rebuilding the capital's existing structures, such as the bazaar, citadel and city walls, while his wife Gawharshad (1378–1457) continued a tradition of female patronage in her commission of a religious complex just outside Herat in 1417 (**1**). A decentralization of funds under Shahrukh enabled more princes and members of the elite to become patrons during and after his reign. This led to a greater focus on patronage of the portable arts, which could express equal brilliance and craftsmanship but at lower (if still immense) expense.

Following the courtly traditions of Persian culture, great emphasis was placed on the education of princes, who were taught at court about proper statecraft, religion, philosophy, astronomy, astrology and literature. As with preceding rulers of the region, Persian was the primary language of the court and the elite, and the preferred medium for historical texts as well as for literary prose and poetry. Timurid princes such as Ulugh Beg (1394–1449) (**2**), Baysunghur (1397–1433) and Sultan Husayn (1438–1506) (**4**) became notable patrons in their principalities of Samarqand and Herat, and were known for their own skills in disciplines like astronomy, poetry and calligraphy. Contemporaries describe court banquets where guests enjoyed musical performances, poetry recitals, and literary discussions and competitions while feasting on food and wine served on and in lavish dishes (**3**). (LA)

1. Fragmentary 12-pointed star tile (in two parts)
This tile is part of a group collected by the Hon. Colonel E. Yate (who served on the Afghan Boundary Commission from 1884–86) from the minarets of the *musalla* (prayer hall) of Gawharshad (wife of Shahrukh), after they had been pulled down in 1885. Inscriptions on the surviving minaret identify the celebrated architect Qivam al-Din Shirazi (d. 1438) and the structure's date of completion (AH 841 or AD 1437/8). Gawharshad was buried there in 1457.

c. 1432
Musalla of Gawharshad, Herat, Afghanistan
Stonepaste, painted in white, green, manganese-brown and turquoise glaze
Height 15 cm, width 18 cm, thickness 1 cm; height 21 cm, width 15.5 cm, thickness 1 cm
1907,1011.1, 1907,1011.2

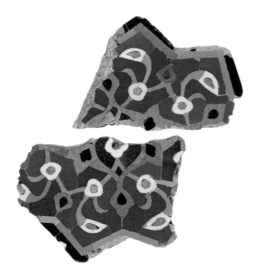

3. Dish with ibex among foliage

Timurid blue-and-white ceramic wares like this dish are indicative of a Chinese-inspired aesthetic that was increasingly becoming standard in the Persianate visual repertoire, even though Iranian potters never matched the quality of Chinese porcelain with stonepaste. Individual features, such as the scalloped waves along the rim, the scrolling peonies, and the Chinese cloud bands in the centre of the dish, have been adapted from Chinese prototypes probably of the Xuande style, while the ibex draws from local subjects.

c. 1450–75
Iran
Stonepaste, painted in blue on an opaque white glaze
Height 10 cm, diameter 42.6 cm
1982,0805.1

2. Cup with dragon handle

While this jade cup does not reflect the finest craftsmanship, it carries importance because of its association with the Timurid prince 'Ulugh Beg Küragan' (Ulugh Beg, Son-in-Law), once governor of Samarqand. Jade held significant value as a talisman in post-Mongol Iran and Central Asia, where the material could also be sourced. With its distinctive chi (Chinese hornless dragon) handle, the cup also betrays Chinese inspiration and may have imitated a Chinese original. A second inscription on the silver repair extols God's generosity in Ottoman Turkish and suggests the object was appreciated over centuries and across geographical borders.

c. 1420–49
Probably Central Asia
Nephrite jade, carved and inscribed, with later silver repair
Height 7.3 cm, width 19.5 cm, depth 12.4 cm
Brooke Sewell Permanent Fund, 1959,1120.1

4. Jug

This vessel, which once would have had a lid and been attached to a dragon-shaped handle, belongs to a large group of virtually identical globular vessels produced under the Timurids from the mid-to-late 15th century. Its inscription includes the titles of the Timurid prince Sultan Husayn, who ruled Herat from 1470–1506, and the jug is signed and dated at the base by Muhammad ibn Shamsi of Ghur, part of the Khurasan region near Herat.

Dated 11 April AD 1498 (middle of Sha'ban AH 903)
Afghanistan, probably Herat
Brass, cast and inlaid with silver and gold; metal chain attached
Height 13 cm, diameter 12.5 cm
1962,0718.1

1. *Albarello*

Part of the distinctive Ilkhanid Sultanabad group of slip-painted ceramic wares, this *albarello* is decorated in several registers, the widest of which feature lotuses, each enclosed within what may be a Buddhist-inspired teardrop-shaped frame. A transparent blue glaze gives the jar a deeper colour, in contrast to the more typical grey-green slip-painted wares. Sultanabad wares often display Chinese-inspired motifs, believed in many cases to have been transferred to the Iranian context through the medium of Chinese or Central Asian textiles.

14th century
Iran
Sultanabad ware; stonepaste, painted in grey-green and white slip under a transparent blue glaze
Height 33.3 cm, diameter 15 cm
1952,0214.5

2. Mosque lamp with lotus decoration

Outlined in red against a blue background, the large lotuses on this mosque lamp bear a resemblance to the Ilkhanid interpretation of the Chinese lotus on the Sultanabad *albarello*. One of the finest examples of the more uncommon Mamluk mosque lamps without inscriptions – most bear dates or the names of Mamluk sultans or emirs (see p. 127) – this lamp has been associated with the *madrasa* (religious college) of Sultan Hasan (r. 1347–51, 1354–61) in Cairo.

c. 1350–60
Egypt
Yellowish colourless glass, free blown, applied, and enamelled in red, blue and white; tooled on the pontil
Height 38.5 cm, diameter 25.5 cm (max)
Donated by Sir Augustus Wollaston Franks, 1881,0909.3

Opposite
3. Chinese and Iznik dishes with grapes

Chinese porcelain was traded widely from at least the 9th century, and by the 16th century a Chinese-inspired idiom was becoming increasingly standardized in the Islamic lands. Ming blue-and-white porcelains such as the dish illustrated here (left) were collected and held in high esteem at the Safavid and Ottoman courts. The motif of three grape bunches among vine leaves on this dish became one that inspired Iznik potters imitating porcelain in blue-and-white fritware in the 1530s and 1540s (right). Unlike its Chinese prototypes, however, the Ottoman piece includes turquoise decoration and lacks a scalloped rim.

1403–24
Jingdezhen, Jiangxi Province, China
Porcelain, painted in blue under a transparent glaze
Diameter 41 cm
Bequeathed by Mrs Walter Sedgwick, 1968,0422.27

c. 1530–40
Iznik, Turkey
Stonepaste, painted in blue and turquoise under a transparent glaze
Height 8.9 cm, diameter 41 cm
Donated by Mrs Essie Winifred Newberry, 1949,1115.10

Islam and China in the post-Mongol period

While evidence of contact between the Islamic lands and East Asia dates back to at least the 1st century BC, the early allegiance of the Ilkhanate in Iran and Central Asia to the Great Khanate, the centre of which moved from Mongolia to China under Qubilai Khan (r. 1260–94), laid the foundation for a significant relationship between China and Iran. This was rendered possible not only by the Mongol umbrella that now connected these regions and the area in between, but because – as a nomadic people – the Mongols still recognized the importance of trade with and between settled societies. Merchants, for instance, were protected by the *Pax Mongolica*, which ensured peaceful travel and trade along the so-called 'Silk Road' (actually composed of several routes bearing many products besides silk) linking China to the Middle East. The Mongols' religious tolerance also facilitated their assimilation into China and Iran and allowed skilled Muslims to hold important posts in both empires.

Some of the greatest evidence of cultural transmission between China and the Islamic world can be seen in the motifs and designs present in the visual repertoire of the two regions (which includes fantastical animals such as dragons and phoenixes, cranes, cloud bands and cloud collar motifs, and flowers such as lotuses and peonies); East Asian object forms and artistic techniques and materials, such as Chinese paper, celadon and blue-and-white porcelain wares, and light colour washes, are also evident in the Islamic sphere (**1–3**). The meanings linked to these motifs, forms and styles, however, often did not transfer from one context to the other. Similar imagery could exist simultaneously in several regions while signifying different things, or be filtered in its transmission across geographical boundaries.

This was not an entirely one-sided equation: trade goods made the journey from the Islamic lands to China, including Islamic metalwork and glass, some of which featured Chinese-inspired decoration (**4**). Notably, inspiration also travelled in two directions, as illustrated by a Ming blue-and-white porcelain tray stand found in Damascus

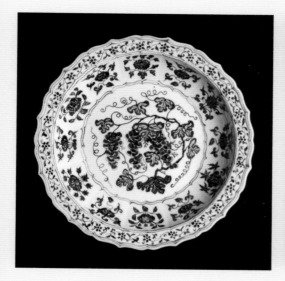

4. Footed bowl

This footed bowl is one of a number of Mamluk glass vessels that have been found in China, probably exported there soon after production. It was acquired in London by Julius Spier, who ran a trading company dealing with China. The inscription repeats the Arabic word *al-alim* ('the learned'). Large lotus flowers contained within roundels show the connection to East Asia pre-dated the bowl's journey to China.

Mid-13th century
Syria
Yellowish colourless glass, free blown, applied, enamelled in red, blue, green and white, and gilded; tooled on the pontil
Height 29.8 cm, width 20 cm, depth 21.5 cm
Donated by Constance Spier through The Art Fund (as NACF), 1924,0125.1

5. Chinese and Mamluk tray stands

Inspired by the form of Mamluk tray stands, such as this example inscribed with the names and titles of Sultan Muhammad ibn Qalawun (r. 1293–1341) (right), the potters of Jingdezhen reproduced the shape and decorative scheme in blue-and-white porcelain. Chinese porcelain was regularly exported to the Middle East. This porcelain tray stand (left) was found in Damascus.

1403–24
Jingdezhen, Jiangxi Province, China
Porcelain, painted in blue under a transparent glaze
Height 17.4 cm, width 18.4 cm, depth 17.2 cm
Funded by the Brooke Sewell Bequest, 1966,1215.1

c. 1320–41
Egypt or Syria
Brass with silver inlay
Height 23.7 cm, diameter 23.2 cm
1897,0510.1

**6. Haji Noor Deen
(Chinese, b. 1963), *Ya Rahim*
('O Merciful')**

In this contemporary scroll,
the Chinese calligrapher Haji
Noor Deen blends Chinese and
Islamic calligraphic traditions into
an original fusion, combining one
of the 99 Arabic names of God
(centre) with the work's date and
artist's seal (at left) in Chinese
characters. A renowned master
of Arabic calligraphy, Noor
Deen in 1997 became the first
Chinese Muslim to be awarded
the Egyptian Certificate of
Arabic Calligraphy.

2000
Black ink on paper, mounted
on cream silk
Height 230 cm, width 102 cm
Brooke Sewell Permanent Fund,
2005,0117,0.1

that copies the shape of a Mamluk one in inlaid
brass (**5**). Fragments of similar Ming tray stands
have been excavated at the Jingdezhen kiln sites
in Jiangxi Province in China, where high-quality
porcelain for the home and export markets has
been produced for several thousand years.

Moreover, among the non-Chinese merchants
and communities living in China under Mongol rule,
Muslim merchants comprised the largest group,
alongside Christians, Jews, Brahmins and
Manichaeans, settling in Quanzhou in Fujian
Province. A strong Muslim minority enjoyed power
at the Ming court in Beijing; many mosques were

built, and blue-and-white porcelains and bronzes
were inscribed in Arabic script with poetry or
Qur'anic text, written in a fluid style typical of
Chinese-Arabic.

Today, the work of the Chinese Muslim master
of Arabic calligraphy, Haji Noor Deen, showcases
the complementary nature of Chinese and Islamic
calligraphic traditions in a fusion of his own
design (**6**). (LA)

Timeline

1501–1722	Safavid dynasty; rule of Isma'il I (r. 1501–24); beginning of Safavid rule in Iran; declaration of Twelver Shi'ism as the state religion; Safavid capital at Tabriz
1514	Battle of Chaldiran; Ottoman victory over Safavids
1517	Egypt and Syria incorporated into the Ottoman domain
1520–66	Rule of Sultan Süleyman the Magnificent; greatest extent of Ottoman Empire
1524–76	Rule of Tahmasp I; Safavid capital moved to Qazvin
1526–1828	Mughal dynasty; rule of Babur (1526–30)
1529	First Siege of Vienna by Ottoman forces
1533–1603	Rule of Elizabeth I
1557	Inauguration of the Süleymaniye mosque complex in Istanbul by the Ottoman master architect Sinan
1578–1603	Rule of Ahmad al-Mansur, Morocco
1579–1627	Rule of Ibrahim 'Adil Shah II of Bijapur, India
1588–1629	Rule of Shah Abbas I; high point of Safavid power; capital moved from Qazvin to Isfahan
1591	Occupation of Timbuktu by Moroccan forces
1605–27	Rule of Jahangir
1628–58	Rule of Shah Jahan
1638	Visit of Moroccan ambassador Jaudar to England
1652	First coffeehouse opens in London
1658–1707	Rule of Awrangzeb
1666–94	Rule of Shah Suleyman I
1683	Second Siege of Vienna by Ottoman forces
1722	Afghan invasion of Iran and capture of Isfahan; Safavid rule thereafter in name only
1732–47	Rule of Nadir Shah Afshar; from 1732 regent for the Safavid Shah Tahmasb II, from 1736 Shah in his own right
1739	Sack of Delhi by Nadir Shah Afshar
1750–79	Rule of Karim Khan Zand; ruling most of Iran from his capital in Shiraz
1779–1925	Qajar dynasty, beginning with northern and central Iran in 1779, followed by the addition of southern Iran in 1794 and Khurasan in 1796
1789–1807	Rule of Selim III; beginning of European-inspired reforms in the Ottoman Empire
1797–1834	Rule of Fath Ali Shah
1808–39	Rule of Mahmud II; *tanzimat* ('reform') period, including the adoption of the fez and European-style clothing
1812–13	Ottoman victory over First Saudi State in Arabia; recapture of Mecca and Medina
1848–96	Rule of Nasir al-din Shah
1851	Foundation of the Dar al-Funun, the first Western-style technical art college in Iran
1858	Mughal dynasty abolished by the British following the 1857 Indian Uprising
1873	Nasir al-Din Shah's first visit to Europe
1887	Occupation of Harar by Ethiopian forces

4 The age of empires 1500–1900

Three major dynasties dominated the Islamic world between the 1500s and the early 20th century: the Ottomans (1281–1924), the Safavids (1501–1722) and the Mughals (1526–1858). After the Ottoman sultan Mehmed II (r. 1444–81) (1) wrested Istanbul (then known as Constantinople) from the Byzantines in 1453, succeeding Ottoman sultans, followers of the Sunni branch of Islam, ruled from their capital in this city until the abolition of the sultanate in 1922. At its height under Süleyman the Magnificent (r. 1520–66), the Ottoman Empire was vast, encompassing much of the Near East, North Africa and southeastern Europe.

On the Ottoman's eastern border in Iran, the Safavids, a dynasty founded by Shah Isma'il (r. 1501–24), emerged as formidable rivals, proclaiming Shi'ism as the state religion in their first capital of Tabriz. At one point ruling over Iran, modern Iraq, parts of present-day eastern Turkey and Syria, Bahrain, the Caucasus, Central Asia, Afghanistan and Pakistan, the Safavid Empire would eventually address its threatened borders to the west (by the Ottomans) and the east (by the Shaybanids) by moving its capital further inland to Qazvin and then Isfahan under Shah Abbas I (r. 1588–1629). At the empire's height under rulers such as Shah Tahmasp I (r. 1524–76) and Shah Abbas, Iran witnessed an efflorescence of artistic patronage, which was complemented and continued beyond their reigns in a vibrant courtly culture of feasting and entertainment interlaced with political strategy. The Safavid dynasty met its demise with the fall of Isfahan to Afghan tribes in 1722, after which Iran underwent a period of political instability until the rise of the Qajar dynasty (1794–1925), which became known for its iconic royal imagery and flourished particularly under the reigns of Fath Ali Shah (r. 1797–1834) and Nasir al-Din Shah (r. 1848–96).

In India, among the major Islamic powers of this period (including the sultanates of Delhi, Bengal and the Deccan), the great Mughals (1526–1858) continued the Turko-Mongol and Persianate legacy of the Timurids of Iran and Central Asia, reigning over much of modern India, Bangladesh and Pakistan until this region became part of the British Empire.

The coming together of these three major rival dynasties in the 17th century – the Ottomans, the Safavids and the

1. Medal of Mehmet II
On conquering Constantinople in 1453, Mehmet was keen to preserve the Byzantine legacy of the city and to this end he collected Greek manuscripts and Christian relics. His interest in the west also encompassed Italy and this led to artists visiting his court, including the painter Gentile Bellini, who spent two years in Istanbul between 1479 and 1481. Bellini painted a portrait of Mehmet (now in the National Gallery in London) and also made him a portrait medal. Bellini's medal provided the inspiration for the medal shown here, which was made by Bertoldo di Giovanni (c. 1420–91). It is thought that Bertoldo's medal may have been commissioned as a gift by Mehmet's Florentine contemporary Lorenzo de Medici (1449–92).

1480–81
Florence, Italy
Bronze, cast
Diameter 9.3 cm
Donated by Henry Van den Bergh through The Art Fund (as NACF), 1919.1001.1

2. *The Princes of the house of Timur* (detail)
In this celebrated painting produced by Mughal artists of different generations (possibly Mir Sayyd Ali and Abd al-Samad), the Mughal emperor Humayun, surrounded by his Timurid ancestors, receives his descendants, which include the Mughal emperors Akbar, Jahangir and Shah Jahan. This grandiose scene illustrating Timurid-Mughal genealogy emphasizes the great regard in which the Mughals held their ancestors.

c. 1550–55
Kabul, Afghanistan (with additions in India in c. 1605 and 1628)
Ink, opaque watercolour and gold on cotton
The Art Fund (as NACF),
1913,0208,0.1

Mughals – is sometimes described as 'the gunpowder age', referring to the new military technology that allowed succeeding rulers to maintain their vast domains. Within each of these empires, however, lay complex and sometimes individual political and social structures and, while Islam was the dominant religion, peoples of other faiths – including Christians, Jews, Zoroastrians, Hindus, Buddhists, Jains, Sikhs and others – continued to participate and prosper in society.

The combination of enormous wealth and enlightened patronage within the three empires resulted in a legacy of magnificent architecture and a remarkable flourishing of the arts. Artists and artisans often travelled between the major centres of Istanbul, Isfahan and Delhi (as well as the Deccan), an interconnectedness that is reflected in the visual culture of the Ottomans, Safavids and Mughals alike, each empire exhibiting distinctive court and urban styles reflecting a unique synthesis of local and external ideas. (LA/VP)

3. Portrait of Shah Abbas I with a falcon

The Safavid Shah Abbas I was a popular subject among Mughal artists, who either depicted him as inferior next to his Mughal contemporary, the emperor Jahangir, or, as in this example, as a ruler of great stature, accompanied by attributes of royal status and power, such as the falcon, his sword and fine clothing, and the halo around his head.

Single-page painting mounted on a detached album folio
Late 17th century
India
Ink, opaque watercolour and gold on paper
Height 45.8 cm, width 31.8 cm (page); height 17.1 cm, width 9.6 cm (image)
1920,0917,0.44

4 | 1 The Ottoman era

The Ottomans are named after Uthman (r. 1281–1324), the leader of one of a number of Turkic tribal confederations in Asia Minor in conflict with the Byzantines. These wars, which continued over close to two centuries, ultimately resulted in the capture of Constantinople (to be renamed Istanbul), in 1453 by Mehmed II 'the Conqueror' (r. 1444–81). One of Mehmed's first actions in the city, once a bastion of Christendom, was to turn the church of Hagia Sophia into a mosque.

The major preoccupation of the Ottomans was with the enlargement of their empire. Selim I 'the Grim' (r. 1512–20) took Egypt and Syria from the Mamluks in 1517 and, following the battle of Mohács in 1526, his successor Süleyman the Magnificent (r. 1520–66) (**3**) brought much of Hungary under his rule (although his next step westwards, the siege of Vienna in 1529, failed). Footholds were established in southern Italy, and the Barbary Corsairs brought Ottoman rule to North Africa. The campaigns in Iran resulted in a major defeat of their Safavid rivals at the battle of Chaldiran in 1514, one of the results of which was the capture of large quantities of booty that included Chinese porcelain. These conquests brought not only treasures but also craftsmen and artists, including the celebrated Iranian painter Shahkulu, taken by Selim I from Tabriz in 1526 along with tilemakers, and who was to become the head of the court artists in Istanbul.

The sections that follow (pp. 157–73) offer a series of snapshots into different aspects of the arts under the Ottomans, a major feature of which was the establishment of a court style – a coherent vocabulary of design to be used on objects made across the full extent of the empire from pottery to *firmans* (administrative edicts) to brocaded textiles. The objects also reflect the multi-ethnic nature of the population of the empire and its tolerance of other religions: Armenians were prominent as craftsmen and patrons; there was a Greek aristocracy based in Istanbul; and the Jewish community, enlarged by Jews fleeing from persecution in Spain and Portugal in the 15th and 16th centuries, played an important role in banking. The 18th century saw European expansion into Ottoman-held territories as well as administrative and military reforms led by Selim III (r. 1789–1807) that included an initiative to bring French weavers to the workshops of Üsküdar (p. 165, ill. 3). Two other important aspects of daily life during the Ottoman era with a connection to the arts were the *hammam* (bathhouses), and the drinking of coffee (see pp. 172–73); fondness for the latter spread to Europe, ultimately turning the humble coffee bean into a major item of global trade. (VP)

1. Banner

Carried on the field of battle, this magnificent banner has, as its central motif, the bifurcated sword known as *Dhu'l faqar*, which according to Muslim tradition was taken as booty from the battle of Badr in 624. This sword has particular association with the Prophet's son-in-law Ali, the last of the 'Rightly Guided' caliphs (r. 656–61), who was also the first of the imams of the Shi'a (see pp. 60–61). Characteristic of the Ottoman representation of this sword, its incurving hilt is in the form of dragons' heads. There are bold inscriptions in Arabic script, some in mirror writing; on the blades are verses from the Qur'an (4:95–96):

Those who strive and fight has he distinguished above those who sit by special reward....

The Ottomans were followers of Sunni Islam and, in conformation with the Sunni creed they practised, the roundels around the sides of the banner state boldly the names of the Prophet Muhammad and the four 'Rightly Guided' caliphs who succeeded him: Abu Bakr, Umar, Uthman and the aforementioned Ali.

Late 17th century
Ottoman Turkey
Silk banner with metal thread
Width 204 cm, length 335 cm
As 1980,Q.211.a

2. Tombstone

In addition to recording and commemorating a person's death, Ottoman gravemarkers also indicated – by the type of headdress placed at the top of the stone – the status of the deceased. In this case he was Seyyid Ahmed Beg, former harbourmaster of Kuti (?), and at the head of the stone is a turban. The main part of the inscription in Ottoman Turkish reads:

[He] performed more than 60 years of faithful service to the Ottoman State and [he was], *in his retirement, at the Sultan's command, attached to the Imperial Ottoman Navy, which had been ordered to cleanse the Mediterranean of traitors of the Greek Community who at that time were in revolt. While the Imperial Ottoman Navy was on those shores he died a martyr.*

Dated 27 August 1823
(20 Dhu'l-Hijja AH 1238)
Ottoman Turkey
Limestone
Height 195 cm (max), width 39 cm
OA+.7403

3. *Tughra* of Süleyman the Magnificent

This magnificent example of the royal signature known as a *tughra* was made for Süleyman the Magnificent (r. 1520–66). It bears his name, Süleyman Shah, and that of his father, Selim, and the phrase 'the one who is always victorious'. It was once at the head of a document, the introductory line of which is visible written in the Ottoman chancery script known as *diwani*. Each sultan chose the precise form of his *tughra* on the day of his accession from specimens prepared in advance. The design enclosed within the signature, consisting of spiralling shapes in gold and blue, is an element of the Ottoman court style. It can be seen again on an Iznik bottle dated 1529 (see p. 169).

1520–66
Ottoman Turkey
Ink, opaque watercolour and gold on paper
Height 43.5 cm, width 62 cm
Donated by E. Beghian,
1949,0409,0.86

4. Scribe's box

This box is likely to have been made for a scholar or calligrapher for storing books or the equipment needed for writing. It is typical of furniture made for the Ottoman elite: the wooden structure is inlaid with a range of contrasting materials that emphasize the elegance of the geometric designs. A feat of Ottoman craftsmanship, the inlay is made from mother-of-pearl, tortoiseshell and ivory. Boxes similar to this one were also made to house Qur'ans.

17th century
Turkey
Wood, tortoiseshell, mother-of-pearl, metal, ivory
Height 36.5 cm, width 66 cm
1991,0717.2

5. Porcelain bowl

Chinese porcelains decorated with inlays of precious and semi-precious stones were particularly popular at the Ottoman court. In this complex technique, the surface of the porcelain has been chiselled to prepare it for rubies set in gold fittings. Most other examples of similar objects are found in the treasury of Topkapı Palace. This bowl was given by the Ottoman sultan Abdül Hamid II (r. 1876–1909) to the archaeologist Sir Austen Henry Layard in 1877, who was also ambassador to the Ottoman Empire.

1540–90 (bowl); 1570–1600 (Ottoman embellishments)
Jiaging porcelain
Height 6 cm, diameter 12 cm
Donated by George Salting,
1904,0714.1

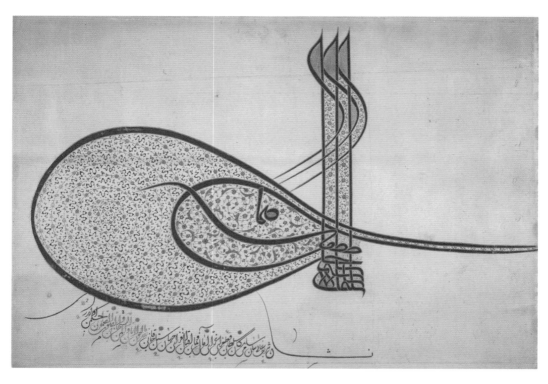

4 | 2 Iznik: potters and patrons

Iznik, a town southeast of Istanbul, was the main centre of Ottoman ceramic production. Between the 1480s and about 1700, an extraordinary range of high-quality wares in different styles were made using stonepaste painted with coloured pigments under transparent glazes (**1–4**). The demand for the pottery initially came from the court. The earliest objects were much inspired by imported Chinese porcelain, so favoured by the sultans and captured in great quantities from the Safavids at the battle of Chaldiran in 1514. During the 16th century, different designs and colours were introduced, culminating, in about 1550, in the introduction of a bright iron-rich red, known as Armenian bole (**3**). A key element of Ottoman design both on the pottery and in the other arts of the period is the conscious juxtaposition of two groups of elements traditionally known as *rumi* and *hatayi*. Motifs denoted as *rumi* are characterized by vegetal or 'arabesque' ornament, which had appeared in the arts of the Saljuqs of Rum (denoting Anatolia, where they ruled from 1077 to 1307). *Hatayi* (the Arabic for Chinese), highlighted the inclusion of Chinese decorative elements such as cloud scrolls and peonies (VP).

1. The Abraham of Kütahya ewer

This ewer, dated in Armenian 11 March 915 (AD 1510), is a key object in the history of Iznik pottery. It is decorated in blue and white in a style known as 'Baba Nakkaş ware after the name of an artist who worked at the *kitabkhana* of Mehmed II (d. 1446), and who is known to have made illustrations in this style. On the ewer's base is an Armenian inscription indicating that it commemorates a certain 'Abraham, servant of God, of Kütahya'. Kütahya in Anatolia was an important Byzantine town captured by the Saljuqs in the 11th century; later, under the Ottomans, it became an important cosmopolitan city with a significant number of resident Armenian Christians. Known in the 18th century as a centre for ceramic production, pottery may have been made in Kütahya from as early as the 16th century.

Dated 1510
Iznik, Turkey
Stonepaste, painted in blue under a transparent glaze
Height 17.1 cm
Bequeathed by Miss Edith Godman, G.1

2. Iznik basin

Large basins such as this one, known as *ayak tasi*, may once have been accompanied by ewers and used for ablutions by members of the Ottoman court. The main element of the design consists of a serrated edge leaf known as *saz*, combined with rosettes and overblown floral motifs based on Chinese peonies. This style and colour scheme, with its delicate turquoise and green, are typical of Iznik pottery of the middle of the 16th century, the point of reference for which is the Dome of the Rock mosque lamp dated AH 956 (AD 1549) (see p. 65).

c. 1540–60
Iznik, Turkey
Stonepaste, painted in blues and greens under a transparent glaze
Height 27.3 cm, diameter 42 cm
Bequeathed by Miss Edith Godman, G.66

3. Iznik dish

From about 1550, the style of Iznik pottery was to change dramatically. Naturalistic floral designs were introduced along with a brilliant red. Included among the flowers is the tulip, which was brought to Europe by the Austrian ambassador to the Ottoman court, Ogier Ghiselin de Busbecq. Along with the peony, the chrysanthemum and the hyacinth, the tulip formed part of the distinctive Ottoman visual language, and was applied to ceramics, textiles and works of art in other media. The design around the rim of this bowl is based on the Chinese 'rock and wave', a *hatayi* element.

c. 1550–60
Iznik, Turkey
Stonepaste, painted in blue, green and red under a transparent glaze
Diameter 31 cm
Bequeathed by John Henderson, 1878,1230.497

4. Dish with Greek inscription

In the 17th century the sources of patronage began to change as the industry could no longer solely rely on the court. Greek patrons commissioned vessels such as this one, the Greek inscription reading: 'Lord, Lord, do not turn your face away from us.'

Dated 25 May 1666
Iznik, Turkey
Stonepaste, painted in green, black and red under a transparent glaze
Diameter 26.1 cm
Donated by Sir Augustus Wollaston Franks, 1887,0211.3

4 | 3 Ottoman tiles

Until the mid-1550s, Ottoman production of tiles was limited (**1**) and the ceramic workshops at Iznik largely concentrated on vessels. A major change took place as a result of the commission of tiles for the Süleymaniye, the mosque complex built by Süleyman the Magnificent's architect, Sinan (d. 1588), inaugurated in 1557. Tiles on buildings were initially placed modestly over doorways or windows, or highlighting a *mihrab* (niche) in a mosque. As the fashion developed, however, they soon covered entire walls (**2**), such as in the Harem of Topkapı Palace or the mosque of Rüstem Pasha. The demand on the Iznik workshops was enormous. The use of tiles became a hallmark of Ottoman architecture all over the empire, from Istanbul to Aleppo and, for example, in the towns of the Balkans such as Skopje and Sarajevo. While the main centre for the production of tiles continued to be Iznik, there were local workshops in Jerusalem, Damascus (**3**), Diyarbakır in Anatolia, and elsewhere. (VP)

1. Hexagonal tile
This tile is part of a group known to have decorated the Çinili Hamam in Istanbul, a building commissioned by the Ottoman admiral Hayrettin Barbarossa (d. 1546) and designed by Sinan. Tiles in this colour scheme are rare, and the painterly designs of ducks and the serrated-edge *saz* leaves suggest that court artists were involved in the design.

1540s
Turkey, probably Iznik
Stonepaste, painted in blues under a transparent glaze
Height 28.5 cm, width 24.5 cm
Donated by Sir Augustus Wollaston Franks, 1892,0613.69

2. Panel of four tiles

These tiles, made during the
height of the Iznik tile industry,
once formed part of a much
larger panel covering the
wall of an unknown building.
The designs are a glorious
hybrid, exemplifying the
combination of *rumi* and *hatayi*
elements: vegetal 'arabesque'
forms, overblown peonies and
the ubiquitous *saz* leaf. The
iron-rich, brilliant red slip, thickly
applied so that the surface of the
tile becomes tactile, dominates
the colour scheme.

1550–1600
Iznik, Turkey
Stonepaste, painted in greens,
blue and red under a transparent
glaze
Height 21 cm, width 21 cm
(each tile)
Bequeathed by Miss Edith
Godman, G.77

3. Damascus tiles

Fine pottery and tiles had been
made in Syria between the
12th and mid-15th centuries
(see pp. 119, 130–31), but the
industry declined, only to be given
new life following the Ottoman
conquest in 1517. Damascus
became a major provincial city
of the empire, but it was in
particular the refurbishment of the
Dome of the Rock in Jerusalem,
which Süleyman undertook in
the 1550s, that was to provide
the catalyst for the Syrian tile
industry. It is thought that once
they had finished their work in
Jerusalem, the tilemakers moved
to Syria, where new buildings
were springing up, driving the
demand for tiles. While these
Syrian tiles echo in design their
Iznik counterparts, they are
distinguished by the delicate use
of greens and turquoises without
the inclusion of red.

c. 1550–1600
Damascus, Syria
Stonepaste, painted in greens and
blue under a transparent glaze
Height 29 cm, width 37.5 cm
(each tile)
Bequeathed by Miss Edith
Godman, G.98.a–d

4 | 4 Selim III and reform

Upon his accession to the throne, Selim III (r. 1789–1807) (**1, 2**), a reformer keenly interested in Europe, initiated a number of visionary reforms to modernize the administration and economy of the Ottoman Empire in the late 18th century. Regulations known as *nizam-ı-cedid* (the 'new order') were issued, touching upon administrative, fiscal as well as military reform. The latter included the foundation of a new infantry corps trained, equipped and dressed in European style, the building of new barracks and shipyards and the creation of military, naval and civil engineering schools.

Selim's reign also saw the desire to reinvigorate local manufacture and industry in the face of increasing foreign imports. Edicts promoting the use of local textiles and regulating the dress code of all classes were issued and new factories were established along modern lines, including paper and glass workshops in Beykoz and textile workshops in Üsküdar (**3**).

At the same time, Selim was an avid patron of the arts, a talented poet and an accomplished musician and composer. During his reign, music acquired a greater status than previously; the first opera performance in the Ottoman Empire took place in 1797 and a new system of musical notation was commissioned, which continues in use today.

Selim was also known for his mystical inclinations. He had close associations with the Mevlevi order of dervishes, founded by the followers of Jalal al-Din Rumi, a 13th-century Persian poet, Islamic theologian and Sufi mystic. Selim refurbished the Mevlevi lodge (*tekiye*) in Galata, and he wrote musical pieces that were performed as part of the order's observances.

Selim's reforms and the increasing influence of Western powers on Ottoman affairs antagonized the traditional janissary military troops, the conservative *ulama* and the tenured notables, leading to political instability that culminated in his deposition, imprisonment and subsequent murder on the orders of his successor Mustafa IV. (ZKH)

1. Sabre

This fine sabre or *kilij*, with a gold-inlaid damascened blade, once belonged to Sultan Mustafa III (r. 1757–73), Selim III's father. It bears an inscription commissioned by Selim in recognition of the respect he had for his father and in the hope of divine assistance for a prosperous reign:

May this sword of watered steel, a relic of Mustafa Khan, Be a source of blessing, in consideration of its lines of writing in gold. Sultan Selim, firm in nature, sound in heart, Is the descendant of emperors going back to Adam's time. Because he esteems this memento of his father Oh God… With the breeze of Thy divine assistance, in the flower-garden of Sultan Selim May the hyacinths of his good fortune and his hopes be ever in blossom.

1789–1807
Istanbul, Turkey
Inlaid horn and metal
Length 95.2 cm
Funded by P.T. Brooke Sewell, Esq., 1953,0515.1

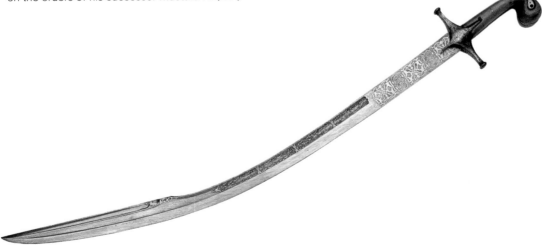

2. Postcard with a portrait of Selim III

The depiction of sultans' portraits was a well-established tradition in the Ottoman world. Postcards with portraits of Ottoman sultans such as this were produced in Istanbul in the late 19th and early 20th centuries by Max Fruchtermann, an Austrian entrepreneur who had been living in Istanbul since 1867, for both the local and tourist market. Selim III is portrayed here wearing a fur-trimmed kaftan and a turban with a jewelled aigrette. His portrait is framed by an oval with the dates, in French and Ottoman Turkish, of his birth, accession to the throne and death.

Early 20th century
Istanbul, Turkey
Printed paper
Length 14 cm, width 9 cm
Donated by Leila Ingrams,
EPH-ME.878

3. Woman's robe

This 'triple-skirt' robe (*üçetek entari*), with scalloped edges and long sleeves, is made of a richly woven silk fabric with a pattern of alternating stripes, floral sprigs and bands of gilt-copper thread. Known as *Selimiye,* this type of fabric was named after Selim III, who established textile dyeing, weaving and embroidery workshops in the neighbourhood of Üsküdar on the Asian side of Istanbul and who brought in weavers from France to create new lightweight fabrics with a European flavour that could rival foreign imports.

Late 18th–early 19th century
Istanbul, Turkey
Silk, cotton and gilt-copper-wrapped thread
Length 134 cm, width 212 cm
(sleeves extended)
As 1974,16.2

4 | 5 Ottoman embroidery

Textiles played an important role in all aspects of Ottoman life, both at court and in the homes of the ordinary inhabitants of the empire, as garments, accessories, house furnishings and animal trappings. Textiles also figured prominently during festivities and ceremonial occasions. Many were embellished with fine needlework. Embroidery in the Ottoman world was regarded highly, more like an art form than a craft.

Patterns and stitches varied based on the type of object being embroidered, the material it was made of, the wealth and status of the embroiderer and owner, their urban or rural origin, their social and religious affiliation, not to mention their personal tastes and preferences. While most embroidery was executed in coloured silks and cottons on cotton and linen fabrics, metallic threads, spangles and beads made of glass, coral or turquoise and pearls were also used, on materials including leather, silks and woollen fabrics.

The designs consisted mostly of floral and vegetal motifs (**3**). Yet patterns and colour palettes evolved over time, mirroring changes in other Ottoman art forms, and incorporating new elements in terms of technique and design (**1**). The 18th century, for example, saw the introduction of representations of architectural elements, and notions of perspective and shading, and the 19th century saw the increased use of metallic thread.

Embroidery was practised both on a domestic and commercial level. Women embroidered in their homes, making articles for their own personal use or for sale, while men worked in workshops embellishing materials destined for tents, horse trappings, boots and weapon covers and containers. The court workshops produced a variety of embroideries for use within the Sultan's palaces, to be used as gifts and for ceremonial occasions (**2**). (ZKH)

1. Sleeveless coat
This coat (*džube*) of purple velvet, decorated with braiding and couched work in metal-wrapped thread, was made as a marriage gift for a Christian Orthodox bride in Prizren, Kosovo. It would have been presented by the groom and worn by the bride at the wedding and subsequently at festive occasions. The 19th century saw the increasing popularity of military-style fashions, rich in braiding and couching, techniques also traditionally present on ecclesiastical textiles. Such styles were adapted to suit regional clothing traditions and adopted by the elite, the use of costly metallic threads a highly visible status symbol.

Mid-19th century
Prizren, Kosovo
Silk, cotton and silver (seen from the back, and with details of couching at the side and front)
Length 111.5 cm
2012,8037.1

2. Curtain made for the Prophet's mosque in Medina

This elaborately worked silk curtain was commissioned for the mosque of the Prophet Muhammad at Medina by Sultan Mahmud II (r. 1808–39), following his re-taking of the two holy cities of Mecca and Medina in 1812–13 from the emirs of the First Saudi State. The sultan's commission upheld the long tradition of presenting luxurious textiles to Mecca and Medina. At the same time, through the dominant presence of Mahmud's insignia (*tughra*) and the careful choice of Qur'anic verses in the embroidery, the curtain served as a means to legitimize the sultan's position as the rightful caliph of all Muslims and to reassert his role as the guardian of Islam's two holiest cities.

1808–39
Ottoman Empire, Istanbul or Cairo
Silk, silver and gold
Length 251 cm, width 206 cm
Donated by the Khalili Family
Trust, 2016,6030.2

3. Prayer cloth

Used by a woman to indicate the direction of Mecca, and known as a *qibla* cloth, this textile is composed of recycled panels of fine embroidery with floral motifs, assembled together and bordered with multicoloured woven bands and ribbons. Unlike a prayer mat, it would not have been placed on the floor, but hung on a wall. Textiles that were used invariably deteriorated. Yet embroidered panels were deemed too precious to dispose of and were salvaged and repurposed in new ways. The value attached to them was not only economic, but also symbolic. The old pieces were believed to carry forth blessings (*baraka*) that were transferred to the newly created object and its owner.

Assembled *c.* 1860–80
Place of production unknown
Silk and cotton
Length 138 cm, width 84 cm
2016,6016.1

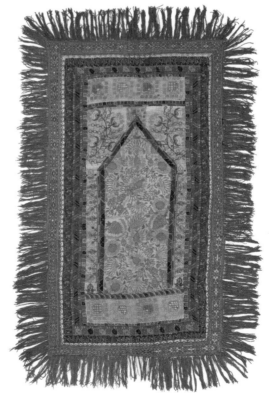

4 | 6 Armenian communities under the Ottomans

One of the characteristics of the Ottoman Empire was the tolerance exhibited towards non-Muslims. *Dhimmi*s were non-Muslims, principally Jews and Christians, who were granted special legal status. A significant religious minority community with this status was that of the Armenians (**1**). Not only did they play a noteworthy role in commerce but also in the arts where they were closely involved in the ceramics industries of Iznik and Kütahya. The ewer made for Abraham of Kütahya (see p. 160), dated to 1510, as well as a significant fragmentary bottle dated to 1529 and made for Bishop Ter-Martiros (**2**), were both made by Armenian potters working in Kütahya. This city had a relatively large and thriving Armenian population during the Byzantine and Ottoman periods (**3**); a colophon of an Armenian manuscript dated 1391 states that there was a church there. (VP/ZKH)

1. The 'Translators tile'
This tile depicts 'the Translators', who translated the Bible into Classical Armenian in AD 413. Four Armenian saints are depicted: Sahak, Nerses, Grigor and Mesrop, who founded of the Armenian alphabet in AD 406 and is shown quill in hand and with a tablet upon which the first letters of the Armenian alphabet are inscribed. The scene served as the frontispiece of the *Dictionary of the Armenian Language* printed in Venice in 1734.

18th century
Kütahya, Turkey
Stonepaste, painted in polychrome colours under a transparent glaze
Height 26 cm, width 19 cm
Donated by Oscar Charles Raphael, 1932,0615.2

2. Bottle

Decorated in designs used in the sultans' *tughra*s (p. 158), this bottle is inscribed on the neck and base in Armenian:

Bishop Ter-Martiros sent message to K'ot'ayes. May the Mother of God intercede for you: send one water-bottle (surahi) here. May Ter-Martiros hold it with pleasure….

May this water-bottle [be] a gift from K'ot'ays to the Monastery of the Holy Mother of God.

Dated 1529 (978 in Armenian)
Iznik, Turkey
Stonepaste, painted in blue under a transparent glaze (broken at the top)
Height 23 cm, diameter 18 cm
Bequeathed by Miss Edith Godman, G.16

3. Model garments for a bridal trousseau

This collection of 87 model garments for a bridal trousseau was once used by an Armenian seamstress as dress samples for clients. It includes items catering for the tastes of wealthy urban brides and comprises examples of Armenian, Iranian and Georgian fashions. Among the pieces included are undergarments, trousers, dresses, jackets, shawls, belts and veils as well as coverlets and accessories. Armenian presence was strong in the Ottoman, Persian and Russian empires and their traditions of attire incorporated different local dress elements, creating a very urban cosmopolitan style.

1850–1900
Armenia or Iran
Silk, cotton and wool
Box: length 26.5 cm, width 18 cm, height 11 cm; largest textile: length 37 cm, width 73 cm; largest dress: length 22 cm, width 24 cm
As1934,1023.1

4 | 7 Life in the bathhouse

Furthering the tradition of Roman baths, *hammams* continued to be established throughout the Islamic period. Their popularity was probably linked to the fact that they provided Muslims with facilities to perform full body cleansing before Friday prayers. Many *hammam*s were in fact built in close proximity to mosques and religious shrines or formed part of religious and educational complexes, the revenue they generated forming an important source of income for the latter. The Ottoman period saw the foundation and endowment of many *hammams* both in Istanbul and in the regional administrative centres. A legend states that Damascus had 365 baths, one for each day of the year.

Ottoman baths differed from their Roman counterparts in that the emphasis was not on steam but on running water. A typical *hammam* consisted of three rooms: the *sıcaklık* or *hararet* (hot room), used for soaking up steam and getting scrub massages; the warm room, used for washing with soap and running water; and the *soğukluk* (cool room), usually a large hall with stone benches used for changing, refreshments, relaxation and socialization.

Hammams were not exclusive to men: some complexes contained separate baths for women and children (**3**), others had different opening times for them. Visits to the *hammam* played an important social function and formed part of all preparations marking significant life-cycle rituals such as births, circumcisions and weddings and accompanied all religious feasts and celebrations. Bathing accoutrements included towels and wooden clogs among other things (**1, 2**). Ottoman *hammam*s fascinated Europeans: no traveller's account from the region in the 19th century was devoid of a description of a visit to a *hammam*. These descriptions, whether accurate or fanciful, positive or negative, fuelled foreign imagination and led to numerous visual depictions of *hammams* in Orientalist paintings, and led to the establishment of Turkish baths in various European cities. (ZKH)

1. Pair of bath clogs
Wooden bath clogs, more commonly known as *nalin* in Turkish or *qabqab* in Arabic, were used by men and women in the *hammam* to avoid slipping on the wet floor. While men's clogs were relatively plain with a very low heel, women's could be quite elaborate. Embellished and inlaid examples such as this pair were usually a marker of a woman's elevated social standing and position. Coupled with the fact that the wearer would have needed the support of an attendant to walk in them, the wearing of these clogs would have served to highlight her position.

19th century
Turkey
Wood, pewter, mother-of-pearl, leather, silk velvet, gilt-metal-wrapped thread
Height 26 cm, length 24.5 cm, width 19 cm
Bequeathed by Henry Christy, As.1553.a–b

2. Embroidered hand towel

Large towels for use in the *hammam*, either to dry the body or to drape around it for modesty, and smaller hand-towels (*peşkir*) used to dry the hands after refreshments were served (at home and in the bath's *soğukluk*), had bands of delicate embroidery at each of their narrow ends. Finely embroidered examples were produced for bridal trousseaus both in workshops and domestically. Towels and napkins displayed in a *hammam* provided an opportunity for women to exhibit their skills as embroiderers, with young girls known for their needlework skills often being sought as brides by women keeping an eye out for prospective partners for their sons and brothers.

c. 1830–50
Turkey
Cotton, silk and silver thread
Length 163 cm, width 60 cm
2014,6013.10

3. Portrait of a woman and child going to the *hammam*

This painting of a woman and small boy going to the *hammam* shows the woman carrying a container, covered or wrapped with a red cloth decorated with metallic thread. This would have contained the things she needed at the *hammam*: the various towels (one for each of the rooms and one, known as a *peştemal*, to drape around the body), a change of clothes, bath clogs, a bath bowl used for rinsing, soap, a mirror and a comb, as well as containers of henna, perfume and other cosmetics.

1620
Turkey
Folio from an Ottoman costume album (see pp. 240–41)
Ink, opaque watercolour and gold on paper
Height 20.7 cm, width 13.7 cm (page)
Bequeathed by Sir Hans Sloane, 1928,0323,0.46.122

4 | 8 Coffee and coffeehouses

In the 14th century, a *shaykh* of the Shadhiliyyah Sufi order, Ali ibn Omar al-Shadhili, upon his return from Ethiopia to Mocha in the Yemen, introduced his companions to a beverage made from boiled coffee grounds. This drink enabled the members of the order to ward off sleep and enhanced their state of mind during *dhikr* performances. Eventually coffee diffused beyond the confines of the religious orders into the secular sphere and was enjoyed by ordinary members of the community. Its use spread along trade and pilgrimage routes throughout the Ottoman Empire, reaching Istanbul in the early 16th century. Beyond the empire's borders, coffeehouses were established in Isfahan and Qazvin in Iran in the early 17th century.

Coffeehouses emerged as places where people with different social, ethnic and religious affiliations could meet on an equal footing. Coffee was not always well received by religious and political authorities, and decrees were frequently issued to ban its use on the basis that it endangered health and morals and that the gatherings where it was consumed threatened the established order. Yet the passion for coffee prevailed, decrees were revoked and people continued to gather in public and in private to enjoy it. A range of objects from roasters (**1**) to cups (**2**) and pots (**3**) became associated with coffee drinking.

Through exposure to the Ottomans, coffee soon caught the attention of Europeans, first as a scientific and botanical curiosity but then as a trade commodity and as an aspect of an exotic culture that many were intrigued by and some keen to embrace. The fondness for the drink quickly spread across Europe, with coffeehouses opening in Venice in 1615, in Marseilles in 1644, in Vienna in 1651 and in London in 1652. European powers attempted to control the highly profitable trade in coffee by establishing plantations in the areas under their control where the climate and soil were suitable, particularly in what are now Java, Colombia and Brazil. Coffee production and export spread and eventually the Ottomans lost their monopoly. The coffee bean had become a global commodity. (ZKH)

1. Coffee roaster and stirrer

Coffee roasting was essential in the preparation of coffee. Coffee beans were freshly roasted every time a fresh brew was called for, the smell rising from the roasting *pan* whenever the beans were stirred part of the sensory experience. This coffee roaster (*mahmassa*), shaped like a large spoon with a long handle, has wheels to enable easy removal from a floor-level fire. The roasted coffee beans were then left to cool before being pounded in a mortar or ground in a mill and brewed.

Early 20th century
Aleppo, Syria
Iron and copper alloy
Roaster: length 78 cm, width 22 cm; stirrer: length 67 cm, width 7 cm
As 1975,07.17.a–b

2. Painting of a coffee brewer

This painting depicts a coffee brewer (*kahveci*) wearing an apron and bearing two cups of coffee. At the Ottoman court, one individual was responsible for the preparation of the coffee that was served to the sultan. There were many different ways of preparing and brewing coffee and each sultan had a specific favourite. This painting comes from an album containing 124 paintings, by an unidentified artist, representing Ottoman sultans, court officials and military figures (ill. 3 on p. 171 is a page from the same album). Popularly known as costume albums, they were produced to satisfy the deep interest and fascination of Europeans with Ottoman social organization, manners and customs.

1620
Turkey
Ink, opaque watercolour and gold on paper
Height 20.7 cm, width 13.7 cm (page)
Bequeathed by Sir Hans Sloane, 1928,0323,0.46.98

3. Coffee pot

This coffee pot, produced in Kütahya, is of a type particularly popular in the 18th century. It was made to hold one or two servings of coffee. Inspired by the decoration on Chinese and Japanese ceramics, utilitarian items including coffee pots and coffee cups were mass-produced in Kütahya and exported to Europe as the fascination with coffee grew and its associated paraphernalia were adopted.

18th century
Kütahya, Turkey
Stonepaste, painted in polychrome colours under a transparent glaze
Height 15.8 cm
Bequeathed by John Henderson, 1878,1230.554

4|9 A marriage of cultures

The establishment of the British East India Company in 1600 and the Dutch East India Company in 1602 allowed both nations to procure luxury goods such as silk, porcelain, tea, ivory and spices directly from a number of ports around the Indian Ocean and amass unprecedented wealth for their governments' treasuries. Within this context, the Ottomans, Safavids and Mughals formed trade relations and diplomatic alliances with European partners to further their own political ambitions. A pair of Iranian blue-and-white ceramic shoes (1) were probably made in response to the growing European demand for Chinese porcelain, but they also allude to Safavid Iran's significant cultural influence and the role it played in global trade with Europe in the 17th century. A different trade story is narrated by an Iraqi Jewish bridal outfit (2) produced in the late Ottoman period, and which encapsulates the spirit of globalization in the mid-to-late 19th century. Many Baghdadi Jews were wealthy entrepreneurs, involved in worldwide trade networks through the East India Company, and they established communities in the trading ports of Surat, Bombay and Calcutta. It was here that women incorporated and adapted the sari blouse as part of their bridal and ceremonial Iraqi garments. (FS)

1. Ceramic blue-and-white shoes
These life-size ceramic shoes were produced in 17th-century Safavid Iran for the European market, although they are not based on European fashions but on a style of heeled shoe worn by upper-class men in the capital of Isfahan and other Iranian cities at the time. Captivated by this style, Western Europeans visiting Iran brought back heeled leather shoes and boots to their home countries and the trend quickly spread in menswear fashion in Holland, England and elsewhere. However, these particular shoes were not made to be worn. In 17th-century Holland, couples were presented with pairs of beautifully painted ceramic shoes as wedding gifts to wish them good luck, so perhaps they were commissioned for this purpose.

1610–1640s
Kirman, Iran
Stonepaste painted in blue under a transparent glaze
Length 24 cm, height 13 cm, width 8 cm (each shoe)
Donated by Sir Augustus Wollaston Franks, 1887,0617.3

2. Jewish bridal outfit

This outfit, worn in about 1865 by Esther Manasseh, a Sephardic Jewish bride living in Ottoman Baghdad, reveals a cosmopolitan outlook and desire to stand out. Made from expensive Syrian or French brocade embellished with gilt lace trim, the figure-revealing dress has a pleated bustle, deep décolleté and lavishly ornamented slashed sleeves, reflecting the Ottoman fashions of the day. Unusually, Esther also wore a richly embroidered Indian sari blouse or bodice under a semi-transparent chemise (the chemise here is not the original), a style of ceremonial dress worn by the Baghdadi Jews of India. Esther must have placed a special overseas order for her exclusive wedding ensemble, complete with a pair of wide, loose trousers and a head-covering.

1860–65
Baghdad, Iraq
Silk, cotton and gilt lace
Length 131 cm, width 147 cm
(dress); length 29 cm, width
55 cm (bodice)
Donated by Mrs R. E. Rea,
As1971,09.2–3

1. Portrait of Shah Abbas I

This painting of Shah Abbas I (r. 1588–1629), attributed to Bishandas, a respected court artist of the Mughal emperor Jahangir (r. 1605–27), is a rare contemporary portrait of the Safavid ruler. It is believed to be a study for a larger painting recording the 1613–19 embassy of Khan Alam, the Mughal ambassador, to the Safavid court in Isfahan. Such portraits served as important tools for diplomacy, providing visual annotations on the physical and psychological attributes of rulers and ambassadors.

Single-page painting mounted on a detached album folio
c. 1618
India

Ink, opaque watercolour and gold on paper
Height 36 cm, width 23.8 cm (page); height 18.1 cm, width 9 cm (image)
1920,0917,0.13.2

2. Portrait of Nasir al-Din Shah

This portrait of the Qajar ruler Nasir al-Din Shah (r. 1848–96) was painted by Muhammad Isma'il, a renowned artist and lacquer painter of the mid-19th century. Its influence is confirmed by the existence of at least three copies of the image made in the later 1850s. In contrast to the naturally but subtly rendered portrait of Shah Abbas I (ill. 1), this work evokes the realism of photography,

a fascination of the shah's. The hand of the artist is revealed, however, through his signature ('painted by the most humble Khanazad Isma'il') on the sofa's gilded edge.

Single-page painting
Dated AD 1853/4 (AH 1270)
Isfahan, Iran
Ink and opaque watercolour on paper
Height 33 cm, width 21.1 cm
1947,0210,0.1

Iran: from the Safavids to the Qajars

The advent of the Safavid dynasty in Iran marked more than the rise of a new power in an ancient land; it permanently altered the religious landscape of the country. Although descendants of the Sunni Shaykh Safi al-Din (1253–1334, of Ardabil), the Safavids adopted Twelver Shi'ism and declared it the official religion of the state from their first capital in Tabriz. The dynasty's founder, Shah Isma'il I (r. 1501–24) rose to power by subduing the Aqqoyunlu in northwestern Iran with the support of the Qizilbash (or 'Crimson headed', for their red caps), Turkman tribesmen who also followed Twelver Shi'ism. Within ten years, Shah Isma'il expanded his domain to include all of modern Iran.

At their height, the Safavids also ruled over modern Iraq, Bahrain, the Caucasus, Central Asia and parts of Turkey, Syria and Pakistan, but the empire's boundaries would face threats to the west and east from the Ottomans and Uzbek Shaybanids, respectively. This led to the decisions to move the capital further inland, first to Qazvin under Isma'il's son, Shah Tahmasp (r. 1524–76), and then to Isfahan in 1598 under Shah Abbas I (r. 1588–1629), the most acclaimed of the Safavid rulers and among them the greatest patron of the arts (1). Shah Abbas transferred his capital to a new location, building an urban centre adjacent to the medieval city of Isfahan. His new city centre expressed Safavid identity through its grand architectural layouts of mosque, palace and marketplace and a distinctive programme of tilework. Moreover, he transferred Armenians from Old Julfa in Azerbaijan to a new quarter in Isfahan where they enjoyed a monopoly on the silk trade, and enabled global trade with Europe, India and East Asia. These initiatives fostered a cosmopolitan aesthetic in Safavid artistic production from manuscript and single-page painting to portable arts and architecture, most of which emanated from the royal *kitabkhana*, or workshop-atelier; artistic patronage eventually expanded to include the urban elite and merchant class.

After the reign of Shah Abbas, two notable royal pavilions with significant decorative programmes (the Chihil Sutun and Hasht Bihisht) were built during the reigns of Shah Abbas II (r. 1642–66) and Shah Sulayman I (r. 1666–94). The Safavid state came to an end with the 1722 invasion of Isfahan by Afghan tribes. Subsequently, Nadir Khan Afshar (r. 1732–47) became the the de facto ruler of Iran. Nadir Shah's rule ended with his assassination and the rise of Karim Khan Zand (r. 1750–79), who ruled from Shiraz in southern Iran. In 1794, the rival Qajar tribe, who had consolidated power in the north of Iran since 1779, murdered the last Zand ruler, founding the Qajar dynasty under Agha Muhammad (r. 1794–97, adding Khurasan in 1796), who was assassinated in 1797 and succeeded by his nephew Fath Ali Shah (r. 1797–1834). Ruling from Tehran, Fath Ali Shah built numerous palaces and official buildings but is most known for his iconic image as expressed through life-size oil paintings. While the long tradition of manuscript painting in Iran did not end, it declined in the face of this newly favoured large-scale royal imagery and the development of the printing press and photography. The latter was introduced to Iran under the renowned Nasir al-Din Shah (r. 1848–96) (2), who had created the Dar al-Funun, the first technical art college in Tehran in 1851, and who first travelled to Europe in 1873. Other arts that flourished under the Qajars include lacquer and other portable objects made for both courtly and religious contexts, reflecting a variety of tastes and subjects and exhibiting continuities from earlier periods. (LA)

4 | 10 Shi'ism in Iran

Twelver Shi'ism became cemented in Iran under the Safavids and remains the official religion of the country to this day. As great patrons of art and architecture, the Safavids commissioned numerous religious as well as secular monuments and were responsible for important donations of objects to Shi'a shrines, notable among these a donation of Chinese blue-and-white porcelains by Shah Abbas I (r. 1588–1629) to the shrine of the eponymous Shaykh Safi al-Din in Ardabil. In many ways, religious and secular imagery became merged in the Safavid arts, with similar visual language used to express both either separately or together, as in the case of Qur'anic and Persian literary texts appearing on the same object or architectural surface (**2, 3**).

Since the time of the Safavids, the most powerful expression of Shi'a devotion to the *ahl al-bayt*, or 'People of the House' (the Prophet Muhammad, his daughter Fatima, his son-in-law Ali, and grandsons Hasan and Husayn), was and continues to be the ritual of *Ashura*, a religious procession and performance commemorating the martyrdom of Husayn, the Prophet's grandson, who died at the battle of Karbala against the Umayyad caliph Yazid I on 10 Muharram AH 61 (10 October AD 680) (**1**). Such processions re-enacting Husayn's martyrdom take place throughout Iran, with men bearing *alam*s, or standards, in different symbolic shapes, such as the sword of Ali (**2**), the hand representing the five members of the *ahl al-bayt*, or the peacock, as in the case of a Qajar standard (**4**). In the Qajar period, such public displays of devotion became increasingly popularized in the form of ceremonial processions or ritual theatre productions accessible to everyone, often performed with a reciter against a portable backdrop or *parda* ('curtain') that could be transported easily from one location to another (see pp. 224–25). (LA)

1. Water jug

While this faceted jug may represent an example of European objects being copied by Persian potters, its fabric and palette in black and blue are a Persian adaptation of Chinese blue-and-white porcelain wares. A Persian inscription scribbled on the inside of the vessel also reveals a distinctly Shi'a sentiment against the Umayyad caliph Yazid I (r. 680–83), who led the battle against Husayn at Karbala: 'drink some water and curse Yazid'.

Dated AD 1697/8 (AH 1109)
Iran
Stonepaste, painted in black and cobalt blue under a transparent glaze
Diameter 8.8 cm (base), height 11.5 cm
Bequeathed by Miss Edith Godman, G.324

2. Standard

Symbolizing in shape the *Dhu'l faqar*, the sword of the Prophet's son-in-law Ali, this standard was meant to be carried in Shi'a religious processions, particularly in Muharram for *Ashura*. It belongs to a pair in the British Museum and is inscribed with the names of the Fourteen Immaculate Ones (Muhammad, his daughter Fatima, and the Twelve Imams). 'God is mighty' appears in Arabic in the roundel at the tip of the standard.

Late 17th century
Iran
Gilded brass with openwork inscriptions and decoration
Height 127.5 cm, width 26.7 cm, thickness 4.5 cm
Donated by Sir Augustus Wollaston Franks, 1888,0901.17

3. Tile depicting a *mihrab* with hanging lamp

Decorated with a stylized image of a hanging mosque lamp under a *mihrab* arch, this tile may have served as a cenotaph.

The 'throne verse' from the Qur'an (2:255) and the names of Shi'a imams frame the tile, while the Persian band of text above the Arabic inscription along the base includes verses after the poet Hafiz: 'Reflect by the graveside after death and observe how, from the flames of my heart, smoke emerges from the shroud'.

17th–18th century
Iran, possibly Kirman
Stonepaste, painted in blue and black on an opaque white glaze
Height 69 cm, width 41 cm
OA+.10639

4. Peacock standard

An enthroned and veiled figure as well as numerous other figures, *jinn* and animals are engraved on this steel *alam* in the form of a peacock. The presence of such a diversity of life around the central figure suggests he might represent King Solomon, who also features in the Qur'an as a prophet and just ruler who spoke the language of birds and animals.

19th century
Iran
Steel, engraved with some gilding and gold overlay; turquoise eyes
Height 89 cm
Donated by Imre Schwaiger through The Art Fund (as NACF), 1912, 0716.1

4 | 11 Kingship and authority

Like many others before them, the Safavid and Qajar rulers of Iran legitimized their authority by connecting themselves visually to ancient and legendary kings in the decoration of objects as well as architecture. Such themes permeated the Persianate visual repertoire seen at the elite levels but also within popular culture. With Shi'ism firmly installed as the state religion, figures such as Solomon, revered by all People of the Book, were a natural model of kingship and just rule. Solomon features in the Qur'an as a prophet who spoke the language of birds and animals and who ruled over all creatures with wisdom and justice. A Qur'anic reference to Solomon on a steel plaque dated to the end of the Safavid shah Sulayman I's reign (r. 1666–94) invites another strategic connection to Solomon through their shared name (2). Solomon also appears on the lid of an ornate goldsmith's box that might have been used in the presence of a royal or elite patron (3).

Iran in the late 19th century witnessed a particularly strong revival in Achaemenid and Sasanian iconography on tiles, other ceramics, metalwork, carpets and in architectural design, perhaps a direct reflection of the interest shown in these periods by the Qajar ruler Nasir al-Din Shah (r. 1848–96). Two tiles in the British Museum collection depicting an enthroned ruler identified as the legendary Persian king Jamshid belong to a class of architectural ornament carved from stone or made from moulded and underglaze-painted ceramic tiles (1). Artists and craftsmen may have copied such images using models reproduced in contemporary guides to the ancient monuments. The most famous *in situ* examples are in the Narinjistan ('Sour-Orange Garden') and Afifabad, both residences of the politically active Qavam family in Shiraz and dating to the late 1800s. (LA)

1. Tile depicting an enthroned ruler

An inscription on the base of his throne identifies this seated ruler as the legendary Jamshid (*Jamshid-i Jam*), described in the *Shahnama* ('Book of Kings') as the fourth king of the world. Represented in an archaizing style referencing the Achaemenid reliefs of Persepolis, this tile belongs to a 'revival' genre of architectural ornamentation found in private residences in Tehran and particularly Shiraz (the buildings shown at upper left and right might possibly represent sites in one of these locations). Another tile in the British Museum collection depicts this identical image in reverse, on carved alabaster.

c. late 19th century
Shiraz or Tehran, Iran
Stonepaste, moulded and painted in polychrome colours under a transparent glaze
Height 30 cm, width 31 cm, thickness 2.5 cm
Bequeathed by Woodward, 1981,0604.2

2. Plaque, possibly made as a door fitting

The *thuluth* inscription on this plaque refers to the Qur'anic story of Solomon and Bilqis, Queen of Sheba, at the moment when the queen receives Solomon's message (27:30):

It is from Solomon and it is this: In the name of God, the Merciful, the Compassionate.

Such openwork steel plaques represent an important development in metalwork production in the 16th and 17th centuries, when they appeared on mausoleum doors or cenotaphs. They were also incorporated into Shi'a *alam*s (standards).

Dated AD 1693/4 (AH 1105)
Iran
Openwork steel
Height 34.3 cm, width 25.4 cm
OA+.368

3. Goldsmith's box

Exhibiting a 19th-century taste for lacquer-painted objects, this elaborate goldsmith's box includes an equally embellished set of gold-inlaid steel tools for weighing jewellery, such as scissors, tweezers, measuring spoons, three weighing scales of different sizes, an extendable rule, a file and a set of weights. The top of the lid depicts King Solomon enthroned and surrounded by *peri*s (winged spirits), *jinn*s, courtiers and animals, including the hoopoe, his wise messenger bird. Underneath the lid, Joseph before Potiphar's wife appears among other enthroned figures. Inside the lid, a hinged mirror with glass on both sides features the Prophet Muhammad's son-in-law Ali and his sons, Hasan and Husayn, with angels.

c. 1840
Iran
Painted and varnished wood with steel balances, weights and tools inlaid in gold
Length 64.5 cm, depth 37 cm, height 16 cm
Donated by Frank Cook Esq., 1927,0525.1

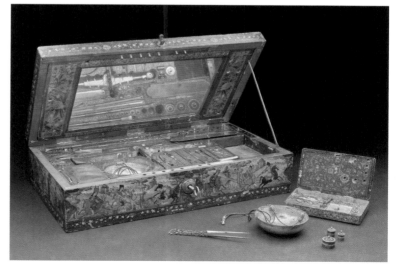

4 | 12 Courtly life

European travellers to Isfahan in the 17th century marvelled at the lavish gatherings hosted by Safavid rulers in designated royal pavilions in the palace grounds. Two such pavilions, the Chihil Sutun ('Forty Columns', completed in 1647, restored in 1706) and the Hasht Bihisht ('Palace of the Eight Paradises', built in 1669), constructed under Shah Abbas II (r. 1642–66) and Shah Sulayman (r. 1666–94), respectively, still stand today as evidence of the captivating settings in which Perso-Shi'a kingship and authority were legitimized through the performance and perpetuation of a modified Persianate tradition of feasting and courtly entertainment. In addition to the sumptuous food and drink guests enjoyed throughout several courses, while entertained by court musicians and dancers and surrounded by rich textiles, furnishings and opulent clothing, the architectural setting ensured a hierarchy of seating and gazing, all orchestrated masterfully to emphasize the wealth and power of the shah to foreign rulers and dignitaries.

Paintings inspired by contemporary illustrated manuscripts and large murals adorned the walls of these pavilions in architectural niches and on large tile panels decorating arches or dadoes above and below the line of sight. These displayed historical meetings or battles as well as literary or generic images featuring love and desire, depending on the location (**2**). The appearance of *cuerda seca* tiles arranged as elements of a large-scale picture in the palaces of Isfahan shows that a Timurid tradition continued into the Safavid period, but with a new focus on pictorial over abstract themes (**1**, **2**). By the Qajar period, the visual imagery of palace pavilions had developed into one that continued the tradition of images set into architectural niches, but which particularly favoured life-size iconic royal portraits, strategically located in areas where they would convey the strongest message of power (**3**). (LA)

1. Tile depicting a hunter
This tile once formed part of an outdoor scene on a larger panel (similar to the spandrel in ill. 2 opposite). It is modelled after contemporary early 17th-century arts of the book, textiles or carpets. The complete scene most likely would have adorned a palace or private mansion.

c. 1600–1650
Isfahan, Iran
Stonepaste, painted in yellow, turquoise, cobalt blue, green, black and opaque white with manganese purple in the *cuerda seca* (dry-cord) technique
Height 22 cm, width 17.5 cm, thickness 3 cm
Donated by Mrs Essie Winifred Newberry, 1949,1115.8

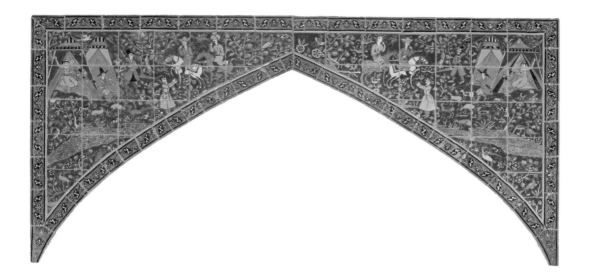

2. Architectural spandrel from a palace or private residence

This spandrel consists of two parts composed in mirror image depicting a courtly outdoor scene with pitched tents and a princely entourage. Each side shows a woman spinning thread and a man playing a *ney*, or Persian flute. Others welcome a crowned princely figure riding into camp with his attendant. Two men wear wide-brimmed European hats. Although this spandrel has been associated with the Royal Palace Stables of Shah Abbas II's palace in Isfahan, its original context has yet to be confirmed.

c. 17th century with later repairs
Isfahan, Iran
Stonepaste, painted in yellow, turquoise, cobalt blue, green, black, opaque white and light greyish-blue glazes with manganese purple in the *cuerda seca* (dry-cord) technique
Height 167.7 cm, width 350.5 cm
Donated by Charles Greenway, 1st Baron, 1937,1217.1

3. Qajar portrait of a prince and his page

In this portrait, a prince in military uniform is identified by his extravagant robe, medal and ornaments. His page holds a matchlock gun with an embellished stock and lock plate. Although the prince has not been specifically identified, he could be one of the 50 sons of the Qajar ruler Fath Ali Shah (r. 1797–1834). Life-size oil-on-canvas iconic portraits depicting important figures in bold but flat colours were particularly popular under the Qajars and were often displayed in the architectural niches of private palaces or residences.

c. 1840
Tehran, Iran
Oil on canvas
Height 183 cm, width 91.5 cm
Bequeathed by Mr and Mrs T. Sayid-Ruate, 1947,1108,0.1

4 | 13 Feasting and hunting

An inscription on an underglaze-painted ceramic dish dated AH 1088 (AD 1677–78) speaks to its function as a serving dish, calling for blessings upon those who partake of it (**1**). As the numerous extant ceramic and metal wares from the Safavid period show, feasting was an important aspect of courtly life and continued a long Persianate cultural tradition of the balance of *bazm u razm* (feasting and fighting), where fighting led to victory, which would then be celebrated with great pomp and circumstance that, in turn, reinforced the ruler's power and authority.

In 17th-century Safavid Iran, feasting played a key political role in helping rulers synthesize ancient Persian traditions of kingship with Shi'a concepts of centralized authority. The wealth and variety of luxury inlaid metal wares and underglaze- and lustre-painted ceramic dishes in public and private collections paint a colourful picture of feasting among the Iranian elite. Their images and inscriptions, forms and techniques also reveal the diverse cultural transmissions present in Iran, travelling to and from East Asia, Europe and India (**3**, **4**). Paintings from this period also suggest that such wares were used actively not only by the courtly elite, but by Sufi dervishes (**2**), some of whom might have been connected to the Safavids, who were themselves descended from the Sufi Shaykh Safi al-Din of Ardabil. (LA)

1. Dish with cypress tree and pheasants

The decoration on this dish reflects a combination of elements seen on other ceramic wares, such as those made in Kirman depicting spiky flowers and blades of grass; elements such as the cypress tree and surrounding pheasants reflect the arts of the book and carpets. The inscriptional band, comprising text scratched into a black ground, represents a style popular throughout the 16th century. It reads:

May this dish always be full of blessin]gs from licit [halal] *riches*

May it always be in the company of fortunate people

May this dish never be empty of blessings

In all months and years, whoever eats [from these blessings]

May their body be healthy from pain and [bal]

Dated AD 1677/8 (AH 1088)
Kirman, Iran
Stonepaste, painted in black and blue with green and red slip under a transparent glaze
Diameter 22 cm (base), diameter 40.5 cm (rim)
Bequeathed by Miss Edith Godman, G.308

2. Dervishes gathering in the wilderness

In this composition, combining elements of tinted drawing with bold colour, dervishes appear in various states of drowsiness, prayer, contemplation, washing, preparing intoxicants and drinking. The drawing's most striking difference from earlier versions of this subject is the inclusion of blue-and-white wares, which stand out against the muted landscape. These might allude to a donation of Chinese blue-and-white porcelains by the Safavid ruler Shah Abbas I (r. 1588–1629) to the Ardabil shrine in Iran, suggesting dervishes may also have used them.

Single-page painting mounted on a detached album folio
c. 1640
Isfahan, Iran
Ink and opaque watercolour on paper
Height 41.9 cm, width 26.9 cm (page); height 26.9 cm, width 19.3 cm (image)
1920,0917,0.300

3. Bottle

While clearly inspired by Chinese porcelain wares, many blue-and-white ceramic objects produced in 17th-century Iran reveal an interest in adapting this aesthetic to local Persian tastes. This bottle represents one of over 20 such vessels with similar moulding and only slight variations of subject matter, which here comprises courtly themes: a youth in European dress being offered wine by a young woman on one side, and a man in European dress hunting animals with a rifle on the other. Such figures may represent the cosmopolitan atmosphere of Isfahan.

17th century (bottle); 19th century (spout)
Mashhad, Iran
Stonepaste, moulded and painted in blue and black on an opaque white glaze; metal spout
Height 34.8 cm, width 20 cm, diameter 12 cm
Bequeathed by John Henderson, 1878,1230.618

4. Ewer

This ewer illustrates the synthesis of a 17th-century Persian taste for Chinese blue-and-white porcelain with elements of Indian metalwork, as suggested by the pointed bulbous body, splayed foot and high handle. Its attribution to Mashhad stems from a link between its maker, Mahmud Mi'mar Yazdi, and Kamal al-Din Mahmud Yazdi, whose name appears on the dome covering the tomb of the Shi'a Imam Riza in Mashhad (for repairing it). Mahmud's colleague Zari was most likely the potter responsible for this vessel's decoration, which reveals inspiration from contemporary Chinese export wares, known as 'Kraak porcelain' from the Dutch, after their popularity in the Netherlands. The inclusion of signatures on such works testifies to the talent and status of the artists who made them.

Dated AD 1616/7 (AH 1025) (ewer); 19th century (spout)
Mashhad, Iran
Stonepaste, painted in cobalt blue under a transparent glaze; metal spout
Height 24.8 cm, diameter 18 cm
1902,0521.1

4 | 14 Sufism and love

A covenant with the Beloved is mine, which I have forever
I hold the well-wisher of his street in the same manner as my life
By the cypress of Chigil I behold the purity of the khalwat *[intimacy]*
of my heart
From the moon of Khotan, I have the splendour of my eye and the lustre
of my heart
O learned pir *[Sufi master]! Don't forbid me the wine-house*
For in abandoning the wine bowl I have a promise-breaking heart
There is a cypress in my house under whose shade
I do not long for the garden's cypress and the meadow's box tree
It is fit that I should boast like Solomon about [your] ruby [lip's] signet
When the great name [of God] may be, what fear have I of Satan
But after long abstinence such as this, Hafiz became a notorious profligate
What worry have I, while in this world I have [Amin al-Din] Hasan. Hafiz

Love – of all subjects, perhaps the most universal to humankind – features strongly in the visual culture of Iran throughout history (**1–4**). Love also constitutes an important station along the Sufi *tariqa* or 'path', in which further divisions exist among levels of intimacy, yearning and *ishq*, or 'passionate love'. In Persianate culture, the line between Sufism and love is a fine one, as attested to by the abundance of literature recounting stories of love, sometimes attained, but often ill-fated or unrequited, and the annihilation of self in search of love (**3**, **4**). These tales were frequently illustrated in manuscripts and on the surfaces of objects, textiles and architecture, the most extraordinary among them composed or adapted from oral or Qur'anic tradition in the medieval period by poets such as Nizami (1141–1209) and the scholar and mystic Jami (1414–92) (**3**). Love was also explored in its earthly and mystical dimensions in *ghazals*, or short rhyming love poems, such as the one by the renowned Iranian poet Hafiz (1315–90) quoted above and inscribed on an inlaid brass ewer (**4**). (LA)

1. Lacquered pen box
With a renewed support for Sufism under the Qajar dynasty (1794–1925) in Iran, scenes from the daily life of Sufi dervishes as well as portraits of venerated Sufi saints and masters became a popular subject for the decoration of lacquered objects, such as this pen box (Persian *qalamdan*). The subject was believed to imbue the object with *baraka* (blessings and protection). On the top of the box, two youths and an older dervish visit a Sufi master for guidance.

19th century
Ink on papier mâché under a lacquered varnish
Height 4 cm, width 4 cm, length 23 cm
1964,1218.5

2. Swan-necked bottle
This type of glass bottle, with its globular body and long, swirling, curvilinear neck, takes its name from the tear-shaped opening at the mouth. Persian folklore identifies the purpose of these *ashkdans*, or 'tear holders', as the place for lovers to collect the tears and sorrows of their distant beloved.

18th–19th century
Iran, possibly Shiraz
Transparent blue glass, free blown, tooled and worked on the pontil
Height 38.5 cm, diameter 10.5 cm (max); height 26.8 cm (neck); diameter 8.7 cm (base)
Donated by Sir Augustus Wollaston Franks, 1877,0116.44

3. Royal textile fragment depicting Persian lovers

This rich but fragmentary textile depicts figures and scenes from three celebrated romances of unattainable love in Persian literature: the stories of Layli and Majnun, originating in Arabic folklore; Khusraw and Shirin, from different sections of the *Khamsa* (Quintet) of Nizami (1141–1209); and Yusuf and Zulaykha, deriving from the Qur'an but a well-known version of which was written by Jami (1414–92). Alternating with the images are verses from the poet Hafiz (1315–90), referring to courtly textiles such as the ruler's banner or standard (*raya*) and 'cloak of sovereignty' (*qaba*). Along with the quality of fabric, this suggests the textile was destined for a royal figure, perhaps at the court of Abbas I.

16th century
Iran
Red and white silk double cloth
Height 32.5 cm, width 17.5 cm
Funded by Edmund de Unger, Esq., 1985,0506.1

4. Jug inscribed with Persian poetry

The small, globular body with a low, slightly splayed foot-ring seen on this jug, or *mashraba*, is the most common shape found among surviving Timurid metalwork. Its 16th-century date demonstrates the continuity of Timurid-style artistic production in Herat beyond that dynasty's time. Such vessels originally included a Chinese-inspired dragon-shaped handle and a cover. Along a small band around its body, verses by Hafiz (quoted at the beginning of this section) allude to the object's function as a container for wine.

Dated March/April AD 1513 (Muharram AH 919)
Herat, Afghanistan
Brass, inlaid with silver and gold
Height 13 cm, diameter 12 cm (max); diameter 8.4 cm (rim)
Bequeathed by John Henderson, 1878,1230.732.a

4 | 15 Textiles from Qajar Iran

During the Qajar period (1779–1925), urban dress styles were, at times, dictated by shifts in palace fashions, most profoundly during the reign of Nasir al-Din Shah (r. 1848–96), the dynasty's longest-ruling monarch. A great admirer of Western aesthetic tastes as a result of his diplomatic travels to Europe, Nasir al-Din Shah introduced innovations in Iran such as postal services, passports, streetcars, gas lighting, photography, museums, military music, European-style clothing (**1**), fireworks and modern furniture. This also helped to stimulate an increased presence of European travellers, merchants, tailors and dressmakers in the region. Children's clothing was also impacted by the fashion trends of the time, since their garments tended to be miniature versions of what adults wore (**2**). The impact on dress was also felt from the East; for example, highly coveted Kashmir shawls were imported from India as early as the 1780s, and their patterns were copied by weavers and embroiderers in Kirman, southeast Iran (**1**).

Religious minorities in Qajar Iran, such as the Zoroastrians who lived mainly in the provinces of Kirman and Yazd, were required to identify themselves through dress. Zoroastrian men were permitted to wear only yellow, brown and tan-coloured clothing, narrow trousers and twisted turbans. The women dressed in distinctive garments made from narrow strips of contrasting fabric remnants, because they were not allowed to purchase textiles by the yard under Iranian law (**3**). (FS)

1. Woman's coat-dress and button detail
This silk coat-dress is cut in a Western-influenced style, with tailored shoulders, sleeves and waist. This is counterbalanced by the silk-embroidered patterns of curling *boteh* (paisley) motifs in pinks and reds, which are wholly Iranian in taste. The paisley and floral designs are probably inspired by motifs on Kashmir shawls, which were copied by embroiderers and weavers in Kirman. The original owner is unknown and one can only infer that it was either made for an Iranian woman with a taste for European fashions or a European woman living in Iran who appreciated Iranian embroidery.

c. 1900
Kirman, Iran
Silk
Length 156 cm, width 145 cm
As 1966,01.530

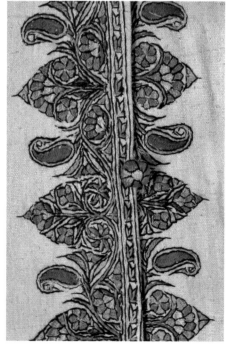

2. Child's outfit

This outfit, comprising a chemise, split skirt and leggings, was made for a girl of three and reflects shifting fashion trends in Iran during the reign of the Qajar ruler Nasir al-Din Shah (r. 1848–96). Skirts, though voluminous, had become progressively shorter during the course of the 19th century until the Shah himself introduced a modified version of the tutu skirt at court, following his visit to a ballet in Paris in 1873.

1880–1900
Iran
Cotton, silk and metal buttons
Length 40.5 cm, width 92 cm (chemise); length 29 cm, width 23 cm (waistband); length 45 cm, width 19.5 cm (leggings, each)
As1981,19.12 (chemise),
As1981,19.10 (skirt),
As1981,19.19.a–b (leggings)

3. Zoroastrian woman's outfit

Probably made for a wedding trousseau, this embroidered ensemble comprises a loose-fitting tunic and a pair of baggy trousers made up of seven different colours of silk. The tunic colours in green and red silk were considered auspicious and continue to be worn by Zoroastrian women on special occasions in present-day Iran. In 1936, under Reza Shah Pahlavi (r. 1925–41), all women were compelled to adopt Western-style dress.

1850–1900
Yazd or Kirman, Iran
Silk and cotton
Length 100 cm, width 97 cm (tunic); length 92 cm, width 63 cm (trousers, each leg)
As1966,01.556 (tunic),
As1966,01.559 (trousers)

4 | 16 Tribe and tent: the Turkmen

The Turkmen are of mixed Turkic and Iranian descent, living mainly in Turkmenistan and adjacent areas of Uzbekistan, Tajikistan, Iran and Afghanistan. Once predominantly nomadic, many Turkmen began settling in cities, towns and collectivized farms from the late 1920s, when their freedom of movement was restricted under Soviet rule. The Turkmen comprise numerous tribes such as the Teke, Yomut, Ersari, Chowdur, Salyr, Saryk and Goklen.

Nomadic Turkmen women were in charge of assembling and dismantling the external structures of entire yurts (tents) as part of the regular cycle of seasonal migration. They furnished them with woven, felted and embroidered textiles with designs that reinforced tribal identities and were a source of familial prestige. Spaces within a Turkmen yurt are divided by gender. The women's side included the kitchen area, utensils, woven storage packs for clothing (**3**) and the bedding pile with floor felts (**1**), quilts and mattresses. The men's side contained sacks of food provisions such as grain, rice and salt, and the women's loom.

Until the age of four or five, nomadic Turkmen children were dressed in protective over-shirts made and embellished by their mothers to guard them against the 'evil eye' or 'eye of envy' (**2**). The hems were deliberately left unfinished to ensure the child's long life and the mother's fertility. Some over-shirts incorporated triangular amulets called *dogha* or *tumar* on the back, at times containing slips of paper with Qur'anic verses or prayers. Other protective elements include metal charms inset with carnelian and cowrie shells. (FS)

1. Double-sided Yomut floor felt

Turkmen floor felts are constructed collectively by women and girls, as young as eight, from several families. One experienced felt-maker acts as supervisor and is in charge of setting out the pattern in blocked segments. The Turkmen tribes of northern Iran, in this case the Yomut, make double-sided or reversible felts. One side is called the 'holiday' or special occasion side and the other is for everyday use (shown here with ram's horn motifs).

1960–70
Iran
Wool
Length 156 cm, width 96 cm
As 1973,09.66

2. Teke child's over-shirt

The twisted black and white cotton cord stitched onto the back of this over-shirt (*kurta*) represents a type of snake native to the Karakum Desert of Turkmenistan, and serves as a charm against snakebites. The matted human hair stitched alongside also serves an amuletic purpose, as hair embodies the power of growth and symbolizes the life force of a person. The protective cotton triangle (*dogha*), too, is a defence against the 'evil eye'.

1930–1950
Turkmenistan
Silk, cotton and human hair
(shown from the back)
Length 37.5 cm, width 43 cm
2008,6025.22

3. Teke ceremonial mantle or cloak

A woman's mantle (*chyrpy*) with false vestigial sleeves is draped over the shoulders or head, and a heavily embroidered one such as this was worn at weddings and other special occasions. Young women wore dark colours, including blue, black and red. Middle-aged married women wore yellow *chyrpys*, while white ones were a prerogative of the elderly. Embroidered with horn and tulip motifs, the latter symbolize abundance, fertility and life.

1880–1930
Turkmenistan
Silk and cotton (shown from the back)
Length 119 cm (incl. fringe), width 65 cm
As1993,27.16

1. 'Jahangir weighing Prince Khurram on his sixteenth birthday'

This manuscript page depicts an event that took place on 31 July 1607, as described in the *Jahangirnama*, the memoirs of the Mughal emperor Jahangir (r. 1605–27). This was the first of a new kind of royal ceremony, in which the emperor or his sons were weighed against precious metals, textiles or treasure to be distributed to the poor. The ceremony took place at an auspicious hour calculated by astrologers, and holy men held the ropes of the scales while reciting blessings and prayers. Here, the young prince Khurram, the future emperor Shah Jahan, sits on one of the scales as Jahangir gauges his weight against bags of gold.

c. 1615–25
Mughal India

Ink, opaque watercolour and gold on paper
Height 44.3 cm, width 29.5 cm (page); height 30 cm, width 19.6 cm (image)
Bequeathed by Percival Chater Manuk and Miss G.M. Coles through The Art Fund (as NACF), 1948,1009,0.69

2. Sultan Ibrahim Adil Shah II holding castanets

This portrait of Ibrahim Adil Shah II, ruler of the Shi'a sultanate of Bijapur (1579–1627), is attributed to Ali Riza, an artist active in the first half of the 17th century. Set within a dark, verdant landscape before a distant white palace, the composition alludes to his love of music and artistic patronage. The castanets (*kartal*s) in Ibrahim's left hand recall those used in Hindu devotional temple music, while the green cloth in his right may derive from the *mandil*, or cloth, depicted in Safavid and Ottoman royal imagery. His luxurious clothing, possibly made from textiles imported from Gujarat, further underscore his royal status.

Single-page painting mounted on an album folio
c. 1610–20
Bijapur, Deccan, India
Ink, opaque watercolour and gold on paper
Height 17 cm, width 10.2 cm
1937,0410,0.2

Islam in South Asia

The earliest presence of Islam in South Asia – the area encompassing India, Pakistan, Bangladesh, Sri Lanka, Nepal and Bhutan, which had been largely ruled or populated by people of Buddhist, Hindu and Jain faiths – dates back to the 7th century, when Arab traders reached the west coast of India. In the following century, the armies of the Umayyad dynasty reached Sindh and the Punjab (in modern-day Pakistan), but it was really with the arrival of the Ghaznavids in the 11th century, followed by the Ghurids in the 12th, that Islam became firmly established in the subcontinent, comprising present-day India, Pakistan and Bangladesh. Both of these dynasties came from Central Asia, the former Turkic and the latter of eastern Iranian or Tajik origin, and both embraced Persianate culture, a legacy they passed on to their successors in India. The most prominent of these were the rulers of Delhi, a series of five sultanates established in 1192 and lasting until 1526.

Over time, the sultans of Delhi extended their control across India from Sindh to Bengal and the Deccan; at its height under the Turko-Indian Tughluq dynasty (1320–1414), their domain covered most of India. By the 14th century, however, several governors in the further reaches declared independence and formed their own states. In Bengal, three such states broke free of the Delhi Sultanate in 1338 and came under a single political umbrella as the Bengal Sultanate, led by Shamsuddin Ilyas Shah (r. 1352–58), founder of the Ilyas Shahi dynasty (1352–1490, with a brief interruption). In the Deccan, the Bahmanid Sultanate was established in 1347; in the late 15th century, it split into the five smaller kingdoms of Ahmadnagar, Bijapur (2), Berar, Bidar and Golconda, all of which emerged as important centres of artistic patronage and production, particularly of manuscripts and metalwork.

Persianate culture also permeated these sultanates, many of which were Shi'a and closely connected to Safavid (1501–1722) Persia.

Meanwhile in Delhi, a Central Asian prince named Babur had swept in from Ferghana (in modern Afghanistan), capturing the city and establishing the Mughal dynasty in 1526 (1). Tracing their lineage back to the Timurids and the Mongols (from whom their modern name derives), the Mughals reigned over vast stretches of the subcontinent until it became part of the British Empire in 1858.

The visual and material cultures of South Asia in the Islamic period reflect visual traditions as layered as the region's history, created by local and foreign artists and craftsmen over centuries of patronage by both indigenous and foreign rulers, many of whom came from equally layered religious and cultural backgrounds. Thus elements of Turko-Mongol, Persianate, European, Buddhist, Hindu, Shi'a, Sunni and Christian traditions, among others, can be found in the literature, music, arts and architecture of the region. (LA)

4 | 17 Power and authority in the sultanates

Following the Muslim conquest of northern and western Bengal in 1198, several dynasties emerged after breaking from the Delhi Sultanate. The Khalji rulers (1290–1320), one of the tributaries of the Sultanate, chose Gaur as their capital. In 1338, the Bengal Sultanate emerged under the leadership of the Ilyas Shahi dynasty, one of three states that split from the Delhi Sultanate. From its seat in Pandua (West Bengal), the Bengal Sultanate ruled over a region comprising today's Bangladesh, the Indian state of West Bengal and the Arakan region of Myanmar. Gaur continued to prosper until 1575, its architecture displaying a distinct regional style (**1**).

The south-central plateau of the Deccan (from Sanskrit *dakshina*, meaning 'southern') was under the rule of Hindu kings before the unsuccessful attempts at its conquest by the Khaljis and Tughluqs of the Delhi Sultanate. The Bahmanid Sultanate in the Deccan, founded in 1347 by the Tughluq commander Zafar Khan, then divided into five smaller states in the late 15th century, setting the stage for the rich cultural products in the 16th and 17th centuries of Ahmadnagar, Bijapur, Berar, Bidar and Golconda. The Mughals gained control of the region between 1600 and 1687, until the Asaf Jahis regained Deccan's autonomy in 1724, ruling from Hyderabad until 1948.

Several Deccani rulers had strong ties with Safavid Persia, with a notable taste for Persianate artistic, literary and musical traditions at their courts. Similarly to contemporary Mughal, Safavid and Ottoman rulers, Deccani sultans also sought the spiritual tutelage of prominent Sufis or other mystics as an aspect of legitimization of their authority (**2**). In both the Deccani and Bengal Sultanates, a diversity of cultures and faiths permeated the visual ethos of these regions as they adapted or synthesized local and foreign elements including Chalukya, Timurid, Persian and Arab, Maratha, Habshi, *nayakwari*, Brahmin, as well as Shi'a, Sunni, Hindu and Christian faiths. (LA)

1. Inscription frieze
The Arabic text on this architectural frieze, likely commemorating the construction of a mosque, praises Yusuf Shah (r. 1474–81), one of the Ilyas Shahi rulers of the Bengal Sultanate:

The great and exalted Sultan...,
son of Barbak Shah, son of
Mahmud Shah, may God
perpetuate his kingdom and
sovereignty....

The Bengali calligraphy style displays exaggerated vertical letters that terminate in arrow-like forms. The inscription could be from the Qutb Shahi mosque in Pandua or the facade of the Tantipara mosque in Gaur. The original positions of such inscriptions are often unknown, as they were removed and collected from the 18th century onwards without record, following the abandonment of cities.

Dated 26 March AD 1480
(14 Muharram AH 885)
India, possibly Qutb Shahi mosque, Pandua, or Tantipara mosque, Gaur
Basalt, carved
Height 49.5 cm, length 265.5 cm
Donated by Col. William Franklin, 1826,0708.2.a–e

2. 'Ibrahim Adil Shah II Venerates a Sufi'

In this painting by Ali Riza (active 1600–50), Sultan Ibrahim Adil Shah II of Bijapur, the same ruler who appears in ill. 2 on p. 192, is shown as a disciple presenting a bejewelled golden spittoon and inscribed gilded flask to his master or *pir*, a Sufi shaykh. Displayed prominently on a canopied dais (*takht*), and fanned by an attendant wearing a pair of jewelled pendants, the spiritual guide may represent the Sufi saint Sayyid Muhammad Husayni Gesu Daraz (1321–1422), of whom Ibrahim was a devotee. Such an image alludes to the significant relationship that existed between prominent Sufis and the court (although many Sufis also questioned connections with rulers of the material world).

1620–27
Bijapur, Deccan, India
Ink, opaque watercolour and gold on paper
Height 42 cm, width 29.5 cm (page); height 16.2 cm, width 14.4 cm (image)
Brooke Sewell Permanent Fund, 1997,1108,0.1

4 | 18 Commercial and royal networks and traditions

The two objects shown here encapsulate only a few of the intriguing complexities of the visual and material cultures found in both Sultanate and Mughal India. The first, a commodity of Indian Ocean trade, illustrates the journey of a gravestone produced by stone carvers in the Gujarati port city of Cambay for export to the Yemen, where it became personalized and dedicated to the deceased (**1**). It belongs to a group of inscribed memorials produced in Cambay for foreign patrons, including nobles, religious dignitaries, officials and wealthy merchants from Iran, the Arabian Peninsula and the Near East. The headstone's carving also reflects a pre-existing tradition of marble carving at Cambay for Jain and Hindu patrons. The second work, a highly prestigious commission probably by a Mughal patron, is a jade terrapin exhibiting both Hindu and Islamic characteristics, leading to suggestions that it was commissioned by a Hindu Mughal aristocrat for a temple or by a Mughal prince for his royal garden (**2**).

Inheriting layer upon layer of traditions over time, space and media, they stand as genuine cultural palimpsests, recounting or alluding to fascinating stories – both real and imagined – of courtly and common people, faith and folklore, and the role of artists and craftsmen (who could simultaneously work for patrons of different faiths and cultures), posing questions about the contexts in which they were produced. (LA)

1. Gravestone

Although purportedly found in the Yemen, this double-sided inscribed gravestone was initially manufactured in Cambay (Khambat), a port city situated in the western Indian state of Gujarat. The inscription includes blessings and Qur'anic verses in Arabic, many of which (e.g., the *basmala*) commonly appear on funerary architecture. The name of the deceased (Abu'l Hasan Ali ibn Uthman) appears on one side of the panel, but the accompanying date is not legible. The gravestone displays a number of features associated with the 'Cambay style', in particular the mosque lamp motif. Gravestones carved in Cambay were popular abroad, especially in Arabia and the Yemen, in the 13th and 14th centuries.

1300–1500
Made in Cambay, Gujarat, India
Marble, flat-carved in relief
Height 86 cm, width 38 cm
Donated by Messrs Newman, Hunt and Christophers, 1840,0302.1

2. Terrapin

This carving of a terrapin is identifiable as a female of the *Kachuga dhongoka* species native to the River Jumna, which joins the Ganges at the sacred Hindu city of Prayag, fortified and renamed Allahabad ('the city of God') by the Mughal emperor Akbar (r. 1556–1605). Given the highly skilled carving and the extraordinary life-size scale, this object was most likely commissioned by an elite Mughal patron, possibly for a local Hindu temple by Mirza Raja Jai Singh I of Amber/Jaipur or his son Jai Singh II, both Mughal aristocrats related to the court by marriage; the terrapin would have been placed under a bell struck to announce the worshipper's presence to the deity Shiva. Another suggestion is that the patron was Prince Shah Salim, the future Mughal emperor Jahangir, a keen patron and collector of jade carving who was fascinated by natural phenomena.

Early 17th century
Mughal India, found at Allahabad
Jade (nephrite)
Height 20 cm, length 48.5 cm,
width 32 cm, weight 41 kg
Bequeathed by Thomas
Wilkinson, through James Nairne,
Esq., 1830,0612.1

One of the last Timurid princes based in Iran and Central Asia, Babur fled his home in Ferghana in Uzbekistan after losing it, along with Samarqand, to the Uzbeks. From Kabul, he launched his conquest of the Delhi Sultanate, defeating its ruler Ibrahim Lodi in 1526 and occupying lands stretching to Bihar in eastern India. Under his grandson and successor, Akbar, the Mughals became the principal rulers of India, extending their domain to Bengal in the east, Gujarat in the west and Ahmadnagar in the Deccan. The Mughals were prolific patrons of the arts and architecture. Heir to the dynastic Turko-Mongol and cultural Perso-Islamic legacies, Mughal visual culture reflects a synthesis of these traditions with European–Christian and local ones.

Emperor Akbar, a famously illiterate but enlightened statesman, owned a vast library, the contents of which he knew well because they were read to him. His interest in philosophy, history and religion from diverse cultures attracted writers, thinkers and artists to his court. His openness to other views was also reflected in his ruling elite, which comprised Turks, Iranians, Indian Hindus and Afghans, and in his *Din-i Illahi*, a world view he developed out of the synthesis of aspects of Hinduism, Buddhism, Islam and Christianity, the latter arriving in India by way of Jesuit missionaries in the 16th century. After Akbar's death in 1605, his son Jahangir maintained the vast empire he inherited while becoming a devoted artistic patron and connoisseur with a keen interest in recording the natural world. Jahangir was succeeded by his son Shah Jahan (r. 1628–58), patron of the celebrated Taj Mahal in Agra, who continued stretching the boundaries of the empire into the Deccan. This region was eventually dominated by the last of the 'Great Mughals', Awrangzeb (r. 1658–1707), after which the empire began a decline that ended with the British Empire's formation in 1858. (LA)

1. Jug inscribed with the name of Jahangir

Jade appealed greatly to Mughal rulers, among them the emperor Jahangir, who was also a keen collector of Timurid objects. This jug, the later inscription of which includes verses alluding to the Fountain of Life and the Qur'anic figure of Khizr, and which also bears an inscription noting its acquisition by the emperor at Fatehpur Sikri, a former Mughal capital, represents one such object. Its form imitates the metal jug known as a *mashraba*, a Timurid favourite that inspired imitations in other media such as jade and ceramics, as well as in other cultural contexts such as Ming China and Safavid Iran, where similarly carved jugs were produced in porcelain and inlaid metal, respectively. The inscription reads:

This cup of jade, choice gem, is [the cup] of Jahangir Shah, [son of] Shah Akbar. Let the water of life be in his cup, so that it may be the water of Khizr, the immortal one.

15th century, with Mughal inscription dated AD 1618/9 (AH 1028)
Iran or Central Asia
Jade (nephrite), carved
Height 10.3 cm, diameter 13 cm
Bequeathed by Oscar Charles Raphael, 1945,1017.257

2. Tablet for a bench

This inscribed panel matches the description of a marble slab commissioned by the emperor Jahangir to improve the appearance of a bench in the garden of his son Shah Jahan's residence at Ahmadabad in Gujarat. Recounted in his memoirs, the tablet was created when Jahangir ordered stonecutters to inscribe a poem that had come to mind as he contemplated a royal garden in Ahmadabad; the resulting tablet was set into a bench in that garden. The verse appears in two central cartouches in a Persian *nasta'liq* script:

The seat of the Shah of the seven worlds, Jahangir, son of Akbar Shahanshah [King of Kings].

The context for the poem's composition and the date appear in cartouches above and below it, with Timurid-inspired floral ornament decorating the interstices.

Dated AD 1617/8 (AH 1027)
Mughal India
Marble, carved
Height 56 cm, width 33.5 cm, thickness 7.3 cm
On loan from the Society of Antiquaries of London, 1956,0519.4

3. Drinking cup inscribed with the name of Shah Jahan

Carved in a half-gourd shape, this jade cup bears the name of the Mughal emperor Shah Jahan, with the following text appearing twice below the rim, on opposite sides:

Article of the King of Kings, the World Conqueror, Shah Jahan, Second Lord of the Conjunction 1057

The inscription emphasizes Shah Jahan's lineage from Timur, founder of the Timurid dynasty (1370–1507), who used the title Lord of the Conjunction.

Dated AD 1647/8 (AH 1057)
Mughal India
Carved jade
Length 17.8 cm, width 12 cm, height 6 cm
Bequeathed by Oscar Charles Raphael, 1945,1017.259

4. Rashid Rana (Pakistani, b. 1968), *I Love Miniatures*

This portrait of Shah Jahan, which blends together elements of historical formal portraits of the ruler in an innovative contemporary technology presented in a Europeanizing gilt frame, acts as a threshold between multiple realities. Pixels or 'dots' forming the image recall modern pointillism, but also the traditional miniature technique of *par dokht* taught at the artist's training ground, the National College of Arts in Lahore. Upon closer examination, the pixels reveal miniature images of commercial billboards in Lahore, provoking a conversation (or confrontation) between the legendary Mughal ruler and ordinary people of the present.

2002
Diasec digital print, gilt frame
Height 55.3 cm, width 46.4 cm, depth 5.4 cm (with frame); height 35 cm, width 25.5 cm (image)
Brooke Sewell Permanent Fund, 2011,3053.1

4 | 20 *Pan* and tobacco

The consumption of stimulants such as alcohol, the chewing of *pan*, or betel, and the smoking of tobacco were common among courtiers and the elite in India. *Pan* and tobacco reflect both the continuity of indigenous practices and the adaption of new or foreign elements into the rituals of both north India and the Deccan. Composed of thin slices of the areca palm nut mixed with a lime paste and spices, all wrapped in a betel leaf, *pan* has long been a part of Indian court ceremonial and the offering of *pan* or a *pandan*, the container for betel, to a courtier would have been a great honour. *Pandans*, along with wine cups and bottles and fruits, appear in images depicting courtly couples on terraces. In later periods, the offering of *pan* at an audience indicated the end of the event.

Tobacco arrived in India in the late 16th century by way of the Portuguese, who brought it with them to Goa from the New World. By the 17th century, smoking tobacco through a water-pipe (*huqqa*, or hookah) was a widespread practice. The hot-water chamber of the pipes were initially made from coconut shell, while later on they were made of decorated glass or metal. An account of a nobleman of Iranian origin, who had travelled to Bijapur on behalf of the Mughal emperor Akbar describes a first encounter with tobacco and a description of a *huqqa*. (LA)

1. Betel container

This octagonal lidded container or *pandan* would have been used to store betel nut. Its name, which dates to the Sultanate and Mughal periods in India, is composed of the Hindi word *pan* and the Persian suffix -dan ('holder'), even though *pan* was not consumed in Iran. A scrolling floral pattern adorns the surface of the container, which is topped by a domed lid and closed with a metal clasp.

c. 1650–1700
Mughal India
Brass, beaten, engraved with glass paste and inlaid silver
Height 10.2 cm, width 14.6 cm
Funded by P.T. Brooke Sewell, Esq., 1956,0726.18.a-b

1. *Huqqa* base

This globular *huqqa* base with a slightly flared neck would have held a long stem supporting a brazier and smoking pipe. Its shape resembles contemporary bases made in the *bidri* technique (see pp. 202–3), but its poppy ornament – painted in gold with details scratched away from the surface – reflects a motif that derived from a decorative repertoire in both the Deccan and Mughal India. The popularity of poppies as a motif has been linked to the mixing of opium with tobacco.

c. 1700
Mughal India
Green glass, gilded
Height 19 cm
Bequeathed by Louis Clarke,
1961,1016.1

4 | 21 *Bidri* ware

One of the most distinctive arts of the Deccan is *bidri* ware, which refers to an inlay metalworking technique found on courtly objects such as bottles, ewers, basins, trays, *pan* (betel) boxes, *huqqa* bases and other emblems of rank (**1**, **2**). *Bidri* ware is cast from an alloy of mainly zinc mixed with copper, tin and lead. An object's surface was then incised with ornament, usually consisting of floral, vegetal or geometric motifs, and inlaid with silver or brass in sheet or wire. Finally, a paste containing sal ammoniac was applied briefly and then removed; this darkened the base metal, producing its characteristic black sheen, which in turn brought out the shine of the inlay.

Although *bidri* ('from Bidar') ware is named after the Bahmanid capital of Bidar, with which it is historically associated, its origins remain unclear; some accounts suggest an Iranian connection via north India. Dating is mainly by stylistic comparison to Deccani paintings and textiles, in which *bidri* ware or its ornamentation is represented. *Bidri* objects also display shapes and decoration in common with Deccani architecture, which gives them a more localized style, distinguished from the Mughal courtly arts. (LA)

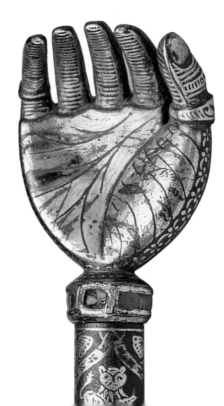

1. Ceremonial staff

Although sometimes described as a backscratcher, this object is more likely a ceremonial staff that once belonged to a courtier or Sufi of high status. Some 17th-century paintings include staffs with folded hand finials not unlike the insignia on this staff, which consists of a hand adorned with rings on the thumb and little finger. On its other end, the staff terminates in the head of a *makara*, a Hindu sea creature. Both terminals are attached to stilettos that can be removed from the shaft.

18th century
Bidar, Deccan, India
Zinc alloy inlaid with silver and gold, set with rubies and emeralds
Height 39 cm, width of hand 2.5 cm, depth of hand 2 cm
Donated by Sir Augustus Wollaston Franks, 1895,0603.96

2. Bottle

In form and decoration, this long-necked bottle shows elements of Mughal or Persianate inspiration. Such objects as well as images of upright flowers appear in wall niches depicted in Mughal paintings or inlaid in semi-precious stones on Mughal architecture, and their profiles appear as niche shapes in Safavid palaces like the Ali Qapu in Isfahan. These floral motifs may reflect the tastes of visiting Mughal patrons, which could have inspired local Bidari craftsmen to produce objects that would appeal to them as well as to the local market.

18th century
Bidar, Deccan, India
Zinc alloy, inlaid with brass and silver
Height 30 cm, width 17 cm
Bequeathed by John Henderson, 1878,1230.758

4 | 22 The jewelled arts

Along with military campaigns and large-scale cultural patronage, Indian rulers in both north India and the Deccan expressed their wealth, power and status through an important ceremony known as the *darbar*. Audiences could include high-ranking government officials or foreign dignitaries among other guests, who witnessed great opulence and extravagance in both ceremony and the display of objects, the accumulation of which further emphasized the wealth of the ruler. If not used within the royal household, they could be given as gifts to honoured guests (as often in the case of textiles or garments, such as *khil'at*) or destined for donation to a temple or mosque.

Jade, precious and semi-precious stones were among the more visible Timurid legacies also embraced by the Mughals and enjoyed at the courts of the Hindu Rajput rulers, as the subcontinent had its own ancient hardstone traditions and therefore the technology to work with such materials. Highly valued in the Turko-Mongol tradition, jade retained its status as a 'victory stone' and talisman in India; Timurid jades were re-situated within a Mughal context through the inscription of a Mughal emperor's name (see p. 198) or new jades were carved by skilled craftsmen and often inset with semi-precious stones (**1**). Court workshops or *karkhanas* housed artisans of diverse indigenous and foreign backgrounds, all of whom contributed to courtly artistic production and many of whom reached high ranks in their professions. Among these artisans were goldsmiths, who were responsible for the *kundan* technique of setting stones into gold (**2**, **3**). (LA)

1. Dagger with a 'pistol-grip' or 'bird-head' hilt

This ornate ceremonial dagger is characterized by its 'pistol-grip' or 'bird-head' pommel hilt, made of jade carved and inlaid with bunches of grapes and vines composed of rubies, emeralds and amber set in gold.

17th century
Mughal India
Steel, jade, amber, rubies, emeralds and gold; sheath of velvet with silk braid
Height 42 cm, width 9 cm; length of tassel 79 cm
Anonymous gift, 2001,0521.40

2. Dagger with 'eared' or 'cloven-pommel' hilt

This dagger boasts a notched gold hilt decorated with flowers, a cheetah, a harpy and a deer in rubies and emeralds on one side, and three flowers, a lion and a deer on the other, with each quillon ending in a dragon's head. The velvet sheath is decorated in incised gold and the chape set with rubies and emeralds. The jewels have been set in the *kundan* technique. Daggers with 'eared' or 'cloven-pommel' hilts appear in Mughal paintings during the reign of Jahangir (1605–27), often on the person of the emperor himself.

17th century
Mughal India
Steel, rubies and emeralds, gold; sheath of velvet
Length 35.5 cm
Anonymous gift, 2001,0521.35

3. Necklace

The decoration on this necklace with a pendant of diamonds and a teardrop emerald was inspired by both the Mughal art of enamelling (shown on the back of the necklace, right) and the ancient *kundan* technique (specific to the subcontinent) of setting gems into gold (below). In the latter technique, the stones are set by being inserted into highly refined gold (*kundan*) that has been placed over a layer of lac, a natural resin. More gold is then applied around the edges to complete the setting. The combination of enamelling and kundan appears to be an essentially Mughal phenomenon. This object, however, post-dates the Mughal period, and was made in Jaipur, which by the 19th century was the leading centre of enamelling in the region.

19th–20th century, possibly earlier
Jaipur, India
Gold, enamel, pearls, rubies, emeralds and diamonds
Diameter 18 cm
Anonymous gift, 2001,0521.34

4 | 23 Textiles from Pakistan

Textile traditions in present-day Pakistan date back millennia and have been the subject of many exhibitions and publications. Similarly to other parts of South Asia, waves of migration and conquest in the region influenced and shaped the variety of techniques of textile manufacture and embellishment, ranging from simple and complex weaving, dyeing and block printing to felt-making and embroidery. In this section, we highlight just two examples of Pakistani female dress, one from the western province of Baluchistan and the other from the northern province of Khyber Pakhtunkhwa.

In 1870, the vast historic region of Baluchistan was formally divided up between Afghanistan, Iran and India. Today it is the largest and most sparsely populated province of western Pakistan and also occupies areas of southeastern Iran and southwestern Afghanistan. The desert and arid mountainous terrain of Baluchistan is largely inhabited by nomadic and semi-nomadic people, who are organized in numerous ethnic and tribal groups. Although women's dress styles are similar throughout Baluchistan, the densely-worked embroidery produced in the home and in professional workshops is distinguished regionally and tribally through a varying colour palette and the placement and choice of stitches (**1**).

In contrast, the majority of Khyber Pakhtunkhwa is mountainous, with steep valleys terraced into small cultivation fields and villages scattered across the high terrain. Here, wool-weaving, felt-making and fine embroidery (**2**) were traditionally carried out, especially in the Indus and Swat valleys. Like in other areas, embroidered garments, accessories and furnishings were produced in the home for bridal dowries and acted as markers of social status, regional identity and tribal affiliation. (FS)

1. Baluch dress
This striking pistachio green calf-length dress (*pashk*) with richly embroidered sleeve-cuffs, chest panel and A-shaped pocket stitched down the front of the skirt, would have been accompanied by baggy trousers and a head-shawl and represents a style worn all over Baluchistan. Made of silk taffeta, the dress is embellished with exceptionally fine red silk embroidery, mirrorwork, metal spangles and colourful beads and pearls stitched onto a gold-thread ribbon along the neckline. In the past, the pocket was described as a receptacle for embroidery thread, small change, snuff and medicines for older generations of Baluchis. Nowadays, it is used to carry a woman's keys, credit cards and mobile phone.

1900–1950
Baluchistan, Pakistan
Silk, gilt-metal-wrapped thread, metal and glass
Length 112 cm, width 158 cm
As 1966,01.604

2. Dress from the Swat Valley

The combination of shocking-pink embroidery against a black cotton base fabric is typical of the dress traditions in the Swat Valley. This fine example, said to be a wedding dress worn with trousers, is made up of patched sections of embroidery in silk floss with touches of light pink, purple and cream outlined in yellow. The geometric and ram's horn motifs betray a cultural link with Central Asian textile traditions, whereas the smooth darning and straight stitches resemble embroideries of neighbouring Punjab and Afghanistan. The back of the dress is left plain, as it would have been covered with an embroidered head-shawl.

1900–1950
Swat-Kohistan, Khyber
Pakhtunkhwa (i.e. former North-West Frontier Province), Pakistan
Cotton and silk
Length 98 cm, width 151 cm
As1986,09.43

4 | 24 Islam in Southeast Asia

The world's third-largest population of Muslims today resides in the countries of Southeast Asia, with majorities in Indonesia, Malaysia and Brunei and minority communities in the Philippines, Thailand, Cambodia, Myanmar, Vietnam and East Timor. Islam probably spread to the region from as early as the 9th century, initially through maritime trade via India, China and the Middle East and as a result of travelling mystics and religious scholars and the presence of mercantile communities. The first kingdom in Southeast Asia to convert to Islam was the Pasai in the 13th century and Islam spread eastwards quite steadily from then on. The last major bastion to convert were the kingdoms of south Sulawesi in the early 17th century. From illuminated copies of the Qur'an (**1**) to richly decorated textiles and weaponry, the art and material culture of Muslim Southeast Asia is regionally diverse and reflects the multicultural, multi-religious and multi-ethnic domain of the archipelago.

Here, we highlight three artistic forms which, although from Indonesian contexts, have been produced and valued for centuries with regional variations across the Malay Archipelago. The first is batik, the technique of applying a wax resist design onto cotton or silk before dyeing it, which is a renowned textile art of the Malay world (**2**). Secondly, the ceremonial *keris* (or kris), which is a distinctive, asymmetrical dagger with an elaborately decorated sheath and hilt that is worn as an ancestral weapon and spiritual object (**3**). Finally, the tradition of shadow puppet theatre (*wayang*), which was historically performed both at royal courts and in villages to mark important rites of passage and as public entertainment (**4**). (FS)

1. Illuminated Qur'an

Qur'ans from the East Coast of the Malay Peninsula are generally the finest and most technically and artistically accomplished of all illuminated Malay Qur'ans. The example here, open at the beginning of chapter 36 (*Surat Ya Sin*), produced in Kelantan (northeast coast of Malaysia) or Patani (southern Thailand), has delicately illuminated double frames in red, yellow, green and dark blue.

1850–1900
Malaysia or Thailand
Polychrome inks on paper
Height 22.3 cm, width 16.5 cm
(each page)
British Library, BL3702686
and BL3702687

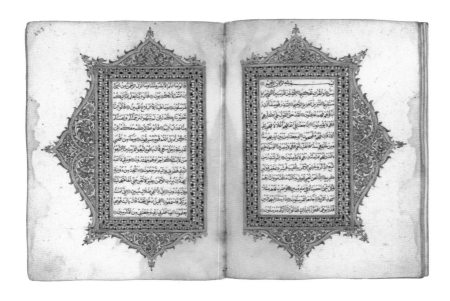

2. Man's batik head-cloth (and detail)

This head-cloth is replete with stylized Arabic script (e.g. *bismillah*, 'In the name of God'), designs derived from Ottoman *tughra*s (royal signatures) and representations of Ali's bifurcated sword, *Dhu'l faqar*. The iconography attests to the strong cultural and political links between maritime Southeast Asia and Ottoman Turkey. Such calligraphic head-cloths were worn by Muslim clan chiefs and lineage heads in West Sumatra and the symbols on them were both amuletic devices and status markers.

c. 1900
Sumatra (possibly Jambi),
Indonesia
Indigo-dyed cotton
Length 91 cm, width 85 cm
As 1992,05.3

3. *Keris* and sheath

Worn by men and women, the *keris* is a ubiquitous feature of Islamic societies throughout island Southeast Asia and has a rich spirituality and mythology attached to it. A blade-smith (*empu*) would have constructed straight or wavy blades in layers of different iron ores and meteorite nickel, which were folded dozens or hundreds of times, creating distinct damascened patterns. The decorated hilt and sheath, made of wood, metal, ivory or gold, are markers of regional identity.

18th century
Solo, Java, Indonesia
Metal, gold and wood
Length 55.5 cm, width 16 cm
Donated by Rev. William Charles
Raffles Flint on behalf of Lady
Raffles, widow of Sir Stamford
Raffles, As 1859,1228.256.a–b

4. Shadow puppet of Prince Panji

This shadow puppet (*wayang kulit*), made of carved, painted and gilded animal hide, represents the legendary Javanese hero Prince Panji. The stories of Panji and his beloved princess, Candra Kirana, date to around the 13th century and spread from Java to the Malay Peninsula, Bali, Thailand and Burma. They are enacted as both shadow plays and masked dances (*topeng*).

In Cirebon *topeng*, on the north coast of Java, Panji symbolizes the 'Perfect Being' of Sufi mystical thought.

1800–16
Java, Indonesia
Animal hide, horn, gold and pigments
Length 58.6 cm, width 17.5 cm
Donated by Rev. William Charles
Raffles Flint on behalf of Lady
Raffles, widow of Sir Stamford
Raffles, As 1859,1228.752

4 | 25 Textiles from Southeast Asia

Textiles in Islamic Southeast Asia display an immense diversity of skill and technique including supplementary and twill weaving, batik, tie-dyeing, embroidery and appliqué work. Textiles pervade secular and religious life, are markers of regional, ethnic and personal identity and are vital elements within significant rites of passage such as births, circumcisions, marriages and deaths. Finer textiles are symbols of social status, wealth and prestige. Here we focus on high-value textiles that were woven and decorated with gold- and silver-wrapped threads (*songket*): a sarong from Brunei (**2**) and a Minangkabau headdress from West Sumatra (**3**).

Shimmering *songket* fabrics are brocades that are woven of silk or cotton threads with supplementary weft patterns of gold- and silver-wrapped threads. Once the preserve of court and the nobility, regional varieties continue to be produced in Indonesia, Malaysia and Brunei as ceremonial shoulder cloths, sarongs and headdresses.

The homeland of the Minangkabau people is on the Indonesian island of Sumatra. The Minangkabau converted to Islam in the 16th or 17th century but maintained their long-established tradition of a matrilineal society; lineage, property and inheritance are the responsibility of senior women. The main elements of female ceremonial dress include a tunic, sarong skirt, shoulder cloth and headdress, which are often made of *songket*, with styles, colours and patterns that are regionally specific from village to village.

Minangkabau textile headdresses are formed from intricately folded lengths of brocaded (and sometimes embroidered) fabric, often forming hornlike shapes (**1**). They are likened to water buffalo horns or the pointed roofs of the matrilineal-owned houses of the region. (FS)

1. A Minangkabau woman
The woman in this 1905–15 studio portrait is dressed in fine *songket* garments and wears a characteristic horn-shaped headdress, although there are many regional variations of how such headdresses are worn.

Tropenmuseum, Amsterdam, TM-10005044

2. Man's sarong
The skirt cloth is commonly worn by men and women in Southeast Asia. It can be worn unsewn, or as in this sumptuous example, sewn into a tube as a sarong. With its profusion of *songket* weaving and rich colour, this sarong would have indicated wealth, prestige and high social and political status. In recent times in Brunei, the shorter a man wore his *songket* sarong over his trousers, the higher his status. At court, members of the core nobility wore their sarongs around 15 cm above the knee, and the positioning of the highly-decorated panel at the back, slightly to the left or right, indicated bachelor or wedded status, respectively.

Early 19th century
Brunei
Cotton and gilt-metal-wrapped thread
Length 71 cm, width 93 cm
Donated by Sir Augustus Wollaston Franks, As 1895,-.71

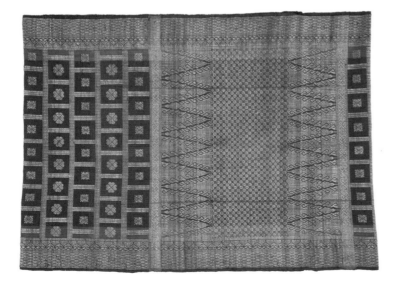

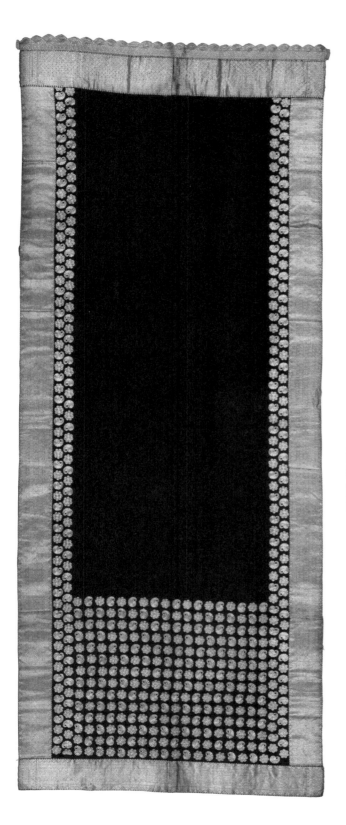

3. Minangkabau headdress

This ceremonial headdress (*kain tangkuluak*) displays far-flung connections. The use of a black woollen ground fabric in hot temperatures, lined with printed European cotton, attests to the influence exerted by Dutch and British traders in the region. Similarly, the paisley and floral motifs couched with silver-wrapped threads derive from Indian textiles. The *songket* and lace borders are locally made, although lace was originally introduced by the Dutch. This headdress was worn wrapped like a turban, with the ends of the lace-edged *songket* fanned to one side.

Late 1930s–early 1940s
Batipuah, West Sumatra, Indonesia
Wool, silk, silver-wrapped thread and cotton
Length 170 cm, width 67 cm
2016,3065.3

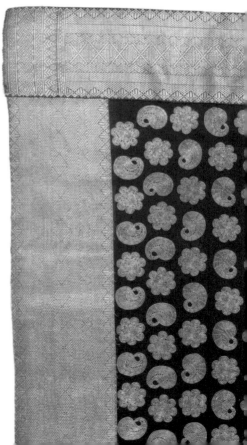

4 | 26 Islam in Africa

Islam has been present on the African continent since the 7th century and is one of the most significant faiths followed there, accounting for around half the total population. The areas of Africa in which Islam is practised have long been central to the wider Islamic world, producing rulers, writers and thinkers as well as connecting to long-distance trade and pilgrimage networks. Harar, the 'city of saints' in the eastern Ethiopian highlands, is an important site of Islamic culture in the Horn of Africa (**1**), while the great urban centres of Timbuktu in Mali and Kano in Nigeria perform similar roles in West Africa.

Arabic was used as the common language of religion, learning and commerce. In areas where paper was scarce, the teaching of literacy and the memorization of the Qur'an was carried out using unbound volumes from which single leaves could be distributed among school pupils (**2**). Literacy in Arabic was, and remains, highly regarded by Muslim and non-Muslim groups across the continent. The script was also used to write local languages from Senegal to Madagascar.

Indigenous African designs and motifs have been combined with the use of Arabic script to form a unique African Muslim iconography and Qur'anic illumination, through local interactions and long-distance trade. This is evident in West African textiles that combine Arabic script and pseudo-script for talismanic and decorative purposes alongside indigenous patterns and motifs (**3**), as well as in Qur'anic illuminations that include well-established textile motifs as verse markers. (WG)

1. Standard

This standard (*alam*) from Harar in Ethiopia carries the *shahada*, the Muslim Profession of Faith: 'There is no god but God; Muhammad is the messenger of God'. It would have been carried at the end of a staff for use in religious processions or military parades. Harar was an independent Muslim city-state with links to Egypt, the Yemen and the wider Indian Ocean until its incorporation into Ethiopia in 1887. It is still considered a holy city of Islam.

c. 1850
Harar, Ethiopia
Bronze
Height 40.5 cm, width 18 cm, depth 4.5 cm
Donated by Mrs Henry Perrin, Af1939,09.8

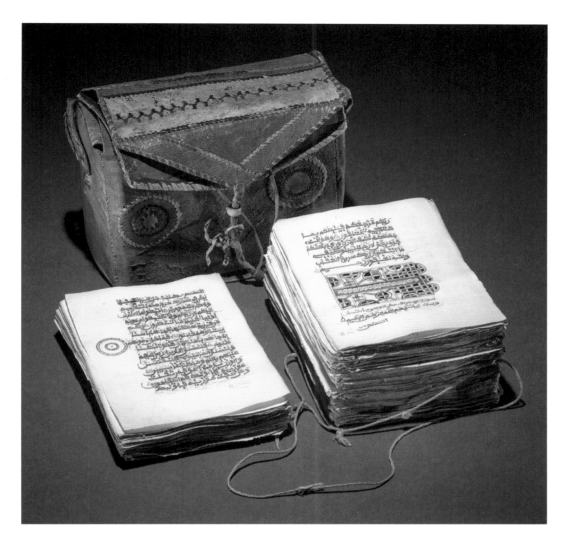

2. Qur'an and carrying case

Until recently, Qur'ans produced in West Africa were generally unbound and carried in leather cases, as here. This manuscript is in the *sudani maghribi* hand, a style developed in the savannah belt south of the Sahara. The rectangular decoration on the right-hand leaf marks the end of a *sura* (chapter), while the circle on the left marks a *hizb* (one-sixtieth of the entire text).

c. 1875–1925
West Africa
Paper, leather and cotton
Height 16.8 cm, width 11.2 cm (page); height 12.5 cm, width 17.3 cm, depth 9 cm (case)
2010,6017.1

3. Textile from Ghana

Okunpa ('good husband') textiles are an example of how 'Islamic' motifs have become part of the wider design repertoire in non-Muslim majority parts of Africa. The pattern, which includes indecipherable Arabic text, is based on batik designs imported since the early 1800s from what is now Indonesia.

Early 2000s
Ghana
Wax resist-dyed cloth
Length 182.5 cm, width 118 cm
Funded by British Museum Friends (Townley Group),
Af2006,15.21

4 | 27 African gold from the sea

As a result of the conquest of the states of the Sudan, the Sultan of Morocco received so much gold dust…that from then on al-Mansur paid his officials in pure metal…and at the gate of his palace 1,400 smiths were daily engaged in making pieces of gold.

In 1994, divers exploring Salcombe Bay off the coast of Devon, England, located evidence of a ship carrying gold from Africa. Known as the Salcombe Cannon Site wreck, over 400 gold coins were recovered, the majority struck by the Sharifs of Morocco, a major power in 16th- and 17th-century North Africa with their capital at Marrakesh. The hoard also contained ingots (**1**) and fragmentary jewellery (**2–4**) along with Dutch pottery, pewter and lead weights, all of which had lain on the seabed undisturbed since the ship had foundered in the 1630s or 1640s. This is indicated by the latest coins in the hoard, struck by the ruler al-Walid (r. 1631–36) in 1631. There are no physical remains of the ship itself and its origin is still a matter for debate. The three possibilities are that it was English, Dutch or belonged to Barbary pirates active along the Devon coast.

The finds open a window onto a fascinating era of international trade and diplomacy on the one hand and the gold trade on the other. The majority of the coins were struck by Moroccan ruler Ahmad al-Mansur (r. 1578–1603) (**5**), a contemporary of Queen Elizabeth I (r. 1533–1603). He was known as *al-Dhahabi*, 'the golden one', on account of his 1591 conquest of Timbuktu, capital of the gold-rich state of Songhay, and celebrated for his wealth (as noted in the quote by the Moroccan historian al-Ifrani (d. 1747) above). There was correspondence between al-Mansur and Elizabeth, who had established the Barbary trading company in 1585. Moroccan ambassadors also visited the English court. England's main exports were cloth and guns, while sugar and gold, as well as ostrich feathers, almonds, dates and aniseed were much in demand at home. (VP)

1. Gold ingot

Ingots could be made from gold in a variety of forms. Taken out of the ground (excavations at the city of Gao have established that gold was extracted there), it would be transported in the form of gold dust to North African cities such as Sijilmasa, an important stop on the African trade route. They could also be made from recycled gold and scientific analysis of the Salcombe hoard has shown that the ingots could have been made from jewellery or coins similar to those in this hoard. It is from ingots that coins are made and the mint master al-Jazna'i who worked at the court of Ahmad al-Mansur writes: 'the ingot must be beaten until it is as thin as a blade. The pieces are cut up into squares first and then rounded into circles…weighed again, then put into piles of twenty and held between the thumb and the index finger.'

17th century
Length 4.5 cm, weight 71.89 g
1999,1207.455
Salcombe Cannon Hoard
acquired with contributions from the Art Fund, Brooke Sewell Permanent Fund and the British Museum Friends (as British Museum Society)

2. Broken and twisted earring

Several earrings of this type were found in the hoard, many of them broken or twisted.

Probably 17th century
Morocco
Length 4.5 cm (max)
1999,1207.482

3. Amulet case cut fragment

Attributed to the Fatimid period, this is one of the earliest pieces of jewellery in the hoard.

c. 10th–12th century
Length 4.4 cm, width 3 cm
1999,1207.466

4. Pendant

A fragment of enamel survives on this European pendant. The mint master al-Jazna'i describes how special refining techniques were needed when melting down gold that contained enamel.

17th century
Possibly Spain
Height 4.3 cm, width 3.6 cm
1999,1207.463

5. Coin

This coin is one of over 100 struck by the Moroccan ruler Ahmad al-Mansur in Marrakesh that were found in the hoard.

Dated AD 1597 (AH 1005)
Diameter 2.95 cm
1999,1207.27

4 | 28 A lyre from Sudan

With the oldest-known example (from around 2600 BC) excavated from the Royal Cemetery of Ur in Iraq, the lyre (known as a *kissar* in northern Sudan and a *tanbura* elsewhere) has great antiquity. The instrument illustrated here is both a remarkable item as a whole, and a conglomeration of single objects, strung with coins, beads, shells and other miscellaneous items.

The coins were mostly minted in Cairo and Istanbul in the second half of the 19th century. This reflects the long-standing links between the Ottomans, Egyptians and regions further south along the Nile, which had only intensified following Egypt's annexation of Sudan in the 1820s. Among them are three British coins (one dated 1861 and two dated 1832), reflecting the growing power of the British Empire in northeast Africa; the lyre was made around the time of the British victory over the *Mahdiyya*, a religious movement that had waged a long and destructive war against the occupying Turco-Egyptians and subsequently their British allies. Testifying to the remarkably wide range of the pieces that adorn the lyre, there is also a coin dated 1804 from the Dutch colony of Sumatra, and a number of cowrie shells, harvested in the Indian Ocean and used as currency across Africa. Similarly, the multicoloured beads that cover almost the entire surface of the arms and crossbeam were used by Europeans as a medium of trade throughout the continent, mass-produced first in Venice and later in France and England.

The variety of objects attached to the lyre points to its ceremonial function. Lyres like this one are played during *zar* ceremonies (*zar* is a belief in the power of spirits and their ability to possess people, originating in the East African slave trade and practised today in Somalia, Djibouti, Eritrea, Ethiopia, Sudan, Egypt, the Arabian Peninsula and southern Iran and Pakistan). Like the objects strung from the lyre, *zar* spirits also have a wide range, including Sufis, *khawajat* (foreigners), Turco-Egyptian officials, Christian Ethiopians, Black Africans, Arabs and women, and the objects may represent offerings, either to propitiate the spirits or as a gift to the musician. (WG)

1. Sudanese lyre

Late 1800s
Sudan
Wood, skin, glass, cowrie shells, metal and animal gut
Height 121.5 cm, width 116 cm
Donated by Thomas Southgate, Af1917,0411.1

Timeline

680	Battle of Karbala and martyrdom of Husayn, grandson of the Prophet
700s	Paper introduced to the Islamic lands by the Chinese; initially used mainly for official documents
900s	Calligraphy standardized by Ibn Muqla through system of proportions and the 'six scripts'
c. 1010	Completion of the *Shahnama* (Book of Kings) in written verse
1258	Mongol invasion of Baghdad and end of Abbasid Caliphate
1400s	Beginnings of album production in Iran
1562	Mughal emperor Akbar's first royal commission, the *Hamzanama* (Book of Hamza)
Late 1500s	Increased production of and demand for single-page drawings and paintings (first in Iran, then India and Turkey)
1800s	Decline in manuscript and album patronage and production in the Islamic world
1976–90	Lebanese Civil War
2007	Turkish government declares two characters (Karagöz and Hacivat) from Turkish shadow puppet theatre cultural assets

5 Literary and musical traditions

The Islamic literary tradition stems from a rich history of storytelling that pre-dates both Islam and the written word. Tales were recited or sung before a courtly or public audience to mark a special occasion, often accompanied by visual backdrops, theatrical performances – including shadow puppet theatre – and music (1). Many stories were eventually written down and inspired elaborately illustrated manuscripts (2, 3).

Oral traditions flourished at the courts of Islamic rulers in a culture promoting *adab*, or refined conduct, a concept emphasized at literary assemblies where courtiers recited poetry, displayed their knowledge and challenged each other with intellectual riddles. Books played an important role in this environment as repositories of knowledge and tools for education. They became objects of art (and of great value) in their own right, evidence of the skill, literary knowledge and taste of their makers, patrons and owners.

Official documents, treatises, histories, biographies and album prefaces, particularly from 16th-century Safavid Iran but also from Ottoman Turkey and Mughal India, shed

1. Sitar

Although its name derives from Persian, the sitar ('three strings') appears to have originated in India. According to tradition, it was introduced to Delhi from Kashmir, where it was associated with Sufi music, and is first mentioned in a Delhi manuscript produced in 1738. By the 19th century, the sitar comprised a key element of music ensembles in northern India and prominent sitar players were highly sought after by courtly patrons.

c. 19th century
Pakistan, possibly Lahore
Red wood and calabash, inlaid with bone, and pierced bone plates; calabash body painted in lacquer and gilt
Height 14 cm, width 57 cm, depth 20 cm
Donated by Miss M.A. North, As1889,0618.2

2. *The Raven addresses an assembly of animals*

This densely populated scene of a raven addressing a gathering of real and fantastic animals probably once belonged to an illustrated manuscript and is attributed to the Mughal court artist Miskin. It carries associations with several literary sources containing moralizing accounts about human conduct, many of them translated or adapted from earlier written sources and oral traditions. Translated from Sanskrit into Pahlavi or Middle Persian, many of these tales ultimately derive from a long-standing Indian oral tradition that was eventually preserved in written form as a book on statecraft called the *Panchatantra* ('Five Occasions of Good Sense').

c. 1590
India
Ink, opaque watercolour and gold on paper; mounted on an album folio
Height 29.2 cm, width 22.2 cm (page)
1920,0917,0.5

3. *Rustam slaying Shaghad after falling into the pit in Kabul*

This painting from a *Shahnama* ('Book of Kings') manuscript illustrates the dramatic final episode in the saga of the legendary warrior Rustam and his faithful horse Rakhsh. Rustam's jealous half-brother Shaghhad conspires with the king of Kabul to lure Rustam into an area prepared with hidden spear-lined pits. Rakhsh is impaled and killed and Rustam fatally injured. Realizing his half-brother's treachery, the wounded Rustam begs him to string a bow for him to ward off predatory animals, enabling Rustam to avenge his own death by pinning his murderer to a tree with his final, well-aimed arrow.

c. 1330s
Iran, probably Tabriz
Ink, opaque watercolour and gold on paper
Height 40.7 cm, width 29.6 cm (page)
Bequeathed by Sir Bernard Eckstein, Bart, 1948,1211,0.25

light on the history of book and album arts in these regions. Surviving manuscripts, albums and workshop materials likewise reveal important information about the production process itself. Persian sources describe the setting of the royal *kitabkhana*, a 'bookhouse' or library-*cum*-workshop. Manuscript-making was a collective endeavour, involving papermakers, scribes and binders, with luxury examples additionally engaging calligraphers, illuminators, painters, rulers and gold-leaf and lapis lazuli washers, among others. In the late 1500s, an increase in non-royal patrons and collectors led to more artists working independently on the open market.

Qur'ans initially comprised the most commonly produced codices, but in the 10th century, paper – first introduced to Central and West Asia in the 8th century – replaced parchment, leading to the refinement of more calligraphic scripts and a higher rate of book production, which included scientific, theological, historical, biographical and literary texts. The portable nature of books also meant that their dissemination, gifting or plunder enabled others to copy their features in a new context. As a result, books could exhibit a synthesis of artistic ideas, styles and techniques representing numerous cultural traditions. In the decades after the Mongol conquests of Iran

4. Album of Indian and Persian paintings and calligraphy

The late 1590s saw a booming market for single-page painting and drawing in Qazvin and Isfahan, with portraits collected and compiled into albums known as *muraqqa*. Such images as well as Persian calligraphic specimens were later admired in India, where a strong culture of collecting and album-making also existed. Assembled in India, this album features the concertina or accordion format (above left), which could be opened to reveal works in an extended horizontal arrangement. It includes the folio illustrated below, pairing an Indian painting of a worshipping woman with a Persian painting of a *rubab* player, elegantly portrayed and signed by the artist Muhammad Ja'far.

16th–18th century (album); 18th century (worshipping woman); *c.* 1590 (*rubab* player)
India and Iran; India (worshipping woman); Qazvin, Iran (*rubab* player)
Lacquered covers with concertina (accordion-style) binding; ink, opaque watercolour and gold on paper (paintings)
Height 29.8 cm, width 19.7 cm (album)
1974,0617,0.15

and Iraq, manuscripts produced under Ilkhanid patronage exhibited Chinese techniques and introduced the ubiquitous lotus flower motif associated with Ilkhanid painting. Along with Qur'ans, the Ilkhanids commissioned a history of the world favouring their own dynasty as well as copies of the *Shahnama* ('Book of Kings') (3), the Persian epic celebrating ancient Iranian kingship, which they used as a manual for princely conduct and a symbol of legitimacy.

Despite periods of political instability, which could affect manuscript production in imperial capitals such as Baghdad or Tabriz, production continued at other sub-imperial centres like Shiraz, which became a key commerical hub. Baghdad and Tabriz remained capitals under the Jalayirids (1335–1432), who oversaw significant developments in the arts of the manuscript.

The relationship between image and text became less literal, with the former beginning to dominate the page. Drawing enabled another realm of exploration in subject matter and style; this would continue not only in Iran and Central Asia, but also in India and the Ottoman Empire.

Following the Jalayirid model, the Timurids (1370–1405) were also great literary patrons. Many Timurid manuscripts consciously emulated the style of earlier Ilkhanid, Jalayarid and Turkmen manuscripts in order to promote the new dynasty. Timurid courtly manuscripts also represent the highest level of manuscript production in a centralized workshop model.

Production and patronage under the Ottoman, Safavid, and Mughal empires followed Timurid precedents, with each court creating its own dynastic model but participating in an even more interconnected world where artists and manuscripts travelled widely; in all three spheres, the effects of cross-pollination are evident. Persian was the prevailing literary language at court (even if not always the spoken language of the realm), with the exception of the Ottomans, who began to commission texts in Ottoman Turkish in the late 1500s.

The album, or *muraqqa* (Arabic for 'patched'), was a composite compilation of different book arts, often including calligraphy, poetry, drawings, illumination and bookbinding. Its format could vary from the oblong *safina* to the horizontally extending concertina (4). Safavid albums were increasingly produced as an individual work in Isfahan, the new Safavid capital under Shah Abbas I (r. 1588–1629). On occasion, local bazaar artists were commissioned by visiting Europeans to depict portraits of people living in cities like Isfahan and Istanbul, producing a genre of costume albums that give snapshots of the social hierarchies of these places.

Many Ottoman and Indian albums reveal the great appeal of Persianate arts of the book, either following earlier Persian models or incorporating works by or inspired by celebrated Persian artists and calligraphers. While patronage and production declined in these regions after 1800, the legacy of the arts of the book survives in innovative contemporary interpretations and adaptations of historic texts as well as in a continually evolving definition of 'Islamic book arts', as artists produce works in dialogue with their global environment. (LA)

5 | 1 Oral traditions

Transcending boundaries of time and space, politics, culture and class, oral traditions originating in India, Iran, Central Asia and the Arab lands developed and were adapted over time into other languages and contexts. These palimpsests of diverse oral traditions feature epics about real and mythical kings and heroes, as well as romances (see p. 239) and religious narratives about the lives of prophets and saints (p. 59). Their narration activated multiple senses, from hearing the storyteller and accompanying music, to seeing images or a performance, to participating in key moments of the story, such as the beating of one's breast to mourn a beloved character. Such stories have inspired manuscript illustrations, monumental paintings, theatrical settings and contemporary visual culture.

The *Hamzanama*, an epic about the adventures of a hero based on the Prophet Muhammad's uncle Amir Hamza, greatly appealed to the young Mughal emperor Akbar (r. 1556–1605). He enjoyed listening to and reciting its tales at his court so much that in 1562, as his first royal commission, he ordered the production of an illustrated version of the epic (**1**). The exceptionally large-scale format of the pages, which were painted on cloth with a heavy paper backing (each illustration backed with a page of text), suggests the possibility that the pages were not bound as one. Instead, they might have been held before Akbar or another audience during the narration, a practice not unlike the use of large-scale paintings in public performances of the *Shahnama* ('Book of Kings', see pp. 236–37) in 15th-century Iran. Ultimately, this celebrated copy of the *Hamzanama* could be 'activated' by its reception on both a public and private scale, either as part of a recitation by a storyteller or as an intimate viewing experience.

The performative nature of the *Shahnama* was adapted by the Shi'a community to recount the story of the martyrdom of Imam Husayn, the Prophet's grandson, at Karbala (see also pp. 103, 178–79). This tragic event inspired annual re-enactments and ritual theatre productions (*ta'ziya*) that continue to this day. These were performed against an illustrated backdrop (*parda* or 'curtain') that could be rolled up and transported between locations, enabling a reciter to point out relevant scenes and images as he recounted the story.

The ground-breaking work, *Who is this Hossein the world is crazy about?* (**2**), made by contemporary multi-media artist Charles-Hossein Zenderoudi, invites the viewer to reflect upon a universal theme about the quest for truth through the prism of the Karbala story. Stages of the narrative are highlighted across the textile in frames that function both as images and visual pauses for meditation, each scene made of a separate linocut print. This work breaks conventional codes of storytelling by which the Karbala tragedy is traditionally presented both in terms of technique as well as conceptual approach. (LA)

1. The *Hamzanama*

These pages represent both sides of a single folio from the *Hamzanama* ('Adventures of Hamza'), which was inspired by popular legends recited by storytellers about the Prophet's uncle Amir Hamza. The completed work, which took 15 years, encompassed 14 volumes, each illustrated with 100 paintings by both Indian and Iranian artists, fewer than 150 of which survive today. The painting has been attributed to the famed artist Basawan, one of Akbar's finest court painters. In it, the Old Testament prophet Ilyas (also known as Elijah or Elias) rescues the drowning grandson of Amir Hamza, Prince Nur al-Dahr (Arabic for 'Light of the Age').

c. 1558–73
Mughal India
Ink and opaque watercolour on cloth (image side); ink on paper (text side)
Height 73.6 cm, width 57.9 cm
Donated by Rev. Stratton Campbell, 1925,0929,0.1

2. Charles-Hossein Zenderoudi (b. 1937), *Who is this Hossein the world is crazy about?*

The title of this work references an inscription repeated along its border, ending with a spiritual reference to the story of the moth and the flame: 'Who is this flame [candle], for which all souls are moths?' The artist's signature, inscribed as 'the work of the humble Hossein Zenderoudi', in the manner of the great masters, appears in a vertical panel at lower left, within the inscriptional frame.

1958
Linocut print on linen
Height 228.5 cm, width 148.5 cm
Funded by Maryam and Edward Eisler with contributions from CaMMEA acquisition group, the Brooke Sewell Permanent Fund and Dr Farhad Farjam, 2011,6034.1

5 | 2 Turkish shadow theatre

Originally inspired by performances in Egypt, shadow theatre has played an important role in the cultural traditions of Turkey since the early Ottoman period. A fabric screen illuminated from behind was the stage upon which a number of characters emerged to perform lively sketches and plays. The figures were made of coloured animal hide and were moved by means of sticks by a master puppeteer, sometimes with the help of an assistant.

Performances occurred mainly during the evenings in Ramadan, or at weddings and circumcisions. The plays themselves, part slapstick comedy part serious dialogue, followed a prescribed structure (**1**). At the same time they allowed the characters, particularly the two principal ones, Karagöz and Hacivat (**2**), to comment on topics ranging from the banalities of everyday life to more serious social and political matters (although topics such as the Sultan and religion were never discussed). The satirical approach extended in later years to the *Karagöz* newspaper published in Istanbul, in which Karagöz and Hacivat commented on current affairs. With the advent of cinema and television, shadow theatre fell into decline, but in 2007 the Turkish government declared Karagöz and Hacivat cultural assets, marking the recognition of this art form as part of national cultural heritage, and leading to its revival. (ZKH)

This page and opposite, below
1. The story of Ferhat and Shirin
In the play 'Ferhat and Shirin', Ferhat, a poor painter, falls in love with Shirin, whose rich mother objects to their relationship. She sets Ferhat the impossible task of bringing water from a nearby mountain using only a pickaxe. He succeeds with the help of Karagöz in spite of all the obstacles set by Shirin's mother. This story is loosely based on the Anatolian love story of Ferhat and Shirin that, in turn, had its origins in the Persian romance of Khusraw and Shirin recorded in Abu'l Qasim Firdawsi's *Shahnama*. Modified to suit shadow theatre, the story has a happy ending (whereas the literary versions do not). The scene here depicts Ferhat digging a water channel into the hillside (opposite page, below) while Shirin waits for him to return in front of her house (this page).

1970s
Made by Metin Özlen (b. 1940), Turkey
Painted animal hide
Length 46.2 cm, width 24 cm (Shirin's house); length 32.6 cm, width 14.7 cm (Shirin); length 30.7 cm, width 8.5 cm (Ferhat); length 36.8 cm, width 39.7 cm (mountain)
As 1980,09.6.a, 9, 15, 18, 32–41, 55

Right

2. Karagöz and Hacivat

Two characters dominate Turkish shadow theatre: Karagöz and Hacivat. Karagöz (with a rounded beard), represents a man of the people, embarking on doomed ventures to make ends meet. He is illiterate, impulsive, cowardly, rude and deceitful. Yet at the same time he is witty, helpful and behaves like a hero. Hacivat (with a pointed beard), on the other hand, is polite and refined, familiar with Arabic and Persian literature and a variety of subjects ranging from food and gardening to music and social etiquette. His knowledge, however, is superficial and his tendency to reason limits his ability to act, invariably causing arguments with Karagöz.

1970s
Made by Metin Özlen (b. 1940), Turkey
Painted animal hide
Height 33 cm, width 10 cm (Karagöz, excluding moving arm); height 33.2 cm, width 9.7 cm (Hacivat)
As1980,09.1, 3

5 | 3 Making a manuscript

The *kitabkhana*, or royal workshop-atelier, was at the centre of manuscript production and dissemination in the Islamic world. Whether concentrated at the heart of an empire, divided among smaller courts, or even mobile, workshops thrived with the support of royal and wealthy patrons.

The making of a manuscript was a collective enterprise. It required the coordinated efforts of papermakers, paper burnishers, pigment grinders, scribes, calligraphers, illuminators, gilders and other artisans.

Once a work was commissioned, the director of the *kitabkhana*, an artist himself, planned the project, determining the layout and assigning artisans. The paper was made from a pulp (formed from soaked strips of linen and hemp), dried, decorated with gold leaf or marbling, and burnished in preparation for ink (made of carbon boiled with gall nuts). When the scribe (**1, 2**) completed the text (leaving room for illustrations), the book passed to the painters, each of whom performed a speciality, be it faces or figures or battle scenes. The composition was initially drawn with a fine brush or copied from an existing design using a pounce (dusting charcoal powder over a perforated pattern taken from the outline of the original).

Painters created their own pigments, often from costly minerals such as gold, silver, lapis lazuli, cinnabar, orpiment and malachite. The pigments were then fixed to the page with albumen, glue or (after the 16th century) gum arabic.

Once the painting was complete, illuminators and gilders added chapter headings, border designs, frontispieces and colophons. The pages were sewn into a binding with a fore-edge flap tucked under the top cover. Leather bindings could also be tooled and decorated with vegetal or geometric patterns or other motifs originating as drawing on paper (see pp. 232–33), or stamped with medallions or cloud collar points created from moulds. Such bindings exhibited increasingly elaborate designs including bird-and-flower (**3, 4**) and figural imagery in the 16th century. By the 19th century, lacquer bindings replaced leather ones. (LA)

1. Tools of the calligrapher
This diverse assembly represents tools used by Ottoman calligraphers in the 19th century. It includes steel-bladed knives for cutting and sharpening pens and steel scissors of different shapes with gold inlay. The handle of one of the large pairs (shown in the foreground) is composed of two of the 99 names of God, 'the living' and 'the just'. Two ivory *maqta*s (at left and right), used to hold the pen in place while it was being cut, bear the signatures of Resmi and Junaid, who probably belonged to the Mevlevi Sufi brotherhood, as did many scribes and calligraphers.

18th–19th century
Turkey
Steel, ivory, gold inlay
Length 18.5 cm, width 3 cm
(largest scissors)
2002,0819.1–12

2. Seated scribe

Attributed to the celebrated Safavid artist Riza Abbasi, this drawing shows a seated scribe in contemplation, with a *safina* (a long, narrow album) on his knees. A royal seal ('Abbas, the servant of the king of Holiness [Ali]') suggests the work either represents a known figure or was considered valuable enough to collect in a royal album.

c. 1600
Isfahan, Iran
Ink, opaque watercolour and gold on tinted paper
Inscribed 'Riza drew it'
Height 15.7 cm, width 12.4 cm
1920,0917,0.271.1

3. Book cover

This book cover depicts a frog and insects among flowers in its central panel, surrounded by cartouches containing floral and foliate designs.

c. 1640
Iran
Leather, moulded and tooled
Height 32 cm, width 20.8 cm, thickness 0.4 cm
In memory of Anthony Gardner, a gift from the beneficiaries of the Anthony Gardner Estate, 1993,0727,0.1

4. Roses (*gul-i surkh*)

This drawing of insects among roses belongs to a 28-folio album with 55 drawings of plants, flowers, birds and insects. Most of its drawings are attributed to Shafi Abbasi, son of Riza (see ill. 2 above), and two bear seal impressions identified with him. Specializing in birds and flowers, Shafi's work reveals European as well as Indian inspiration.

Dated AD 1632/3 (AH 1042); overall album contents *c.* 1632–74
Isfahan, Iran
Ink on paper; lacquered covers
Height 13.9 cm, width 19.7 cm (drawing); height 28 cm, width 19.7 cm, thickness 2.7 cm (album)
Brooke Sewell Permanent Fund, 1988,0423,0.1.48

5 | 4 Calligraphy

Among the arts of the Islamic world, calligraphy holds pride of place for its connection to the Qur'an, where it is said that God's first creation was the pen (*qalam*) and that the pen recorded all existence onto a safely preserved tablet. By extension, calligraphers and the practise of calligraphy were also held in the highest esteem, as the act of writing beautifully was considered a pious endeavour that reflected the moral virtues of those who pursued it (**3**). Often, calligraphers could be poets or historians as well.

As an artistic tradition, calligraphy was standardized in the 10th century by the Abbasid vizier Ibn Muqla (886–940), who created a system of letter proportions for script measured by rhomboid dots and established the canon of the 'six scripts' (*al-aqlam al-sitta*), which would be elaborated by later masters. Among other scripts, *nasta'liq*, an elegant and rhythmic cursive script developed in the 14th century, is considered the greatest achievement in Persian calligraphy. Not only a vehicle for recording revelation, calligraphy was thus also critical for the development of the literary arts.

A calligrapher's knowledge was passed from master to disciple through a *silsila*, or chain, that connected generations of calligraphers to the model calligrapher and artist, the Prophet's son-in-law Ali. With the guidance of his teacher, a student learned over the course of many years through observation, instruction (which involved teaching the formation of letters, their systems of proportion and their composition, as well as the preparation of materials and tools), practice and revision (**1**), with the ultimate goal of obtaining a diploma (*ijaza*) in order to practise and teach. Pupils studied calligraphic treatises and examined the work of master calligraphers over the centuries; such learning 'by the eye' (*naziri*) provided a foundation for learning 'by the pen' (*qalami*). (LA)

1. Calligraphic exercise in *naskh* and *thuluth* scripts
Alongside training under the tutelage of a master, the calligrapher's individual practice and its constant repetition were essential to his growing career. This example shows one type of practice sheet, where a series of rhombic dots form a framework for the shaping and proportioning of letters in a pairing of two different scripts. The inscribed phrase reads, 'Oh Lord make it easy and not difficult, oh Lord may it be completed in the best way'. Although unsigned, the writing in this exercise recalls the style of the renowned Ottoman calligrapher Mustafa Rakim (1757–1826).

18th–19th century
Ottoman Turkey
Height 12.2 cm, width 23.8 cm
Donated by Oliver Hoare, 2003,0227,0.1

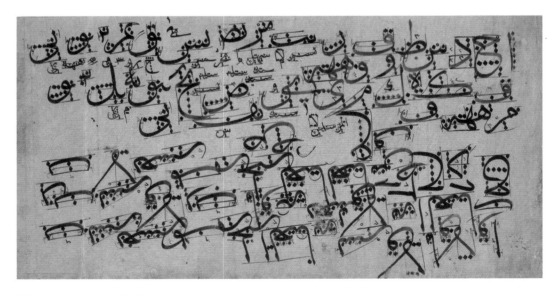

2. Calligraphy

This page of mystical Persian poetry was penned by the renowned Safavid calligrapher Mir Imad (d. 1615), who was trained by the disciple of the celebrated Mir Ali of Herat (d. 1556). One couplet is attributed to the 11th-century Sufi poet Abu Sa'id Abu'l-Khayr, who lived in Khurasan. The Persian language and the fluid *nasta'liq* script provided a visual vehicle for the musicality of Persian poetry. Coveted by the Mughals of India, specimens were collected in albums containing both painting and calligraphy, such as the one to which this folio belongs.

Dated AD 1610/1 (AH 1019); album assembled in Mughal India, late 17th–18th century
Iran
Ink, opaque watercolour and gold on paper; lacquer binding (not shown)
Height 42.5 cm, width 29.5 cm (folio)
1974,0617,0.21.79

3. *Ya Bahá al-Abha*

The Arabic phrase *Ya Bahá al-Abha* ('O Glory of the Most Glorious') is one of the most common spiritual invocations used by Bahá'ís to affirm their faith, offer praise or gratitude and seek guidance and support. This calligraphic rendering of it comes from a composition attributed to the Persian Mishkin Qalam ('Musk-scented Pen'; 1826–1912), a well-known calligrapher who embraced the Bahá'i faith while serving as tutor to the Qajar Crown Prince in Tabriz, eventually becoming scribe to Bahá'u'lláh, the Prophet-Founder of the faith.

Signed *Banda-yi Bab-i Bahá, Mishkin Qalam* (Servant of the Gate of Bahá, Mishkin Qalam)
Late 19th–early 20th century
Possibly Acre, Ottoman Palestine (modern Israel)
Ink, opaque watercolour and gold on paper pasted to board
Height 49.5 cm, width 62.5 cm (paper)
2010,6015.1

5 | 5 Drawing

Although calligraphy, with its relationship to the Arabic script and the Qur'an, was considered the highest art form, the art of painting or picture-making was also revered. Seeking to elevate the status of *tasvir*, the act of depiction, commentators especially on Persian painting likened it to writing by emphasizing the connection between the reed pen and the brush and the processes of each, and associating artistic activity with the 'writing' or creation of the world (see pp. 230–31).

The Arabic term *tasvir* does not differentiate between drawing and painting, yet drawing was mostly valued as a preparatory step towards a finished work. This changed in the late 15th and early 16th centuries, when artists practising in Iran began to explore and produce finished drawings. Albums assembled by artists and connoisseurs testify to the important roles of drawing as a preparatory process, as a vehicle for transferring designs to other media, and as an autonomous work. These collections served as pattern books for painters, binders, lacquermakers, saddlemakers, woodworkers and other artisans, or simply for pleasure. They show the dynamic nature of drawing as a medium that invited experimentation, whether through its reaction to the texture or pattern of paper or another surface; through the incorporation of foreign elements, such as Chinese- or European-inspired motifs; or through the exploration of texture and line using only pen, brush and ink.

Demand for drawing grew alongside the demand for single-page compositions and many artists developed signature styles. Requiring few and inexpensive materials, artists could work spontaneously and from nearly anywhere. Most extant drawings survive from 16th- to 18th-century Iran, Central Asia, Turkey and India, and explore subjects including single figures, bird-and-flower (p. 229) or other themes from nature (**1**, **2**), and the mystical, mythical, quotidian or fantastic (**1**, **3**). (LA)

1. Two pheasants in a Chinese-inspired landscape
This skilfully rendered drawing mounted on a detached album folio shows a landscape with a gnarled tree, scrolling fungi and two pheasants among dense foliage. Drawings such as this reveal a Chinese-inspired aesthetic resulting from the Mongol invasions of Iran and Central Asia and especially prevalent in the 15th century in these regions. Drawings were collected in albums and often pasted onto equally ornate folios where they could be admired by princes and other courtly elite.

Early 15th century
Herat, Afghanistan
Ink, opaque watercolour and gold on paper
Height 29.1 cm, width 44.7 cm (page); height 27 cm, width 22.7 cm (drawing)
Bequeathed by Sir Bernard Eckstein, Bart, 1948,1211,0.24

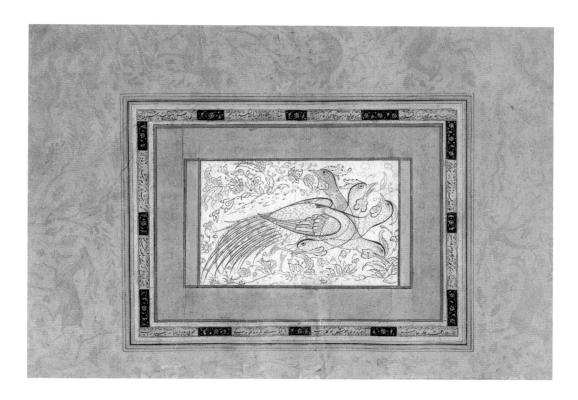

2. Study of a pheasant in motion

This drawing of a bird caught in five states of motion represents a masterful study of movements, while also exhibiting a calligraphic manipulation of line as an anchor for the entire composition. An ascription (albeit false) to Shah Quli (d. *c.* 1556), a Safavid artist who directed the studio of the Ottoman emperor Süleyman the Magnificent (r. 1520–66), and its preservation on an album page framed by verses of Persian poetry further suggest the drawing was admired as an independent work.

Late 16th century
Qazvin, Iran
Ink and gold on paper
Height 44.3 cm, width 30.7 cm
(page); height 10.2 cm, width
15.8 cm (drawing)
1930,1112,0.4

3. Angel riding a composite camel

The fantastic nature of this Mughal drawing is emphasized by the fact that the angel (who holds a bottle of smoking incense) is riding a camel made up of both human and animal figures. Composite animals were a particularly popular convention in northeastern Iran and India in the late 1500s–1600s, formed from a variety of figural types, including humans, demons and real and mythical creatures, all combined into the shapes of common animals such as the horse or camel.

1605–27
Mughal India
Ink, opaque watercolour and gold
on paper
Height 21.4 cm, width 15.3 cm
Bequeathed by Charles
Hazelwood Shannon,
1937,0710,0.332

5 | 6 Beyond the book: the single page

In the late 1500s, during the reign of the Safavid Shah Abbas I (r. 1588–1629) in Qazvin and Isfahan, an increased demand for single-page paintings and drawings boosted the role of the individual artist in Iran. Artistic patronage expanded beyond the court to wealthy merchants and functionaries, who could afford individual works produced quickly and inexpensively and assembled in albums, rather than commission a costly and labour-intensive illustrated manuscript. This was a marked change from when Timurid and early Safavid artists in the *kitabkhana*, or royal workshop-atelier, operated collectively towards the creation of a finished product. Among the most popular subjects depicted in single-page compositions are courtly figures (courtiers and courtesans), musicians, warriors, dandies, female figures of ideal beauty and Sufi dervishes. Some of these represent known personages, while others are generic portraits. Riza Abbasi (1565–1635), a leading artist both at and beyond the court of Shah Abbas, excelled particularly in the depiction of single figures (**2**; and also p. 229).

Patronage of the single page also flourished within the neighbouring Mughal and Ottoman empires, where Persianate painting and calligraphy were coveted and inspired local artists. As important as the court-commissioned manuscripts produced in the Mughal emperor Akbar's imperial workshop, for example, were single-page images collected in carefully assembled albums, depicting portraits of actual people (**1**) as well as detailed observations of landscapes and nature, and in some cases featuring mythical elements (**3**). (LA)

1. Wandering dervish with a dragon-headed staff

This blue-eyed dervish covered in symbolic trinkets may represent an ascetic figure who lived during the Mughal emperor Akbar's reign (1556–1605). In this period, certain branches of Sufism flourished in the Indian subcontinent and displayed practices in common with local mystics. Akbar found resonance with the influential teachings of the famous Andalusian scholar Ibn Arabi (1165–1240; see p. 69), whose mystical thinking distinguished between inner meaning and outer form, suggesting that the latter acts as the shadow or mirror image of the former.

Painting mounted on an album folio
c. 1570s
Mughal India
Ink, opaque watercolour and gold on paper
Height 19 cm, width 12.8 cm
Brooke Sewell Permanent Fund, 1983,0727,0.1

2. Seated youth reading

While this figure's face and the vegetation surrounding him recall other works by Riza Abbasi, features such as the sitter's slender proportions, his seat, and an intriguing Persian inscription suggest that the painting may pay homage to Muhammadi, a 16th-century artist from Herat:

On the order of the prosperous, most noble, most pure Highness, may God prolong his reign, is this likeness of the work of Master Muhammadi of Herat, [God's] mercy be upon him. The lowly, most contemptible of slaves, I opened [painted] this [face], which was honoured and decorated with the most noble seal. The work of the humble Riza-yi Abbasi.

The inscription also references the effaced royal seal below the figure's seat, suggesting the work may have been commissioned by Shah Abbas I.

c. 1625–26
Isfahan, Iran
Ink, opaque watercolour and gold on paper; mounted on a detached album folio
Height 21.9 cm, width 14.7 cm (page)
1920,0917,0.298.3

3. Angel seated on a carpet
The figure in this painting, one of a facing pair of angels, probably derives from a well-known Persian portrait type of a seated woman. The colourful Chinese-inspired scrolling decoration in the background recalls the artistic schools of Bukhara (Uzbekistan) and Khurasan (northeastern Iran and Afghanistan). Persian verses framing the angel emphasize her beauty through a connection to China, which was associated with great beauty in Persian literature and culture.

c. 1555
Bukhara (over-painted in Mughal India)
Ink, opaque watercolour and gold on paper; mounted on a detached album folio
Height 29 cm, width 19 cm (page)
Bequeathed by Percival Chater Manuk and Miss G.M. Coles and funded by the Art Fund (as NACF), 1948,1009,0.54

5|7 *Shahnama*, the Iranian 'Book of Kings'

'Drink up your wine and – as you do so – I
Will tell a story from the days gone by,
A story full of love and trickery,
Whose hero lived for war and chivalry.'
'Sweet moon', I said, 'my cypress, my delight,
Tell me this tale to wile away the night.'
'First listen well', she said, 'and when you've heard
The story through, record it word for word.'

So begins one of the most popular stories from the *Shahnama* ('Book of Kings'), considered the Iranian national epic, written down in 50,000 lines of verse by the Persian poet Abu'l Qasim Firdawsi by around AD 1010. Including countless other tales of semi-mythical kings and warriors, heroes and villains, these verses recount the story of ancient Iran, preserved to the present day in diverse media including manuscripts (**1**, **3**), architectural decoration (**2**), film (**4**) and on walls or curtains (*pardas*) used as backdrops for a narrative recited or sung by a professional storyteller. The *Shahnama* provided a key foundation for the shaping of national identity in Persianate literary and visual culture from the courts to the common people. A template for royal behaviour for the entire eastern Islamic world, it served as a legitimizing tool for foreign rulers who linked themselves visually to the powerful chain of Iranian rulership through courtly commissions and dissemination of the manuscript. In popular culture, its verses and characters continue to share elements in common with the mythology and oral traditions of earlier periods as well as in cultures east and west of Iran, suggesting that geographical boundaries do not necessarily hinder the spread of the spoken word. (LA)

1. The Arrival of Fariburz before Kay Khusraw

Unable to choose between his son Fariburz and his grandson Kay Khusraw as his successor, the mythological Iranian king Kay Kavus promised the throne to the prince who could successfully seize the fortress of Bahman. Victorious, Kay Khusraw ascended the throne and is shown here receiving his rival Fariburz, who kneels to his left. This painting belongs to the 'Big Head' *Shahnama* copied in 1484 for the Turkman Sultan Ali Mirza, who ruled the Caspian province of Gilan.

Dated AD 1493/4 (AH 899)
Gilan, Iran
Ink, opaque watercolour and gold on paper
Height 34.4 cm, width 24.4 cm (page)
1992,0507,0.1

2. Tile depicting a polo match between Siyavush and Afrasiyab

Here the legendary Iranian prince Siyavush and Afrasiyab, the ruler of Turan, play polo. Siyavush had fled to the court of Afrasiyab after a dispute with his father,

the king of Iran. Selections of verses from the *Shahnama* frame the tile, describing the start of the game, the sound of the crowd's cheering reaching the moon, and Siyavush riding into the king's playing field with such speed that he disappears from sight, impressing the Turanian king. Three clover-shaped cartouches at the top contain the name of the potter, Muhammad Ibrahim.

c. 1850
Tehran, Iran
Stonepaste, painted in polychrome colours under a transparent glaze
Height 30.6 cm, width 30.6 cm
Bequeathed by Miss Edith Godman, G.314

3. Rustam sleeping while Rakhsh fights a lion

The legendary Rustam is the greatest hero of the *Shahnama*. Here the warrior and his faithful horse Rakhsh risk a short cut in their effort to rescue the Iranian king Kay Kavus from a demon's captivity. Stopping to rest in a meadow along the way (here depicted as a forest), they unknowingly find themselves in a lion's lair. The lion returns as Rustam sleeps, but Rakhsh protects his master by trampling the lion to death. The manuscript to which this page belonged is believed to have been commissioned by the Safavid ruler Shah Tahmasp (r. 1524–76) for his father, Shah Isma'il I (r. 1501–24), but it was never completed; the painting, too, remains unfinished. Its esteemed artist, Sultan Muhammad, worked at the atelier of the Aqqoyunlu Turkmen in Tabriz before becoming the director of this *Shahnama* project.

1515–22
Tabriz, Iran
Ink, opaque watercolour and gold on paper
Height 31.6 cm, width 20.8 cm
Bequeathed by Sir Bernard Eckstein, Bart, 1948,1211,0.23

4. Ali Akbar Sadeghi (Iranian, b. 1937), *The Sun King XXXI*

Loosely based on the *Shahnama*, the storyline of the animated film in which this celluloid was used centres on a wealthy king who has everything but love. While exploring his palace one day, he discovers a painting of a beautiful woman and falls for her. His search for his beloved includes an encounter with the White Div ('demon') pictured here.

2016
Iran
Animation celluloid with drawn background, mixed media
Height 35 cm, width 30 cm
Funded by the Farjam Foundation, 2016,6042.2

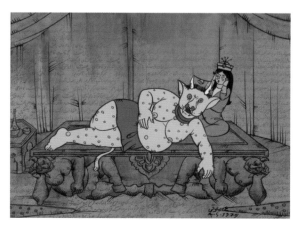

5 | 8 Knowledge and literature

Epics such as the *Shahnama*, romances recounted in the books of the *Khamsa* (Quintet) of the Persian poet Nizami (1141–1209) or the Indo-Persian poet Amir Khusraw Dihlavi (1253–1325), *mirrors for princes* (literature meant to guide and advise future rulers), and biographical, historical and scientific texts comprise some of the many types of illustrated manuscripts produced throughout the Islamic world. Commissioned mainly by royal and elite patrons who could afford to support the team of artisans and the costly materials required in the *kitabkhana*, or workshop-atelier, manuscripts often played a strategic role in times of political transition or instability. Rulers and court officials commissioned and endowed Qur'ans and other literary and scientific manuscripts to charitable institutions such as mosques or *madrasas* (religious colleges) to elevate their own standing before God and their subjects. They also used texts to create legitimizing historical narratives, whether by representing likenesses of themselves in earlier narratives (such as the Ilkhanids did with the Great Mongol *Shahnama*, see ill. 3 on p. 221) or by introducing themselves as subjects of dynastic histories.

The relationship between image and text in illustrated manuscripts appears to have evolved over the centuries, with early texts utilizing images to evoke a culture of learning and knowledge transmission more so than to illustrate a text directly (**1**). Other images supported textual content with visual narratives that expanded upon key moments in a story (**2**, **3**). Over time, especially from the 16th century onwards, the balance of text and image shifted to the image often occupying most of the page (**2**, **3**). (LA)

1. Two doctors administering medicine to a patient
This page comes from an Arabic version of the well-known herbal treatise on medicine by the Greek physician Dioscorides of the 1st century AD. It was translated into Syriac and then Arabic in Baghdad in the 9th century. Arabic copies were widely disseminated and, following the Greek tradition, included illustrations of figures as well as plants. The text addresses septic wounds caused by poisonous bites, the diagnosis of a fractured skull, and intestinal ulcers. The classical tripartite setting and the absence of landscape recall earlier styles of Islamic manuscript illustration. The folio belongs to a manuscript with a dated colophon of AD 1224 in Istanbul's Hagia Sophia library.

Dated AD 1224 (AH 621)
Baghdad, Iraq
Ink and opaque watercolour on paper
Height 32.8 cm, width 24.3 cm (page)
Donated by Sir Bernard Eckstein, Bart, 1934,1013,0.1

2. Bahram Gur hunting with Dilaram

The Sasanian ruler Bahram V (r. AD 420–438) was known for his hunting prowess as Bahram Gur (Persian for a fast-running onager). Boasting to his servant Dilaram that he could transform a stag into a doe and vice versa, he shot the antlers off a stag and formed antlers on a doe by piercing the latter's head with two arrows. Rooted in oral tradition, this tale was recounted and illustrated in several versions. This scene is from the *Hasht bihisht* ('Eight paradises'), one of the five stories included in the Indo-Persian poet Amir Khusraw Dihlavi's version of the *Khamsa*, but it also appears in the Persian poet Nizami's *Khamsa* as well as in the *Shahnama*.

c. 1610–11
Mughal India
Ink, opaque watercolour and gold on paper
Height 41.6 cm, width 26.5 cm
1920,0917,0.258

3. Arjuna and Bhima preparing for battle

This battle scene is from the *Razmnama* ('Book of war'), an abridged Persian translation of the *Mahabharata*, the Hindu epic, ordered by the Mughal emperor Akbar (r. 1556–1605). Here the warriors Arjuna and Bhima confront each other in their chariots, enclosed by war elephants and cavalry. The manuscript to which this folio belongs was commissioned by a Mughal army commander who served both Akbar and Jahangir and who purportedly had a workshop of 20 artists.

c. 1616–17
Mughal India
Ink, opaque watercolour on paper
Height 34.7 cm, width 23.8 cm
Brooke Sewell Permanent Fund,
1981,0703,0.1

5 | 9 Costume albums

Album-making appears to have begun in 15th-century Iran and continued to develop in Safavid Iran and later in Ottoman Turkey and India from the 16th century and well into the 1800s (**1**, **2**; and see pp. 222, 231–35). While many surviving albums and album folios carry courtly associations, one genre – the costume album – attests to a thriving commercial market catering to visiting foreigners. Travellers such as the German physician and explorer Engelbert Kaempfer, who spent almost 20 months in Iran from 1684–85, commissioned local artists to document people, animals and scenes from daily life, which shed light on local Iranian customs and served as a type of 'souvenir book' (**1**). The format of the 'Kaempfer Album' follows European pattern books with two types of people or animals shown on each page and includes some of the traveller's own sketches.

In the Ottoman lands, costume albums in both manuscript and printed form first appeared in the mid-16th century and continued to be produced into the 19th century, when photographic images of Eastern costume entered the visual repertoire. Made by Ottoman painters in Istanbul, such albums were intended for foreign visitors as a sort of insider's guidebook into Ottoman society and were a local response to European-made books depicting Ottoman costume. The same artists also served local patrons or produced other types of painting for different markets.

One of the finest examples of an Ottoman costume album was commissioned by the English merchant Peter Mundy while stationed in Istanbul as a clerk for the Levant Company from 1617–20 (**2**). It follows the format of typical Ottoman costume albums with images arranged according to Ottoman social hierarchy: sultans, men (from courtiers to common people), women and foreigners. It is distinguished by a quality of workmanship commensurate with courtly album production. Moreover, Mundy's images are accompanied by his own comprehensive and sympathetic account of Ottoman society based on both personal experiences and other sources. (LA)

1. Four portraits of women in the Kaempfer Album
The four women portrayed here on facing pages represent a Zoroastrian woman, a Turkish (*Rumi*) woman, an Indian (*Hindu*) woman and a Georgian (*Gurji*) woman, as described by the captions appearing in Persian above each of them. The artist Jani, who completed most of the paintings in the 45-page album, called himself *farangi saz*, or 'painter in the European style', suggesting he may have been responding to European tastes by using European techniques (such as modelling).

Dated AD 1684/5 (AH 1096)
Isfahan, Iran
Ink and opaque watercolour on paper; album bound in brown leather with gilt decoration, with marbled paper inside covers
Height 22.4 cm, width 32 cm, thickness 2.9 cm (album); height 21.4 cm, width 29.9 cm (each page)
Bequeathed by Sir Hans Sloane, 1974,0617,0.1.17–18

2. Portraits of noblewomen in the Mundy Album

The 'single-figure' format of Ottoman costume albums such as the Mundy Album (*A briefe relation of the Turckes, their kings, Emperors, or Grandsigneurs, their conquests, religion, customes, habbits, etc*) drew from single-figure portraits mounted in Persianate albums, suggesting that artists utilized their own traditions while catering to European tastes. These pages come from the section on women; both individuals appear to be noblewomen, one of whom (above) is dressed simply but elegantly in a high headdress, a black overcoat over white robe and trousers, and bath clogs, possibly her way to the *hammam*. Skilfully composed decorative paper cut-outs flank both figures while other floral cut-outs (cyclamen, lilac, roses and tulips) appear on the facing album pages. In its present form, the Mundy Album comprises 60 folios with 59 paintings of figures

and additional découpages, but there appear to be lacunae.

1618
Istanbul, Ottoman Turkey
Ink and opaque watercolour, applied with cut paper; album covered with green leather

Height 20.6 cm, width 14.5 cm, thickness 2.2 cm (album); height 19.8 cm, width 13.2 cm (each page)
1974,0617,0.13.48.v, 49.r, 46.v, 47.r

5 | 10 Modern artists' books

The making of books by Middle Eastern artists represents both a continuity with the well-established tradition of book production in the Islamic world and the tradition established by French artists at the turn of the 20th century, the *livre d'artiste,* or artist's book. It is the Lebanese artist Shafic Abboud, who spent much of his life in Paris, and was a member of the *École de Paris,* who is credited with having produced the first such artist's book, *Le Bouna,* made in 1953 (**1**). While *Le Bouna* is a story that belongs within the folk history of Lebanon, the others illustrated in this section are all linked to poetry telling different kinds of narratives. A striking feature is the close interaction between text and image, demonstrating symbiotic relationships between the artist and the poet. Another Lebanese artist, Etel Adnan, worked with the *leporello,* the concertina book. Here she has delicately inscribed the poem of Nelly Salameh Amri set in the Lebanese Civil War (1976–90), framed by the tragic story of the Greek heroine Antigone who defies her uncle Creon and is put to death (**3**). Iraqi artist Dia al-Azzawi takes his inspiration from the poetry of Adonis, the *nom de plume* of Syrian poet Ali Ahmad Said (b. 1930) (**2**), while Rachid Koraïchi reflects upon the words of Palestinian poet Mahmoud Darwish (1941–2008), in his *Nation in exile* (**4**). (VP)

1. Shafic Abboud (Lebanese, 1926–2004), *Le Bouna*
The story illustrated here comes from a village known as Mhaidthe, northeast of Beirut where Abboud had close connections. It is a macabre tale in which two orphan brothers Helou ('sweet') and Murr ('bitter') fall into the hands of a wicked priest, after which various dramas unfold.

1953
Artist's book printed in Paris (edition 10/20)
Paper, ink
Height 38 cm, width 28 cm (book closed)
Funded by CaMMEA, 2016,6060.1

2. Dia al-Azzawi (Iraqi, b. 1939), *Adonis LX*

Made on the occasion of the 60th birthday of the Syrian poet Adonis (b. 1930), this book illustrates five of his poems. Here the artist has placed extracts within the painting:

The meek of the earth approached, they immersed this age in ragged dreg-drops and tears, they immersed the searching body, away from its warmth….

1990 (edition 1/6)
Original gouache and five hand-painted lithographs
Height 39.5 cm, width 109.5 cm
Brooke Sewell Permanent Fund, 1990,1123,0.1

3. Etel Adnan (Lebanese, b. 1925), *Blessed day*

The use of Arabic script as a form of decoration is known as *hurufiyya* (after the Arabic word for letter). Here Adnan has highlighted individual phrases and placed symbols between the lines. The poem begins:

Today is a blessed day. A day off for the snipers. Antigone addresses the king. She has to die. Today is a blessed day. She has to express questions which carry no anger, no need for revenge….

1990
Paris, France
Height 16 cm, width 190 cm (open)
Brooke Sewell Permanent Fund, 1990,1117,0.1

4. Rachid Koraïchi (Algerian, b. 1947), *Nation in exile*

Koraïchi became friends with the poet Mahmoud Darwish when the latter went into exile in Tunis in 1981. This work is a series of engravings representing Darwish's poems, dramatically combining script and symbols. The poem begins:

*Write down! I am an Arab
And my identity card is number fifty thousand
I have eight children
And the ninth will come after summer
Will you be angry?*

1981
Paris
Paper
Height 76 cm, width 46.5 cm (page)
Donated by Rachid Koraïchi, 2016,6059.11.a–b

5 | 11 Music

The musical traditions of the Islamic world are as rich and varied as the lands and regions where they originate. One of the main distinguishing features of these traditions, however, is the fact they are based on scales different from the chromatic scale associated with Western music. These scales, with their quarter notes and other finer gradations, allowed for more differentiated tonal nuances in singing and in the playing of instruments. Melodies were generally organized in terms of modes with characteristic patterns and scales, rhythmic formulas and intonations, allowing performers to improvise within the framework of the modes. Singers, male and female, including the celebrated Umm Kulthum (1), contributed their individual interpretations of modes and performed emotive renderings of lyrics and poems.

Instrumental music was not generally seen as an independent art form but was intertwined with vocal music, supporting and complementing it. The variety of musical instruments was substantial. These can be broadly divided into the following categories: stringed instruments (2), wind instruments and percussion instruments (3).

Regional music styles were in a constant state of development, borrowing from and mutually influencing each other, while maintaining a classical repertoire in each region, with a preference for particular instruments. Since the 19th century, there has been increased exposure to the various types of western music, leading to new developments in local music styles.

Within Islam itself, there is no prohibition against music in the Qur'an. The recitation of the Qur'an relies on melody, rhythm and vocal ornamentation, as does the call to prayer, *adhan*. Sufi mystical orders relied on melody in their ceremonies and accorded music a privileged place in their religious observances. (ZKH/VP)

1. Chant Avedissian (Egyptian, b. 1951), *Umm Kulthum*

The famous Egyptian singer, Umm Kulthum (d. 1975), is depicted smiling and wearing her trademark dark glasses against a background of Ottoman crescents and stars. Referred to admiringly as *Kawkab al-sharq* ('Star of the East'), Umm Kulthum had an immense repertoire that encompassed religious, sentimental and nationalistic songs. Her improvisations and her ability to create multiple iterations of single lines of text mesmerized audiences, bringing them to tears and drawing them into the emotion and symbolism of the words she sang.

1990s
Cairo, Egypt
Stencils, pigments on recycled cardboard
Height 49.5 cm, width 70 cm
Brooke Sewell Permanent Fund, 1995,0411,0.2

2. Arabian lute

The lute (*ud*) is one of the most popular musical instruments played across the Arab world, Turkey, Iran and elsewhere. Some regard it as the most prestigious in the region. Its name is believed to derive from the Arabic for 'wood', in reference to the strips of wood used to make its rounded body. Arabian lutes are normally larger, and produce a fuller and deeper sound, than their Turkish and Persian counterparts. This example, signed and dated by the maker, Fawzi Monshid (b. 1947), has 12 pegs with doubled strings grouped in six courses that would have been plucked with a plectrum, known in Arabic as a *risha* ('feather').

13 July 1981
Basra, Iraq
Rosewood, cedar, ebony
and bone
Length 79 cm
2017,6003.1

3. Nja Mahdaoui
(Tunisian, b. 1937),
Double-headed drum

The artist Nja Mahdaoui has been described as a 'choreographer of letters'. On this drum he has painted calligrams that echo the shapes of Arabic letters, but are without meaning. This is a hallmark of his style, the focus being on the aesthetic and rhythmic qualities of the letters. Religious ceremonies and public events in Mahdaoui's native Tunisia are often accompanied by percussion performances and he frequently performs his art with musicians and poets. Drums of this type are suspended from the shoulder by a leather strap and are played with two wooden beaters.

1997–98
Painted in La Marsa, Tunisia
Wood and animal skin
Height 46 cm, diameter 67 cm
Af1998,03.1

Timeline

6 The modern world

The 1800s saw the expansion of European empires into the Arab lands of the Middle East. In 1798, Napoleon's forces had occupied Egypt, where they remained for three years, their attempts to take Syria only repulsed by joint Ottoman and British intervention. But it was the First World War (1914–18) that began the seismic shifts that led to the dismemberment of the Ottoman Empire and the end of the close to 1,300-year-old caliphate in 1924. Iran also underwent political turmoil, with the overthrow of the Qajar dynasty in 1925 by Reza Khan (r. 1925–41). He became the first ruler of the Pahlavi dynasty that ruled Iran until the revolution of 1978–79 that established the Islamic republic (1). Afghanistan's complex history saw British intervention (1838–1919), the introduction of a monarchy, Soviet intervention (1979–89) and control by the Taliban (1996–2001).

In the former Arab provinces of the Ottoman Empire, following the First World War, the victorious French and British colonial powers divided up the region according to the Sykes-Picot Agreement of 1916, creating and controlling a series of states across the region (Syria, Lebanon, Iraq, Transjordan and Palestine). Only the Arabian Peninsula remained largely free of European control. The Second World War changed the balance of power dramatically. In its aftermath, European colonial powers began to withdraw from the region and independent states emerged, determined to assert their national identities.

1. Hengameh Golestan (Iranian, b. 1952), *Witness 79* Golestan documented a demonstration of 8 March 1979 in Tehran, when more than 100,000 women flooded the streets to protest against the compulsory wearing of the *hijab*. Her remarkable photographs captured a moment in time in the history of the Iranian revolution, with women from all professions protesting together. They were not printed until 2015.

1979 (edition 3/10)
Tehran, Iran
Black and white photograph
Height 50 cm, width 70 cm
The Art Fund, 2017,6018.2

2. Syrian banknote

On the face (top) of this banknote is Hafez al-Assad (r. 1970–2000). In the centre are three iconic images relating to Syria's history: the Umayyad mosque in Damascus commissioned by the caliph al-Walid on the site of a Roman temple and Christian basilica, and completed after his death in AD 715; an Umayyad dinar; and a cuneiform tablet from the ancient site of Ebla dating to about 2500 BC. The reverse of the note highlights modernity, with images representing the industrialization of the country.

Dated 1997, issued 2013
Syria
Height 7.5 cm, width 17 cm
2016,4016.9

3. Raed Yassin (Lebanese, b. 1979), *The Yassin Dynasty*

At first sight, Raed Yassin has made what looks like a traditional Chinese porcelain vase. Painted upon it, however, is a scene from the Lebanese Civil War (1976–1990) featuring a key battle, the 'Mountain war', that took place in 1983 in the Chouf Mountains between the Christians and the Druze. It was made in Jingdezhen, the porcelain capital of China, along with six other vases that together highlight the main battles that were to change the course of the war.

2013
Jingdezhen, China
Hand-painted porcelain vase
Height 35 cm, diameter 37 cm
Funded by CaMMEA and the Brooke Sewell Permanent Fund, 2016,6037.1

In the following pages we show how Middle Eastern and Central Asian states emphasize their links to their past cultures and historical achievements, while at the same time highlighting their place in the modern world (**2**). For their part, artists find ways both to reflect on their place in society and to comment on the tumultuous politics of the region they inhabit (**3**). (VP)

6 | 1 Palestinian dress

Palestinian embroidered garments and headgear were once markers of regional identity, marital and social status, vocation and, from the late 1930s, political commitment (**1, 2**). Most extant embroidered garments from Palestine date from between the early 19th and mid-20th centuries, spanning the last years of Ottoman rule and three decades of the British Mandate period (1918–1948) until the establishment of the State of Israel in 1948. Richly embroidered female garments were made by Arab women of rural Palestine who lived in over 800 villages scattered throughout the coastal plain and in the hills to the north and east (**3**). In contrast, urban women and men, living in towns such as Jerusalem, Hebron and Nazareth, wore fashions in the style of the Ottoman and British ruling elite. In recent times, political destabilization, displacement and economic hardship have contributed to the erosion of Palestinian textile traditions. Nevertheless, some women continue to make cushions and garments to wear and sell, as Palestinian embroidery has acquired nationalistic significance.

As for male garments, until the 1920s, head-cloths and head-ropes were worn exclusively by the Bedouin of Iraq, Arabia, Palestine, Syria, Lebanon and Jordan, visibly distinguishing them from townsmen who preferred the fez or turban. From the late 1930s, however, plain and checked head-cloths (*keffiyeh*) became unifying symbols of Palestinian national identity following the Arab revolt (1936–1939) in Palestine aimed at British colonial rule (**2**). Subsequently, from the 1960s, the black and white fishnet-patterned *keffiyeh* was strongly associated with Yasser Arafat (1929–2004), former president of the Palestinian National Authority and chairman of the Palestine Liberation Organization. (FS)

1. Set of model Palestinian hats

This set of 18 model hats reflects the importance of headgear as a marker of age and experience, religious affiliation, social hierarchies and vocations in Palestinian towns and villages until the 1930s. Included are hats worn by various Jewish, Christian and Muslim religious officials and scholars, village elders, manual labourers and the urban elite. These types of models were made for tourists, pilgrims and Church missions visiting the Holy Land.

1890s–1920s
Palestine
Silk, wool, fur, cotton, wood and paper
Length 43 cm, width 20.5 cm (pegboard); height 3.5–8.5 cm, diameter 5–5.5 cm (hats)
Donated by the Jerusalem and Middle East Church Association, As 1987,07.6.a–s, As 1987,07.7.a–r

2. The *keffiyeh*

Folded diagonally and held in place with a head-rope (*aqal*), the checked *keffiyeh* has a number of designations across the Arab world, including *ghutra*, *shimagh* and *mashada*. The Bedouin example (left) is woven with indigo-dyed thread and the high-status head-rope shown on the red *keffiyeh* (centre) is bound with gilt thread. The example on the right, with Palestinian flag, was adapted in the 1980s into a woman's neck scarf (as worn in the West Bank and refugee camps in Jordan).

1920–1948 (Bedouin); 1950s–1980s (red); 1940s–1950s (head-rope); 1980s (scarf)
Palestine (Bedouin); Palestine or Yemen (red); Saudi Arabia (head-rope); Palestine or Jordan (scarf)
Cotton, synthetic wool, silk, gilt-metal-wrapped thread
Length 114 cm, width 121 cm (Bedouin); length 127 cm, width 124 cm (red); circumference 119 cm (head-rope); length 152 cm, width 14 cm (scarf)
As 1966,01.290 (Bedouin); bequeathed by Leila Ingrams, 2015,6054.1 (red); donated by Gerald de Gaury, As 1974,05.3 (head-rope); As 1988,06.21 (scarf)

3. Set of dolls in regional Palestinian dress

This set of seven dolls was made for sale at the World's YWCA School at the Aqabat Jaber Refugee Camp in Jericho, which sheltered 30,000 refugees between 1948 and 1967. Made of textile over a wired metal frame, the dolls are identified as follows (left to right): Bethlehem (a married woman), Bethany or al-Azariya, Al-Salt (a Bedouin), Nazareth, an urban Muslim in outdoor veils, Jerusalem (Bait Mahsir district) and Jericho.

Jericho, Palestine, 1950s–1960s
Silk, cotton, polyester, sequins, card and metal wire
Height 19–20 cm
Donated by the Jerusalem and Middle East Church Association, 2012,6014.75–83

6 | 2 Politics and conflict

There is an inextricable link between textiles and politics in the Islamic world. Luxury textiles discussed elsewhere, such as inscribed *tiraz* fabrics from Fatimid Egypt (see p. 10) or sumptuous Ottoman silks (see p. 165), exemplify their use as conspicuous emblems of imperial power and status. Political portraiture in the Islamic world is another long-established medium through which rulers transmitted and asserted their power. In the 20th century, the development and dissemination of technologies such as television, colour photography and colour printing offered new and more affordable opportunities for political propaganda. Printing on textiles also became faster and more economical, allowing a wider distribution of political and religious ideologies. The printed silk scarf illustrated here was produced to promote the notion of a pan-Arab nation or state (**2**). The idea was initially conceived by Arab intellectuals as a result of the growing resentment against Ottoman Turkish rule and, after the First World War, in response to the Western imperialist partition of the Ottoman Empire's Arab provinces.

The time-honoured tradition of carpet weaving has also been affected by modern political realities. Before the collapse of the USSR in 1991, Soviet authorities encouraged carpet weavers to glorify communist heroes through the medium of portrait rugs (**1**). In contrast, Afghan carpet weavers recorded their experiences of the Soviet invasion of Afghanistan (1979–89), and its aftermath, graphically on their pictorial 'war rugs' (**4**). In recent times, artists living in the West, such as Sara Rahbar, have produced works that grapple with war, national identity and belonging (**3**). (FS)

1. Portrait rug of Lenin
This rug was produced to mark the 100th anniversary of Lenin's birth (1870–1924). Before the collapse of the USSR in 1991, Soviet authorities strongly encouraged artisans to glorify communist heroes and socialist ideologies in their works.

1970
Turkmenistan
Wool and cotton
Length 75.5 cm, width 48 cm
Funded by British Museum
Friends, As2002,01.4

2. Scarf with political portraits
This scarf was designed to promote the creation of a pan-Arab union in the 1960s. It features a map of 13 countries of the Middle East and North Africa, with their respective flags, surrounded by portraits captioned in Arabic of leaders who were lauded as heroes of Arab nationalism. From 1958 to 1961, Egypt and Syria formed the United Arab Republic. Syria, Iraq and Egypt proposed another single sovereign state in 1963. Ultimately, these ambitions were never realized.

1963–64
Yemen or Egypt
Silk
Length 80 cm, width 76 cm
As1997,01.9

3. Sara Rahbar
(Iranian-American, b. 1976),
Texas Flowers

Having migrated to the USA after the 1979 Iranian Revolution, Sara Rahbar's works grapple with the entangled relationship between the two countries she calls home. *Texas Flowers* is an assemblage of embroidered motifs from Central Asian *suzani* textiles that are stitched onto a vintage American flag. Once regarded as symbols of love on a bridal *suzani*, the flowers are transformed into revolver chambers surrounding an outline of Texas.

2008
USA/Iran
Silk and cotton
Length 183 cm, width 122 cm
Funded by the Brooke Sewell Permanent Fund, CaMMEA and Maryam and Edward Eisler, 2015,6005.2

4. Afghan war rug

International interest in war rugs spurred female weavers to produce overtly militaristic images of the Soviet invasion and subsequent withdrawal. This 'exit rug', featuring a central map of Afghanistan, celebrates the *mujahideen* victory over the Soviets. Inside the map, rocket launchers and Kalashnikovs point at armoured vehicles and helicopters that are shown in retreat. The inclusion of English words and the rug's portable size would have appealed to foreign consumers.

1989–1990s
Afghanistan or Pakistan
Wool and cotton
Length 94 cm, width 63 cm
Donated by Graham Gower, 2010,6013.24

6 | 3 Contemporary art

Artists of the Middle East often tackle in a direct but subtle way the realities of the region today. Jamal Penjweny, living in the Kurdish region of Iraq, and Chicago-based Michael Rakowitz, for example, both artists of Iraqi heritage, have commented in different ways on the aftermath of the Iraq War of 2003. Among the devastating impacts of the war was the looting of the National Museum of Iraq as well as various historic sites. The most important missing objects were placed on the University of Chicago's 'Lost Treasures from Iraq database', and only a small proportion have been subsequently recovered. Rakowitz's response was to make reproductions of these lost objects out of packaging and Arabic newspapers and he refers to them by their database number (**3**). The reproduction of such objects in modern materials serves both to emphasize the fragility of cultural heritage and to encourage reflection on the nature of the relationship between past and contemporary engagement with artefacts that have survived over millennia, and between cultural memory and present experience. Penjweny, in his ironic *Saddam is Here*, looks at the human cost and the tragedy of contemporary Iraq still living with the effects of the era of Saddam Hussein (**2**).

Saudi artist Manal Dowayan works in a number of different media from photography to installation, and her subject matter is concerned mostly with highlighting issues faced by women in Saudi Arabia. In *Standing and pecking dove* she finds a peaceful way of drawing attention to a time in recent history when women of Saudi Arabia could not travel on their own (**1**). (VP)

**1. Manal Dowayan
(Saudi Arabian, b. 1973),
*Standing and pecking dove***
These birds look like doves of peace but stamped upon them are documents. These were the authorization papers that women wanting to travel out of Saudi Arabia needed to obtain and which had to be signed by a male guardian.

2011
Porcelain
Height 23 cm, width 20 cm (max)
Funded by CaMMEA,
2016,6055.1–2

**2. Jamal Penjweny
(Iraqi-Kurdish, b. 1981),
Saddam is Here**

'They supported him, they cheered for him, they beautified his cruelty and crimes and they simply put him in power to be the godfather of Iraq. Saddam is here. Iraqi society cannot forget him even after his death because some of us still love him and the rest are still afraid of him.' Penjweny's darkly comic photographs, first exhibited at the Venice Biennale of 2013, show ordinary Iraqis acting out their daily lives with the portrait of the former Iraqi president (d. 2006) in front of their faces.

2010 (edition 4/5)
Height 60 cm, width 80 cm
The Art Fund, 2017,6019.4
(one of 12)

**3. Michael Rakowitz
(American, b. 1981),
The Invisible Enemy Should
Not Exist: Jar with Four
Pierced Lugs (IM42587)
(left); Headless Female
Figure Wearing Dress
(IM9005) (right). From
the series Recovered,
Missing, Stolen**

The phrase 'The Invisible Enemy Should Not Exist' is a reflection of *Aj-i-bu-ur-sa-pu-um*, the Babylonian name for the ancient processional way that ran through the Ishtar Gate at Babylon. The jar echoes a type of pottery known as 'scarlet ware' made in about 2800 BC, and includes scenes of feasting and music. The headless figurine is inspired by Sumerian votive statues of about 2500 BC, placed in temples to worship their gods, with interlocked hands representing individuals.

2009
United States
Packaging, newspapers, glue
Height 29 cm (jar); height 2.5 cm, width 5.1 cm (figurine)
CaMMEA and the Modern Museum Fund, 2010,6025.9, 2010,6025.8

6 | 4 Destruction and loss

The two artists featured here each use traditional forms and techniques to tell a story about conflicts that have informed or continue to inform the world of today. Pakistani Imran Qureshi studied at the National College of Arts in Lahore, learning the techniques practised in the painting workshops (*karkhana*) of the Mughal emperor. In contrast to the often idealized natural worlds evoked by the painters of miniatures, there is darkness in Qureshi's renderings. In the work shown here, in a landscape once full of life, the trees are dying, fallen, choked by vines and there are spurts of blood (**1**). His work is about what he sees around him, whether it is on a political or personal level: the destruction of the environment and acts of terror in his native Lahore. Turkish artist Asli Çavuşoğlu, in her delicate red paintings, tells a story about the loss of cochineal, the traditional pigment made from a beetle that lives in the roots of a plant that grows on the banks of the Aras River, which marks the border between Turkey and Armenia (**2**). She is marking two kinds of loss: first, the loss of the beetle's natural habitat through environmental degradation in former Soviet Armenia, and second, the loss of the Armenians, whose skills produced the cochineal dye after the mass killings and forced expulsions of 1915 in the former Ottoman Empire. (VP)

1. Imran Qureshi (Pakistani, b. 1972), ***Where the Shadows are so Deep***
This painting is one of series commissioned for the Curve Gallery at the Barbican Centre in London. Qureshi describes how he decided that he should 'enhance the scale of this huge… space by having something that is very tiny, very small, very miniature.' The actual curve of the gallery is also echoed in the shape of the orange ground on which the trees are growing. The title of the work comes from the poetry of Pakistani poet Faiz Ahmed Faiz (d. 1984).

2015
Gouache, gold leaf, Wasli paper
Height 41.5 cm, width 33.6 cm
Brooke Sewell Permanent Fund, 2017,3001.1

2. Asli Çavuşoğlu (Turkish, b. 1982), *Red/Red* diptych

To make the two different reds here, the artist has used both traditionally produced cochineal and the bright industrial dyes that have replaced it. She works on worn and restored papers and the paintings themselves evoke the floral style that epitomizes Ottoman art.

2009
Istanbul, Turkey
Paper, pigment (Armenian cochineal)
Height 100 cm, width 70 cm
Funded by CaMMEA,
2016,6046.1.1–2

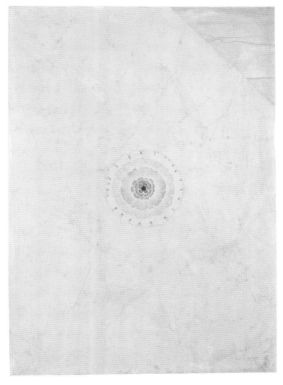

6 | 5 Tradition and modernity

Contemporary performers, designers and artists from across the Islamic world are constantly engaging with their own cultures' long-established visual and artistic forms and finding new and relevant ways to present them to modern audiences. For example, a contemporary style of shadow puppet theatre, Wayang Hip Hop (**1**), has developed in the cosmopolitan city of Yogyakarta, in central Java. Through humour, Wayang Hip Hop adapts age-old Javanese stories and sayings to address contemporary problems and has attracted a new generation of urban Indonesians to this ancient art form. Similarly, across the Indian Ocean, East African printed *kanga* cloths in the 21st century have been designed to deliver messages on issues as diverse as public health education and political allegiances (**2**) to supporting a national football team. Worn primarily as female garments, *kanga*s include proverbs and sayings in Kiswahili that are cleverly combined with colourful designs and have been remarkable mediums of communication for women since the 19th century. In contrast, artists from the Islamic world living in exile or diaspora, far away from their native homelands, such as the Oxford-based Sudanese painter, Ibrahim El-Salahi, often draw upon their past experiences, Islamic roots and memories of their birthplaces and present them in novel ways and forms for global audiences (**3**). (FS/WG)

1. Hip hop shadow puppets of Garry and Patrick
Wayang Hip Hop was created in 2010 by Catur Kuncoro, a third-generation master puppeteer who blends traditional shadow puppetry (*wayang kulit*) with contemporary global youth culture. His puppets, based on the much-loved tradtional clowns of the genre, are dressed in urban streetwear, trainers, caps and bling jewellery and use microphones. Kuncoro and his accompanying singers and rappers address topical issues that resonate with contemporary audiences, such as drug trafficking, economic inequalities and the generation gap, all to the sounds of lively hip hop beats.

2015–16
Yogyakarta, central Java, Indonesia
Hide, horn and bamboo
Length 66.5 cm (Garry, in red); length 83.1 cm (Patrick, in blue); length 51.7 cm (microphone)
Brooke Sewell Permanent Fund, 2016,3035.4.a–b, 2016,3035.3.a–b, 2016,3035.5

2. *Kanga* with an image of Barack Obama

This *kanga*, and thousands like it, were printed in 2008 to celebrate the election of former US President Barack Hussein Obama (b. 1961). His portrait is flanked by maps of Africa and bordered with heart-shaped flowers. Although born in Hawaii, Obama was dubbed the 'son of the soil' by Africans because his father was Kenyan. The jubilation across Africa was palpable following his win, with Obama's images painted on walls, buses and t-shirts, while restaurants, schools and children were named after him. The *kanga*'s Kiswahili inscriptions are most fitting, with 'Congratulations Barack Obama' over his picture and 'God has blessed us with love and peace' printed across the bottom.

2008
Tanzania
Cotton
Length 315 cm, width 107 cm
2008,2034.1

3. Ibrahim El-Salahi (Sudanese, b. 1930), *Tree*

The UK-based Sudanese artist Ibrahim El-Salahi was one of the earliest Modernist painters in Sudan and a founder of the Khartoum School movement. A practising Sufi, his *Tree* series is informed by his spiritual beliefs, personal experiences and native home. The image is of an abstracted *haraz* (acacia) tree, which grows on the banks of the Nile and is leafless during the rainy season, but blossoms when the weather turns dry, symbolizing steadfastness and individuality. *Tree* also echoes the human form and a dervish's patched cloak (*jibba*), which El-Salahi interprets as the diverse 'patchwork' of Sudan itself.

2001
Oxford, United Kingdom
Coloured inks on paper
Height 35 cm, width 26 cm
Donated by Ibrahim El-Salahi,
2010,2037.1

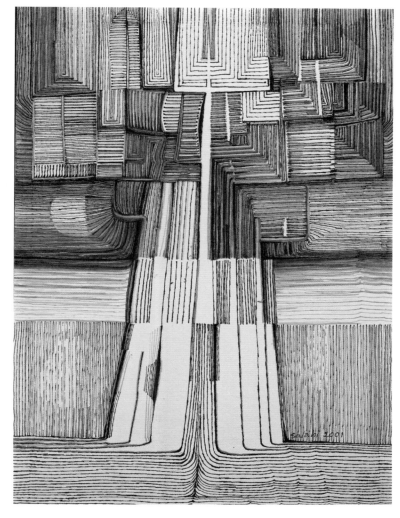

Glossary

Ahl al-bayt ('People of the House') Members of the household of the Prophet Muhammad, understood by the Shi'a including especially, Muhammad, Fatima, Ali, Hasan, Husayn and their progeny.

Ahl al-kitab ('People of the Book') A Qur'anic phrase that refers to Jews, Christians and Muslims who have received divine revelation. The term sometimes extends to Zoroastrians.

Arabesque A 19th-century western art historical term used to describe a motif consisting of a leafy vine scroll that expands with geometric regularity and symmetry. Other related terms include *tawriq* (to burst with leaves), *nabati* (vegetal), and *rumi/islimi* (foliated split palmettes).

Arista/cuenca A technique in which hardwood or metal moulds were pressed onto an unfired tile, creating the design as a series of shallow recesses, known as a *cuenca*. The narrow ridges are called *arista*. The recesses are then filled with coloured glazes which stopped the colours running into each other.

Basmala Qur'anic formula, *bismi'llah al-rahman al-rahim* ('in the name of God, the Merciful, the Compassionate').

Buraq The winged steed on which the Prophet Muhammad is said to have ridden on his miraculous 'night journey' (*mi'raj*) from Mecca to Jerusalem and to the heavens and back.

Caliph From the Arabic *khalifa* ('successor'), the title given to leaders of the Muslim community following the death of the Prophet Muhammad in 632.

Coptic From the Greek *aegyptos* ('Egyptian') and turns into the Arabic *qibti*. The majority indigenous Egyptian Christian community.

Cuerda seca From the Spanish 'dry cord'. A decorative technique used on ceramics, whereby an oily substance mixed with manganese is applied before firing as a separating device to keep different coloured pigments from running into one other and which appears as a dark outline after firing. In Spain and Portugal, an associated technique is *arista*.

Dervish Another word for a Sufi mystic, generally one who has forsaken worldly goods.

Dhimmi (meaning protected person), refers to individuals living in Islamic lands, who were granted special status under Islamic law in return for paying a tax.

Earthenware pottery made from clay, generally used for utilitarian objects glazed or unglazed.

Fritware *See* stonepaste.

Five Pillars (*arkan*) of Islam The five guiding principles for all Muslims, known as the profession of faith (*shahada*), prayer (*salah*), charity (*zakat*), fasting (*sawn*) and pilgrimage to Mecca (*hajj*).

Hadith From the Arabic, meaning 'report', generally translated as 'Traditions'. These relate to the sayings or actions of the Prophet Muhammad or to the corpus of these reports gathered after the Prophet's death.

Hijra From the Arabic for 'emigration' or 'flight'. Refers to the emigration of the Prophet Muhammad from Mecca to Medina in 622, the first year that the Muslim lunar calendar is calculated.

Hajj the annual pilgrimage to Mecca and other sacred sites, which takes place in the last month of the Islamic calendar, Dhu'l-Hijja, and required of every able Muslim once in their lifetime.

Imam From the Arabic for 'leader'. In a Sunni context, refers to one who leads prayers, or a scholar of religious sciences. In a Shi'a context, refers to temporal and spiritual leadership of the community by descendants of the Prophet Muhammad, through the family of the Prophet's son-in-law Ali ibn Abi Talib and his wife Fatima.

Isma'ili A branch of the Shi'a that traced the imamate through Imam Ja'far al-Sadiq's eldest son Isma'il (d. 755), after whom the branch is named. Several subdivisions developed over time including the Tayyibis and the Nizaris.

Jinn According to Qur'an 55:14, spirits created from vapour or smokeless flame, capable of good or bad actions.

Ka'ba the sacred cube-shaped structure at Mecca, which pilgrims circumambulate during the *hajj* or *umra* pilgrimage, and the focus of the *qibla* (see qibla).

Khata'i From the Persian for 'from Cathay' (a term historically used to describe peoples or objects from China or, more abstractly, from East Asia), referring to an apparently Chinese-inspired aesthetic comprising motifs such as lotuses, peonies, scrolling cloud bounds, fantastical animals (including dragons and phoenixes), and highlighting Chinese or East Asian artistic techniques and materials.

Khurasan A term referring both to the modern province located in northeastern Iran, and to the historic broader region extending from northeastern Iran across much of Afghanistan and Tajikistan as well as the southern areas of Turkmenistan and Uzbekistan.

Kufic a simple angular type of Arabic script first used in the 7th century with variants that include floriated and foliated forms.

Late Antique Refers to the end of the Classical period (specifically the Byzantine and Sasanian empires) and the world into which Islam arrived, corresponding to approximately AD 450–650.

Mihrab The niche or recess in a mosque wall, indicating the qibla.

Naskh One of the six calligraphic scripts ('the Six Pens') first developed by the calligrapher Ibn Muqla (d. 940) in the tenth century and which continued to evolve until the thirteenth century.

Nasta'liq An elegant cursive calligraphic script developed in the fourteenth century and used to write Persian, Ottoman Turkish and Urdu.

Persianate A modern term referring to societies, cultures or objects where Persian language and/or artistic and literary traditions play a significant or prominent role.

Qibla The direction of the Ka'ba at Mecca, and the orientation of prayer for Muslims.

Shah The Persian title for 'king', 'ruler' or 'emperor', widely used in Persianate societies.

Shahada The Islamic profession of faith, *la ilaha illa Allah, wa Muhammad rasul Allah* ('There is no god but God; Muhammad is the messenger of God') the first of the Five Pillars of Islam.

Shi'a The second largest denomination of Islam after Sunni, based on the succession of the Caliphate by the family of the Prophet Muhammad and the leadership of the community by imams.

Stonepaste (fritware) A manmade ceramic fabric created by potters in Egypt around the 10th–11th centuries to imitate the fineness of imported Chinese porcelain in which ground quartz or glass is added to clay. Fired to a high temperature, this composite fabric fused into a fine solid body and white surface, which in turn enabled technological innovation in terms of decoration. It is similar to the material known as faience employed by the potters of Ancient Egypt and Iran.

Sufi From the Arabic *suf*, meaning 'wool' (referring to the woollen cloaks worn by Sufis). Denotes one who follows Sufism, or the Sufi Path.

Sufism Refers in the broadest sense to a form of mysticism rooted in Islam and based on the search for enlightenment in attaining oneness with God, a mystical union known as *tawhid*.

Sultan An Arabic term meaning 'ruler', associated with secular authority and used throughout the Islamic world.

Sunni The majority denomination of Islam, based on the succession of the Caliphate.

Sura Chapter of the Qur'an; there are 114 in total. A *sura* is made up of several verses or *ayat* (sing. *aya*)

Thulth (or thuluth) From the Arabic for 'one third', refers to one of the 'six scripts' or calligraphic styles, large in format and used in manuscripts and for architectural inscriptions.

Tiraz From the Persian word for 'embroidery', refers to inscribed cloth made in state workshops, the inscriptions on such fabrics and also the factories themselves.

Transoxiana 'Land beyond the Oxus', known in Arabic as the *Ma wara al-nahr* ('what [is] beyond the [Oxus] river'). Refers to the historic region situated between the Amu Darya and Syr Darya rivers, which includes much of present-day Uzbekistan and Tajikistan and parts of Kyrgyzstan and Kazakhstan.

Twelver Shi'ism A branch of the Shi'a (from the Arabic word for 'twelve') that believes in twelve imams, the first being Ali ibn Abi Talib, the son-in-law of the Prophet Muhammad, and ending with Muhammad, the *Mahdi* or 'expected one'.

Selected bibliography

The publications referenced here represent a selection of works consulted in the preparation of this book. They are intended as an aid to further reading and the list is by no means comprehensive.

Introduction and Chapter 1: A history of histories

Asher, Catherine B., 1992, *The New Cambridge History of India: Architecture of Mughal India*, Cambridge.

Behrens-Abouseif, Doris, 2005, 'Veneto-Saracenic Metalware, a Mamluk Art', *Mamluk Studies Review*, Vol. 9, No. 2, pp. 147–72. (also ch. **3**, **5**)

Behrens-Abouseif, Doris, 2006, 'The Islamic History of the Lighthouse of Alexandria', *Muqarnas*, Vol. 23 pp. 1–14.

Blair, Sheila S., 2006, *Islamic Calligraphy*, Edinburgh.

Blair, Sheila S. & Bloom, Jonathan M., 2006, *Cosmophilia: Islamic Art from the David Collection, Copenhagen*, Chestnut Hill.

Boehm, Barbara Drake & Holcomb, Melanie, 2016, *Jerusalem, 1000–1400: Every People Under Heaven*, New Haven. (also ch. **3**)

Canby, Sheila R., 1998, *Princes, Poets and Paladins: Islamic and Indian Paintings from the Collection of Prince and Princess Sadruddin Aga Khan*, London.

Carboni, Stefano & Whitehouse, David, 2002, *Glass of the Sultans*, New York. (also ch. **3**)

Carey, Moya, 2009, 'The Gold and Silver Lining: Shams al-Din Muhammad b. Mu'ayyad al-'Urdi's Inlaid Celestial Globe (*c*. 1288) from the Ilkhanid Observatory at Maragha', *Iran*, Vol. 47, pp. 97–108.

De Moor, Antoine, Fluck, Cäcilia, & Linscheid, Petra (eds), 2013, *Drawing the Threads Together: Textiles and Footwear of the 1st Millennium AD from Egypt*, Tielt.

Finkel, Irving L. & Seymour, Michael J., 2008, *Babylon: Myth and Reality*, London.

Greenwood, William, 2014, *Kings & Pawns: Board Games from India to Spain*, Edinburgh.

Harper, Prudence Oliver, 1961, 'The Senmurv', *The Metropolitan Museum of Art Bulletin*, Vol. 20, No. 3, pp. 95–101.

Hoyland, Robert G., 2001, *Arabia and the Arabs: From the Bronze Age to the Coming of Islam*, London.

Ibn Battuta, Muhammad ibn Abdallah (d. 1368 or 1377), 2002, *The Travels of Ibn Battutah* (abridged and annotated by Tim Mackintosh-Smith), London.

Ibn Jubayr, Muhammad ibn Ahmad (d. 1217), 1952, *The Travels of Ibn Jubayr* (trans. R. J. C. Broadhurst), London.

Ibn Khaldun, Abd al-Rahman (d. 1406), 1958, *The Muqaddimah: An Introduction to History* (trans. Franz Rosenthal), 3 volumes, Michigan.

Insoll, Tim, 1999, *The Archaeology of Islam*, Oxford.

Irwin, Robert, 2002, *Night and Horses and the Desert: An Anthology of Classical Arabic Literature*, London.

Jahangir, Nur al-Din Muhammad (d. 1627), 1989, *The Tuzuk-i-Jahangiri or Memoirs of Jahangir* (ed. Alexander Rogers & trans. Henry Beveridge), London.

Jones, William, 1783, *The Moallakát, or Seven Arabian Poems Which Were Suspended on the Temple at Mecca*, London.

Kruk, Remke, 2001, 'Of Rukhs and Rooks, Camels and Castles', *Oriens*, Vol. 36, pp. 288–298.

La Niece, Susan, Röhrs, Stefan & McLeod, Bet (eds), 2010, 'The Heritage of 'Maître Alpais': An International and Interdisciplinary Examination of Medieval Limoges Enamel and Associated Objects', *British Museum Research Publication*, No. 182, London, pp. 1–56.

Leaman, Oliver, 2004, *Islamic Aesthetics: An Introduction*, Edinburgh.

Leoni, Francesca (ed.), 2016, *Power and Protection Islamic Art and the Supernatural*, Oxford.

Macdonald, Michael C. A., 2010, 'Ancient Arabia and the Written Word', *Proceedings of the Seminar for Arabian Studies; Supplement: The Development of Arabic as a Written Language*, Vol. 40, pp. 5–28.

Milwright, Marcus, 2010, *An Introduction to Islamic Archaeology*, Edinburgh.

Munro-Hay, Stuart, 1991, *Aksum: An African Civilisation of Late Antiquity*, Edinburgh.

Necipoğlu, Gülru & Payne, Alina (eds), 2016, *Histories of Ornament: From Global to Local*, Princeton & Oxford.

Necipoğlu, Gülru, 2016, 'Early Modern Floral: The Agency of Ornament in Ottoman and Safavid Visual Cultures', in Gülru Necipoğlu & Alina Payne (eds), *Histories of Ornament: From Global to Local*, Princeton & Oxford, pp. 132–155.

Necipoğlu, Gülru (ed.), 2017, *The Arts of Ornamental Geometry: A Persian Compendium on Similar and Complementary Interlocking Figures*, Leiden & Boston.

Pancaroğlu, Oya, 2003, 'Signs in the Horizons: Concepts of Image and Boundary in a Medieval Persian Cosmography', *Res: Anthropology and Aesthetics*, Vol. 43, pp. 31–41.

Prisse d'Avennes, Emile, 1877, *L'Art Arabe d'après les Monuments du Kaire*, Paris.

Rawska-Rodziewicz, Elzbieta, 2017, *Ivory and Bone Sculpture in Ancient Alexandria*, Paris.

Rogers, J. Michael, 2006 (reprint), *Mughal Miniatures*, London. (also ch. **2**, **4**, **5**)

Rutchowscaya, Marie-Hélène, 1990, *Coptic Fabrics*, Paris.

Saliba, George, 1992, 'The Role of the Astrologer in Medieval Islamic Society', *Bulletin d'études orientales*, Vol. 44, pp. 45–67.

Saudi, Mona & Adonis, 2011, *Petra Tablet: The Hand of Stone Draws the Place*, Beirut.

Shalem, Avinoam, 1994, 'The Fall of al-Madā'in: Some Literary References Concerning Sasanian Spoils of War in Mediaeval Islamic Treasuries', *Iran*, Vol. 32, pp. 77–81.

Simpson, St John (ed.), 2002, *Queen of Sheba: Treasures from Ancient Yemen*, London.

Spring, Chris, 2012, *African Textiles Today*, London. (also ch. **6**)

Suleman, Fahmida, 2010, 'Art', in Amyn Sajoo (ed.), *A Companion to Muslim Ethics*, London, pp. 91–104.

Vernoit, Stephen (ed.), 2000, *Discovering Islamic Art: Scholars, Collectors and Collections*, London.

Williams, Jonathan, Cribb, Joe & Errington, Elizabeth, 1997, *Money: A History*, London.

Chapter 2: Faith and pilgrimage

Akbarnia, Ladan with Leoni, Francesca, 2010, *Light of the Sufis: The Mystical Arts of Islam*, Houston.

Allan, James W., 2012, *The Art and Architecture of Twelver Shi'ism: Iraq, Iran and the Indian Sub-Continent*, London. (also ch. **4**)

Daftary, Farhad, 2007, *The Isma'ilis: Their History and Doctrines* (2nd edition), Cambridge.

Flaskerud, Ingvild, 2010, *Visualizing Belief and Piety in Iranian Shiism*, London & New York.

Gruber, Christiane J., 2009, 'Between Logos (*kalima*) and Light (*nūr*): Representations of the Prophet Muhammad in Islamic Painting', *Muqarnas*, Vol. 26, pp. 229–262.

Gruber, Christiane J., & Shalem, Avinoam (eds), 2014, *The Image of the Prophet Between Ideal and Ideology*, Berlin.

Ibn al-Arabi, Muhyiddin (d. 1240), 1911, *The Tarjumán al-Ashwáq. A Collection of Mystical Odes* (ed. & trans. R. A. Nicholson), London.

Kurbage, Youssef & Fargues, Philippe, 1997, *Christians and Jews Under Islam*, London.

Paine, Sheila, 2004, *Amulets: Sacred Charms of Power and Protection*, London.

Porter, Venetia, 2006, *Word into Art: Artists of the Modern Middle East*, London.

Porter, Venetia, 2007, 'Amulets Inscribed with the Names of the "Seven Sleepers" of Ephesus in the British Museum', in Fahmida Suleman (ed.), *Word of God, Art of Man: The Qur'an and its Creative Expressions*, Oxford, pp. 123–34. (also ch. **3**)

Porter, Venetia, 2011, *Arabic and Persian Seals and Amulets in the British Museum*, London.

Porter, Venetia (ed.), 2012, *Hajj: Journey to the Heart of Islam*, London.

Madison, Francis, Stanley, Tim, Savage-Smith, Emilie & Pinder-Wilson, Ralph H., 1997, *Science, Tools and Magic. Parts 1 & 2*, London & Oxford.

Martinez-Gros, Gabriel (ed.), 2015, *Jérusalem, Ville Trois Fois Sainte*, Marseille & Paris.

Reeve, John (ed.), 2007, *Sacred. Books of the Three Faiths: Judaism, Christianity, Islam*, London.

Savage-Smith, Emilie & M. B. Smith, 2004, 'Islamic Geomancy and a Thirteenth-Century Divinatory Device: Another Look', in Emilie Savage-Smith (ed.), *Magic and Divination in Early Islam*, Aldershot, pp. 211–76.

Suleman, Fahmida, 2015, *People of the Prophet's House: Artistic and Ritual Expressions of Shi'i Islam*, London.

Wright, Elaine J., 2009, *Islam: Faith, Art, Culture: Manuscripts of the Chester Beatty Library*, London & Dublin.

Chapter 3: Interconnected worlds, 750–1500

Allan, James W., 1973, 'Abu'l Qasim's Treatise on Ceramics', *Iran*, Vol. 11, pp. 111–20.

Allan, James W., 1979, *Persian Metal Technology: 700–1300 AD*, London.

Allan, James W., 1982, *Nishapur: Metalwork of the Early Islamic Period*, New York.

Allan, James W., 1983, *Islamic Metalwork: the Nuhad Es-Said Collection,* London.

Arberry, Arthur J., 1955, *The Koran Interpreted*, London.

Atil, Esin, 1981, *Renaissance of Islam: Art of the Mamluks*, Washington.

Baer, Eva, 1965, *Sphinxes and Harpies in Medieval Islamic Art*, Jerusalem.

Baker, Patricia L., 1995, *Islamic Textiles*, London.

Bakırer, Ömür & Redford, Scott, 2017, 'The Kubadabad Plate: Islamic Gilded and Enameled Glass in Context', *Journal of Glass Studies*, Vol. 59, pp. 171–91.

Behrens-Abouseif, Doris, 2005, 'Veneto-Saracenic Metalware, a Mamluk Art', *Mamluk Studies Review*, Vol. 9, No. 2, pp. 147–72.

Blair, Sheila S., 2008, 'A Brief Biography of Abu Zayd', in Gülru Necipoğlu & Julia Bailey (eds), *Frontiers of Islamic Art and Architecture: Essays in Celebration of Oleg Grabar's Eightieth Birthday*, Leiden & Boston, pp. 155–76.

Bloom, Jonathan, M., 2007, *Arts of the City Victorious: Islamic Art and Architecture in Fatimid North Africa and Egypt,* London & New Haven.

Caiger-Smith, Alan, 1985, *Lustre Pottery*, London.

Canby, Sheila R., Beyazit, Deniz, Rugiadi, Martina & Peacock, Andrew, 2016, *Court and Cosmos: The Great Age of the Seljuqs*. New York & New Haven.

Carboni, Stefano, 2001, *Glass from Islamic Lands*, London.

Carboni, Stefano, 2007, *Venice and the Islamic World, 828–1797*, New York. (also ch. **4**)

Chaudhuri, Kirti Narayan, 1985, *Trade and Civilisation in the Indian Ocean: An Economic History from the Rise of Islam to 1750*, Cambridge.

Contadini, Anna, 1998, *Fatimid Art at the Victoria and Albert Museum*, London.

Dodds, Jerrilynn D. (ed.), 1992, *Al-Andalus: The Art of Islamic Spain*, New York.

Eames, Elizabeth, 1992, *English Tilers,* London.

Ecker, Heather, 2004, *Caliphs and Kings: The Art and Influence of Islamic Spain*, Washington.

Evans, Helen C. & Ratliff, Brandie (eds), 2012, *Byzantium and Islam: Age of Transition, 7th–9th Century*, New York.

Fluck, Cäcilia, Helmecke, Gisela & O'Connell, Elisabeth R. (eds), 2015, *Egypt: Faith After the Pharaohs*, London.

Ghouchani, Abdullah, 1986, *Inscriptions on Nishapur Pottery*, Tehran.

Gonella, Julia, 2013, 'Three stucco panels from Samarra', in J. Bloom & S. Blair (eds), *God is Beautiful and Loves Beauty*, Newhaven & London, pp. 80–101.

Graves, Margaret S., 2008, 'Ceramic House Models from Medieval Persia: Domestic Architecture and Concealed Activities', *IRAN*, Vol. 46, pp. 227–51.

Gray, Basil, 1938, 'A Fatimid Drawing', *The British Museum Quarterly*, Vol. 12, No. 3, pp. 91–96.

Gray, Basil, 1939, 'A Seljuq Hoard from Persia', *British Museum Quarterly*, Vol. 13, No. 3, pp. 73–79.

Halm, Heinz, 1997, *The Fatimids and their Traditions of Learning*, London.

Hillenbrand, Carole, 1999, *The Crusades: Islamic Perspectives*, Edinburgh.

Ibn Fadlan, Ahmad (d. 960), 2011, *Ibn Fadlan in the Land of Darkness: Arab Travellers in the Far North* (trans. Caroline Stone & Paul Lunde), London.

Ibn Munqidh, Usama (d. 1188), 2008, *The Book of Contemplation: Islam and the Crusades* (ed. & trans. Paul M. Cobb), London.

Institut du Monde Arabe, 2001, *L'Orient de Saladin: l'Art des Ayyoubides*, Paris.

Jenkins-Madina, Marilyn, 2006, *Raqqa Revisited: Ceramics of Ayyubid Syria*, New York & New Haven.

Kennedy, Hugh, 2004, *When Baghdad Ruled the Muslim World*, Cambridge.

Kessler, Rochelle L., McWilliams, Mary A., Pancaroğlu, Oya & Roxburgh, David J., 2002, *Studies in Islamic and Later Indian Art from the Arthur M. Sackler Museum, Harvard University Art Museums*, Cambridge.

Komaroff, Linda, 1992, *The Golden Disk of Heaven: Metalwork of Timurid Iran*, Costa Mesa & New York.

Komaroff, Linda (ed.), 2011, *Gifts of the Sultan: The Arts of Giving at the Islamic Courts,* New Haven.

Komaroff, Linda & Carboni, Stefano, 2002, *The Legacy of Genghis Khan: Courtly Art and Culture in Western Asia, 1256–1353*, New York, New Haven & London.

Krahl, Regina, Guy, John, Raby, Julian & Wilson, Keith (eds), 2010, *Shipwrecked: Tang Treasures and Monsoon Winds*, Washington.

La Neice, Susan, Ward, Rachel, Hook, Duncan & Craddock, Paul, 2012, 'Medieval Islamic Copper Alloys', in Paul Jett, Blythe McCarthy & Janet G. Douglas (eds), *Scientific Research on Ancient Asian Metallurgy*, London, pp. 248–54.

Lentz, Thomas W. & Lowry, Glenn D., 1989, *Timur and the Princely Vision: Persian Art and Culture in the Fifteenth Century*, Washington.

Lowick, Nicholas M., 1985, *Siraf XV: The Coins and Monumental Inscriptions*, London.

MacGregor, Neil, 2012, *A History of the World in 100 Objects*, London.

Marzinzik, Sonja, 2013, *Masterpieces: Early Medieval Art*, London.

Mason, Robert B., 2004, *Shine Like the Sun: Lustre-Painted and Associated Pottery from the Medieval Middle East*, Costa Mesa and Toronto.

Melikian-Chirvani, Assadullah Souren, 1982, *Islamic Metalwork from the Iranian World 8th-18th Centuries*, London. (also ch. **1**, **4**)

Mérat, Amandine, 2014, 'New Research on Medieval Embroideries from Tell Edfu at the Louvre Museum,' *British Museum Studies in Ancient Egypt and Sudan*, Vol. 21, pp. 63–79.

Millner, Arthur, 2015, *Damascus Tiles: Mamluk and Ottoman Architectural Ceramics from Syria*, London.

Northedge, Alastair, 2005, *The Historical Topography of Samarra*, London.

Pancaroğlu, Oya, 2007, *Perpetual Glory: Medieval Islamic Ceramics from the Harvey B. Plotnick Collection*, New Haven & Chicago.

Pancaroğlu, Oya, 2013, 'Feasts of Nishapur: Cultural Resonances of Tenth-Century Ceramic Production in Khurasan,' in Mary A. McWilliams (ed.), *In Harmony: The Norma Jean Calderwood Collection of Islamic Art*, New Haven.

Phillips, Tom (ed.), 1999, *Africa: The Art of a Continent*, London.

Pinder-Wilson, Ralph, 1971, 'An Inscription of Badr Al-Jamali,' *The British Museum Quarterly*, Vol. 36, No. 1 & 2, pp. 51–53.

Porter, Venetia, 2001 (reprint), *Islamic Tiles*, London. (also ch. **4**)

Porter, Venetia & Ager, Barry, 1999, 'Islamic Amuletic Seals: The Case of the Carolingian Cross Brooch from Ballycottin,' in Rika Gyselen (ed.), *La Science des Cieux: Sages, Mages, Astrologues*, pp. 211–18.

Priestman, Seth, 2016, 'The Silk Road or the Sea? Sasanian and Islamic Exports to Japan,' *Journal of Islamic Archaeology*, Vol. 3, No. 1, pp. 1–35.

Raby, Julian, 2012, 'The Principle of Parsimony and the Problem of the 'Mosul' School of Metalwork,' in Venetia Porter & Mariam Rosser-Owen (eds), *Metalwork and Material Culture in the Islamic World: Art, Craft and Text. Essays Presented to James W. Allan*, London, pp. 11–87.

Redford, Scott, 2004, 'On *Saqis* and Ceramics: Systems of Representation in the Northeast Mediterranean,' in Daniel H. Weiss & Lisa J. Mahoney (eds), *France and the Holy Land: Frankish Culture at the End of the Crusades*, Baltimore, pp. 282–312.

Roxburgh, David J. (ed.), 2005, *TURKS: A Journey of a Thousand Years*, London.

Saba, Matthew D., 2015, 'A Restricted Gaze: The Ornament of the Main Caliphal Palace of Samarra,' *Muqarnas*, Vol. 32, pp. 157–98.

Sardi, Maria, 2010, 'Mamluk Textiles,' in Margaret Graves (ed.), *Islamic Art, Architecture and Material Culture: New Perspectives*, Oxford, pp. 7–14.

Scott-Meisami, Julie, 2001, 'The Palace Complex as Emblem: Some Samarran Qasidas,' in Chase Robinson (ed.), *A Medieval Islamic City Reconsidered: An Interdisciplinary Approach to Samarra*, Oxford, pp. 69–78.

Shalem, Avinoam, 2004, *The Oliphant: Islamic Objects in Historical Context*, Leiden.

Soucek, Priscilla, 1999, 'Ceramic Production as Exemplar of Yuan-Ilkhanid Relations,' *RES: Anthropology and Aesthetics*, Vol. 35, pp. 125–41.

Tait, Hugh (ed.), 1991, *Five Thousand Years of Glass*, London.

Tonghini, Cristina, 1995, 'The Fine Wares of Ayyubid Syria,' in Ernst Grube (ed.), *Cobalt and Lustre: The First Centuries of Islamic Pottery*, London & Oxford, pp. 248–93.

Vorderstrasse, Tasha, 2005, *Al-Mina: A Port of Antioch From Late Antiquity to the End of the Ottomans*, Leiden.

Ward, Rachel (ed.), 1998, *Gilded and Enamelled Glass from the Middle East*, London.

Ward, Rachel, 2002, 'Two Ivory Plaques in the British Museum,' in Warwick Ball and Leonard Harrow (eds), *Cairo to Kabul: Afghan and Islamic Studies Presented to Ralph Pinder-Wilson*, London, pp. 248–54.

Ward, Rachel, 2003 (reprint), *Islamic Metalwork*, London.

Ward, Rachel, 2012, 'Mosque Lamps and Enamelled Glass: Getting the Dates Right,' in Doris Behrens-Abouseif (ed.), *The Arts of the Mamluks in Egypt and Syria – Evolution and Impact*, Göttingen & Bonn, pp. 55–75.

Ward, Rachel (ed.), 2014, *Court and Craft: A Masterpiece from Northern Iraq*, London.

Ward, Rachel, La Neice, Susan, *et. al*, 1995, 'Veneto-Saracenic Metalworks: An Analysis of the Bowls and Incense Burners in the British Museum,' in Duncan R. Hook and David R. M. Gaimster (eds), *Trade and Discovery: The Scientific Study of Artefacts from Post-Medieval Europe and Beyond*, London, pp. 235–58.

Watson, Oliver, 2004, *Ceramics from Islamic Lands*, London.

Watson, Oliver, 2004 (reprint), *Persian Lustre Ware*, London & Boston.

Chapter 4: The age of empires, 1500–1900

Askari, Nasreen & Crill, Rosemary, 1997, *Colours of the Indus: Costume and Textiles of Pakistan*, London.

Atasoy, Nurhan & Raby, Julian, 1989, *Iznik: The Pottery of Ottoman Turkey*, London & Istanbul.

Bennett, James (ed.), 2005, *Crescent Moon: Islamic Art and Civilisation in Southeast Asia*, Adelaide.

Bilgi, Hülya & Zanbak, Idil, 2012, *Skill of the Hand, Delight of the Eye: Ottoman Embroideries in the Sadberk Hanim Museum Collection*, Istanbul.

Boggs, Richard, 2010, *Hammaming in the Sham: A Journey Through the Turkish Baths of Damascus, Aleppo and Beyond*, Reading.

Canby, Sheila R., 1999, *The Golden Age of Persian Art, 1501–1722*, London. (also ch. **5**)

Canby, Sheila R., 2009, *Shah 'Abbas: The Remaking of Iran*, London.

Carswell, John, 2006 (reprint), *Iznik Pottery*, London.

Crowe, Yolande, 2002, *Persia and China: Safavid Blue and White Ceramics in the Victoria and Albert Museum 1501–1738*, London.

Crowe, Yolande, 2012, 'The Safavid Potter at the Crossroad of Styles,' in Willem Floor & Edmund Herzig (eds), *Iran and the World in the Safavid Age*, London, pp. 407–24.

D'Amora, Rosita & Pagani, Samuela (eds.), 2011, *Hammam: le Terme Nell'Islam*, Florence.

De Guise, Lucien (ed.), 2005, *The Message & the Monsoon: Islamic Art of Southeast Asia*, Kuala Lumpur.

Desmet-Grégoire, Hélène, 1989, *Les Objets du Café*, Paris.

Diba, Layla S. (ed.), 1998, *Royal Persian Paintings: The Qajar Epoch, 1785–1925*, New York.

Ellis, Marianne & Wearden, Jennifer, 2001, *Ottoman Embroidery*, London.

Gillow, John, 2008, *Indian Textiles*, London.

Haidar, Navina Najat & Sardar, Marika, 2015, *Sultans of Deccan India, 1500–1700: Opulence and Fantasy*, New York.

Hasan, Syed Mahmudul, 1966, 'Two Bengal Inscriptions in the Collection of the British Museum,' *The Journal of the Royal Asiatic Society of Great Britain and Ireland*, No. 3/4, October, pp. 141–47.

Hattox, Ralph S., 1985, *Coffee and Coffeehouses: The Origins of a Social Beverage in the Medieval Near East*, Seattle & London.

Istanbul, 2008, *Reformer, Poet and Musician: Sultan Selim Han III*, Istanbul.

Juhasz, Esther (ed.), 2012, *The Jewish Wardrobe: From the Collection of the Israel Museum, Jerusalem*, Milan & Jerusalem.

Kerlogue, Fiona, 2003, 'Islamic Talismans: The Calligraphy Batiks,' in Itie van Hout (ed.), *Batik: Drawn in Wax. 200 Years of Batik Art from Indonesia in the Tropenmuseum Collection*, Amsterdam, pp. 124–135.

Khalili, Nasser D., Robinson Basil W. & Tim Stanley, 1996 and 1997, *Lacquer of the Islamic Lands. Parts 1 & 2*, London.

Krody, Sumru Belger, 2000, *Flowers of Silk and Gold: Four Centuries of Ottoman Embroidery*, Washington.

Lambourn, Elizabeth, 2004, 'Carving and Communities: Marble Carving for Muslim Patrons at Khambhāt and around the Indian Ocean Rim, Late Thirteenth-Mid-Fifteenth Centuries,' *Ars Orientalis*, Vol. 34, pp. 99–133.

Lambourn, Elizabeth, 2004, 'Carving and Recarving: Three Rasulid Gravestones Revisited,' *New Arabian Studies*, Vol. 6, pp. 10–29.

Lerner, Judith, 1980, 'Three Achaemenid "Fakes": A Re-evaluation in the Light of 19th Century Iranian Architectural Sculpture,' *Expedition*, Vol. 22, No. 2, pp. 5–16.

McWilliams, Mary A. & Roxburgh, David, 2008, *Traces of the Calligrapher: Islamic Calligraphy in Practice, c. 1600–1900*, Houston.

Melikian-Chirvani, Assadullah Souren, 2007, *Le Chant du Monde: L'Art de l'Iran Safavide, 1501–1736*, Paris.

Meller, Susan, 2013, *Silk and Cotton: Textiles from the Central Asia That Was*, New York.

al-Mojan, Muhammad H., 2013, 'The Textiles Made for the Prophet's Mosque at Medina: A Preliminary Study of their Origins, History and Style,' in Venetia Porter & Liana Saif (eds), *The Hajj: Collected Essays*, pp. 184–194.

Natvig, Richard, 1987, 'Oromos, Slaves, and the *Zar* Spirits: A Contribution to the History of the *Zar* Cult,' *The International Journal of African Historical Studies*, Vol. 20, No. 4, pp. 669–89.

Nersessian, Vrej, 2001, *Treasures from the Ark: 1700 Years of Armenian Christian Art*, London.

Paine, Sheila, 2001, *Embroidery from India and Pakistan*, London.

Paris, *Trésors de l'Islam en Afrique de Tombouctou à Zanzibar*, 2017, Paris. (also ch. **3**)

Porter, Venetia, 2000, 'Coins of the Sa'dian Sharifs of Morocco off the Coast of Devon. Preliminary Report,' *XII. Internationaler Numismatischer Kongress Berlin 1997. Proceedings II*. Berlin, pp. 1288–1293.

Raby, Julian, 1987, 'Pride and Prejudice: Mehmed the Conqueror and the Italian Portrait Medal,' *Studies in the History of Art*, Vol. 21, pp. 171–94.

Rogers, J. Michael, 1983, *Islamic Art and Design 1500–1700*, London.

Rogers, J. Michael, 1995, *Empire of the Sultans: Ottoman Art from the Collection of Nasser D. Khalili*, London.

Rogers, J. Michael, & Ward, Rachel, 1988, *Süleyman the Magnificent*, London.

Semmelhack, Elizabeth, 2016, *Standing Tall: The Curious History of Men in Heels*, Toronto.

Sharma, Sunil, 2017, *Mughal Arcadia: Persian Literature in an Indian Court*, Cambridge & London. (also ch. **5**)

Sinha, Sutapa, 2001, 'A Note on the Inscriptions of Bengal Sultans in the British Museum,' in Enamul Haque (ed.), *Hakim Habibur Rahman Khan Commemoration Volume: A Collection of Essays on History, Art, Archaeology, Numismatics, Epigraphy and Literature of Bangladesh and Eastern India*, Dhaka, pp. 133–43.

Stronge, Susan, 1985, *Bidri ware: Inlaid metalwork from India*, London: Victoria and Albert Museum.

Stronge, Susan, 2010, *Made for Mughal Emperors: Royal Treasures from Hindustan*, London. (also ch. **5**)

Suleman, Fahmida, 2017, *Textiles of the Middle East and Central Asia: The Fabric of Life*, London. (also ch. **6**)

Summerfield, Anne & Summerfield, John (eds), 1999, *Walk in Splendour: Ceremonial Dress and the Minangkabau*, Los Angeles.

Taylor, Roderick, 1993, *Ottoman Embroidery*, Wesel.

Ther, Ulla, 1993, *Floral Messages: From Ottoman Court Embroideries to Anatolian Trousseau Chests*, Bremen.

Wearden, Jennifer & Baker, Patricia, 2010, *Iranian Textiles*, London.

Welch, Stuart Cary, 1985, *India: Art and Culture, 1300–1900*, New York.

Zebrowski, Mark, 1997, *Gold, Silver and Bronze from Mughal India*, London.

Zorlu, Tuncay, 2011, *Innovation and Empire in Turkey: Sultan Selim III and the Modernisation of the Ottoman Navy*, London.

Chapter 5: Literary and musical traditions

Akbarnia, Ladan & Dadlani, Chanchal, 2006, *The Tablet and the Pen: Drawings from the Islamic World*, Cambridge.

And, Metin, 1975, *Karagöz: Turkish Shadow Theatre*, Istanbul.

Babaie, Sussan, 2001, 'The Sound of the Image/The Image of the Sound: Narrativity in Persian Art of the 17th Century,' in Oleg Grabar & Cynthia Robinson (eds), *Islamic Art and Literature*, Princeton.

Beach, Milo C., Fischer, Eberhard & Goswamy, B. N. (eds), 2011, *Masters of Indian Painting*. 2 Vols, Zurich.

Blair, Sheila S., 2000, 'Color and Gold: The Decorated Papers Used in Manuscripts in Later Islamic Times,' *Muqarnas*, Vol. 17, pp. 24–36.

Bloom, Jonathan, 2001, *Paper Before Print: The History and Impact of Paper in the Islamic World*, London & New Haven.

Brend, Barbara & Melville, Charles (eds), 2010, *Epic of the Persian Kings: The Art of Ferdowsi's Shahnameh*, London.

Canby, Sheila R., 2005 (reprint), *Persian Painting*, London.

Calza, Gian Carlo (ed.), 2012, *Akbar: The Great Emperor of India, 1542–1605*, Milan.

Cité de la Musique, 2003, *Gloire des Princes, Louange des Dieux*, Paris.

Darwich, Mahmoud & Koraichi, Rachid, 2000, *Une Nation en Exil*, Paris.

Das, Asok Kumar, 2005, *Paintings of the Razmnama: The Book of War*, Ahmedabad & Portchester.

Farhad, Massumeh & Rettig, Simon, 2016, *The Art of the Qur'an: Treasures from the Museum of Turkish and Islamic Arts*, Washington.

Faridany-Akhavan, Zahra, 1993, 'All the King's Toys,' *Muqarnas*, Vol. 10, pp. 292–98.

Ferdowsi, Abolqasem (d. 1025), 2016 (reprint), *Shahnameh: The Persian Book of Kings* (trans. Dick Davis), London.

Fetvacı, Emine & Gruber, Christiane, 2017, 'Painting, from Urban to Royal Patronage,' in Finbarr Barry Flood & Gülru Necipoğlu (eds), *A Companion to Islamic Art and Architecture*, pp. 874–902.

Guy, John & Britschgi, Jorrit, 2011, *Wonder of the Age: Master Painters of India, 1100–1900*, New York.

Hammarlund, Anders, Olsson, Tord & Özdalça, Elisabeth (eds), 2005, *Sufism, Music and Society in Turkey and the Middle East*, Istanbul.

Jenkins, Jean & Olsen, Paul Rovsing, 1976, *Music and Musical Instruments in the World of Islam*, London.

Kynan-Wilson, William, 2017, '"Painted by the Turcks themselves": Reading Peter Mundy's Ottoman Costume Album in Context,' in Sussan Babaie & Melanie Gibson (eds), *The Mercantile Effect: Art and Exchange in the Islamicate World during the 17th and 18th Centuries*, London, pp. 38–50.

Langer, Axel (ed.), 2013, *The Fascination with Persia: The Persian-European Dialogue in Seventeenth-Century Art & Contemporary Art from Tehran*, Zurich.

Muallem, David, 2010, *The Maqam Book: A Doorway to Arab Scales and Modes*, Tel Aviv.

Oral, Unver, 2009, *Turkish Shadow Theatre: Karagöz*, Ankara.

Porter, Venetia, & Barakat, Heba Nayel, 2004, *Mightier than the Sword. Arabic Script: Beauty and Meaning*, Kuala Lumpur.

Roxburgh, David J., 2017, 'Persianate Arts of the Book in Iran and Central Asia,' in Finbarr Barry Flood & Gülru Necipoğlu (eds), *A Companion to Islamic Art and Architecture*, pp. 668–90.

Roxburgh, David J., 2005, *The Persian Album, 1400–1600: From Dispersal to Collection*, New Haven.

Schick, Leslie Meral, 2004, 'The Place of Dress in Pre-Modern Costume Albums,' in Suraiya Faroqhi and Christoph K. Neumann (eds), *Ottoman Costumes: From Textile to Identity*, Istanbul, pp. 93–101.

Seyller, John William, 2002, *The Adventures of Hamza*, Washington.

Simpson, Marianna Shreve, 1993, 'The Making of Manuscripts and the Workings of the *Kitab-Khana* in Safavid Iran,' *Studies in the History of Art*, Vol. 38, pp. 104–21.

Sims, Eleanor, with Marshak, Boris I. & Grube, Ernst J., 2002, *Peerless Images: Persian Painting and its Sources*, New Haven.

Siyavuşgil, Sabri Esat, 1955, *Karagöz*, Ankara.

Thackston, Wheeler M., 2000, *Album Prefaces and Other Documents on the History of Calligraphers and Painters*, Boston.

Touma, Habib Hassan, 1996, *The Music of the Arabs* (trans. Laurie Schwarts), Cambridge & Portland.

Wright, Elaine, 2008, *Muraqqaʿ: Imperial Mughal Albums from the Chester Beatty Library*, Alexandria & Hanover.

Chapter 6: The modern world

Adams, S., 2006, 'In My Garment There is Nothing but God: Recent Work by Ibrahim El Salahi,' *African Arts*, Vol. 39, No. 2, pp. 26–35, 86.

Bonyhady, Tim & Lendon, Nigel with Jasleen Dhamija, 2003, *The Rugs of War*, Canberra.

Mahdaoui, Molka, 2015, *Nja Mahdaoui: Jafr. The Alchemy of Signs*, Milan.

Varela, Miguel Escobar, 2014, 'Wayang Hip Hop: Java's Oldest Performance Tradition Meets Global Youth Culture,' *Asian Theatre Journal*, Vol. 31, No. 2, pp. 481–504.

Weir, Shelagh, 1989, *Palestinian Costume*, London.

General reference works

Abdel Haleem, Muhammad A. S. (trans.), 2005, *The Qur'an*, Oxford.

Bloom, Jonathan & Blair, Sheila S., 1997, *Islamic Arts*, London.

Brend, Barbara, 1991, *Islamic Art*, London & Cambridge.

Ekhtiar, Maryam, Soucek, Priscilla, Canby, Sheila R. & Haidar, Navina Najat, 2011, *Masterpieces from the Department of Islamic Art in the Metropolitan Museum of Art*, New York & New Haven.

Flood, Finbarr & Necipoğlu, Gülru (eds), 2017, *A Companion to Islamic Art and Architecture*, 2 Vols, Hoboken.

Irwin, Robert, 1997, *Islamic Art*, London.

Makariou, Sophie (ed.), 2012, *Les Arts de l'Islam au Musée du Louvre*, Paris.

Stanley, Tim, Rosser-Owen, Mariam & Vernoit, Stephen, 2004, *Palace and Mosque: Islamic Art from the Middle East*, London.

Acknowledgments

The Albukhary Foundation sponsored the making of the British Museum's Albukhary Foundation Gallery of the Islamic World and the complete reinstallation of the Museum's Islamic collections in 2018. Thanks to this generous gift, we were given the extraordinary opportunity to reconceive the interpretation of the Museum's renowned Islamic collections, and to showcase previously unknown or undisplayed works in a new presentation of the visual culture of the Islamic world. Without it, we could not have produced this book, which brings a greater understanding of the Islamic world to a much wider audience. We are therefore grateful to the Foundation and its chairman, Syed Mokhtar Albukhary, and for the support of Syed Mohamed Albukhary, Director of the Islamic Arts Museum Malaysia.

We are also indebted to those at our own institution who championed this project at its different stages, enabling us to bring it to fruition. Neil MacGregor, the British Museum's former director, inaugurated the partnership with the Albukhary Foundation, and Hartwig Fischer, our current director, embraced the project upon his arrival, understanding the potential for its impact. Jonathan Lubikowski, Project Manager for the Albukhary Gallery, ensured the smooth operation of all aspects of the gallery and book project with his tireless commitment and positive energy. We would also like to thank Jonathan Williams, Deputy Director of Collections, and, in particular, Jonathan Tubb, Keeper of the Department of the Middle East, for supporting us and advocating on our behalf throughout.

The stories told by the objects in this book emphasize the vast and diverse nature of the British Museum's Islamic collections and, by extension, of the Islamic world. To share them, we relied not only on our own knowledge and research of the collections, but also on the expertise and advice of numerous academic colleagues and friends both within and outside the Museum. Among these, we would like especially to acknowledge our two external readers, Sussan Babaie and Scott Redford, who selflessly and carefully read the text cover to cover making invaluable comments. We are additionally grateful to those who read, translated or contributed significantly to individual sections, including Aydın Azizzadeh, Julia Bray, Dominic Parviz Brookshaw, Stefano Carboni, Vesta Sarkhosh Curtis, Irving J. Finkel, Annabel Gallop, Abdullah Ghouchani, Melanie Gibson, Rachel Goshgarian, Alexandra Green, Sarah Johnson, Fiona Kerlogue, Bora Keskiner, Susan La Niece, Michael Macdonald, Leslee Michelsen, Beverley Nenk, Oya Pancaroğlu, Monica Park, Seth Priestman, Marika Sardar, Judy Rudoe, Ünver Rüstem, Sunil Sharma, Tim Stanley, Susan Stronge, Dora Thornton, Charles Tripp, Rosalind Wade-Haddon, Oliver Watson, Michael J. Willis, Charles-Hossein

Zenderoudi and Marie Zenderoudi. Other colleagues provided advice and help at various stages, including Muhammad Abdel-Haleem, James Allan, Doris Behrens-Abouseif, Julie Anderson, Richard Blurton, Sheila Canby, Emine Fetvacı, Christiane J. Gruber, Jessica Harrison-Hall, Julie Hudson, Timothy Insoll, Stephennie Mulder, Sam Nixon, Elisabeth O'Connell, Michael J. Rogers, Laurie Margot Ross, Martina Rugiadi, Iain Shearer, Eleanor Sims, Christopher Spring, Rachel Ward, Ayşin Yoltar-Yıldırım and Kathy Zurek-Doule. Any errors remain our own.

We are also indebted to others at the British Museum who have generously shared with us their knowledge, skills, time and ultimately their passion for objects to help achieve this project. Lack of room prohibits us from sharing the true extent of their hard work and dedication, but they are Wendy Adamson, Dean Baylis, Rachel Berridge, Duygu Camurcuoğlu, Michelle DeCarteret, Jennifer Ellison, Stuart Frost, Hazel Gardiner, John Giblin, David Green, Angela Grimshaw, Jeremy Hill, Imran Javed, Sushma Jansari, Nathan Harrison, Loretta Hogan, Verena Kotonski, Imogen Laing, Denise Ling, Rocio Mayol, Aude Mongiatti, Saray Naidorf, Daniel O'Flynn, Miriam Orsini, Jane Portal, Monique Pullan, Tess Sanders, St John Simpson, Matthias Sotiras, Tanya Szrajber, Francesca Villiers, Richard Wakeman, Carol Weiss, Gareth Williams, Thomas Williams, Helen Wolfe, Hannah Woodley, Holly Wright, and Katherine Young. We are also grateful to our interns and volunteers, Naciem Nikkhah, Shazia Jamal and Reem Alireza.

This book is led by its objects, so we owe a tremendous debt to our talented photographers for the time and effort they devoted in the creation of the beautiful images on these pages. We would like to express our appreciation and admiration to Joanna Fernandes, John Williams, Dudley Hubbard, Kevin Lovelock, Saul Peckham and Michael Row.

At Thames & Hudson, we thank Julian Honer and Philip Watson for orchestrating the project, as well as Peter Dawson (of Grade Design), Ben Plumridge, Susanna Ingram and Susannah Lawson. We are grateful to James Alexander for producing the map of the Islamic world. Our sincere gratitude also goes to Claudia Bloch and Sara Forster, who shepherded the book on the British Museum side from its inception to this point in collaboration with Thames & Hudson.

Finally, we wish to extend a special thanks to our families, who have endured many late nights and weekends without us, some of whom will hopefully appreciate the magnitude of Islamic visual culture and the reason for this book's conception when they grow older.

Credits

All images are © The Trustees of the British Museum, apart from: **Introduction 1** Shadia Alem; **2** © Dereje/Shutterstock.com; **4** © Renata Sedmakova/Shutterstock.com; **5** © Pier Giorgio Carloni/Shutterstock.com; **1.6.3** © Victoria and Albert Museum, London; **1.8.1** and **2.0.3** Reproduced by permission of the artists; **2.5.1** Ayman Yossri Daydban; **2.5.4, 2.6.4** and **3.0.6** are all reproduced by permission of the artists; **3.13.3** Bibliothèque nationale de France; **4.24.1** British Library, London, UK © British Library Board. All Rights Reserved/Bridgeman Images; **4.25.1** Collection Nationaal Museum van Wereldculturen; **5.1.2** © Charles-Hossein Zenderoudi/ADAGP, Paris, 2018. **5.10.1** © The Shafic Abboud Estate. Courtesy of Claude Lemand Gallery, Paris. **5.10.2, 5.10.3, 5.10.4, 5.11.1, 6.0.1, 6.0.3, 6.3.1, 6.3.2, 6.3.3, 6.4.1** and **6.4.2** are all reproduced by permission of the artists; **6.5.3** © Ibrahim El-Salahi. All rights reserved, DACS 2018.

Text credits: **p. 12** quote in cap. 5 from Edmund W. Smith, *Akbar's Tomb, Sikandarah* (Allahabad, 1909), 35; **p. 12** quote from Irwin 1997:31; **p. 28** quote from Irwin 1997:25; **p. 34** quote in caption 1 from Jones 1783 (with commentary by Julia Bray); **p. 69** quote in cap. 3 from Nicholson 1911:66–70); **p. 72** quote in cap. 1 from Savage-Smith and Smith 1980; **p. 80** quote from Northedge 2007:271; **p. 80** 'became a paradigm…' quote from Gonnella 2013:81; **p. 80** quote in cap. 1 from Scott-Meisami 2001:78; **p. 84** quote from Irwin 2016:40; **p. 87** 'stretched from…' quote from Metcalf 1997; **p. 112** Ibn al-Athir quote from Hillenbrand 1999; **p. 113** Ibn Sa'id quote from Raby 2102:12; **p. 243** quote in cap. 1 trans. Oliver Watson; **p. 122** quote from Allan 1973:27; **p. 127** quote from Arberry 1955:24–25; **p. 122** quote in cap. trans. Tim Stanley; **p. 214** quote from Bovill 1958:197; **p. 236** quote trans. Dick Davis; **p. 243** quote in cap. 2 from Toorawa 1993; **p. 243** quote in cap. 3 trans. Simone Fatal.

Index

Europe: influenced by Islamic countries 156, 170, 172, 173, 174; influence on Islamic countries 164, 165, 178, 188, 189
evil eye 71, 108, 190, 191
ewers 29, 94, 95, 120, 121, 160, 185, 185

Faiz, Faiz Ahmed 256
Fath Ali Shah 152, 177, 183
Fatima (daughter of the Prophet) 60, 71
Fatimids 77, 78, 106–11, 132
felt 69, 190, 190
Ferghana 193, 198
Firdawsi, Abu'l Qasim 89, 136, 226, 236
France: metalwork 34
frankincense 83
Franks see Crusades/Crusaders
Franks, Sir Augustus Wollaston 11
fritware see stonepaste ceramics
Fruchtermann, Max 165
Fustat (Old Cairo) 106, 108; ceramics 57, 85, 130, 131; drawings 116; textiles 132

Galata, Mevlevi lodge 164
Gaur 194; Tantipara mosque 194
Gawharsdad 144
Gell, Sir William 124
Genghis Khan see Chinggis Khan
Geniza documents 108, 109
geomancy 72, 73
Georgian dress 240
Ghaibi 130
Ghana textiles 213, 213
Ghaznavids 77, 89, 94, 193
Ghazni tiles 88
Ghurids 88, 89, 94, 96, 193
gilding: calligraphy 55, 158, 231; ceramics 136, 140, 141; glass 25, 30, 30, 114, 115, 122, 122, 126, 126, 148, 201; leather and hide 209; manuscripts 221, 228; metalwork 86, 179; painting 154
glass 30–1, 114–15; Byzantine 31; cameo decoration 92, 93; Egypt 25, 122, 126, 126, 127, 146; enamelled 25, 30, 126–7, 126, 127, 146, 148; gilded 25, 30, 30, 114, 115, 122, 122, 126, 126, 148, 201; India 201, 201; Iran 31, 92, 92, 93; Iraq 31, 187; Lebanon 114, 114; lustre-painted 122; millefiori 31, 31; Palestine 114, 114; sandwich 30, 30; Sasanian 30, 31; Sicily 114; Syria 25, 30, 31, 31, 113, 114, 114, 115, 118, 126, 126, 127, 148; Turkey 166; wheel-cutting 31, 31, 92
Goa 200

Godman, Edith 11
Godman, Frederick Du Cane 11
Golconda 193, 194
gold 40, 79, 106, 214; amulets 59, 71; coins 21, 32, 32, 33, 49, 76, 76, 214, 215; dishes and vessels 34, 99, 99; ingots 214, 214; daggers 204; jewellery 107, 205, 205, 214, 214; pendants 107; see also gilding
gold inlay 73, 94, 128, 129, 142, 142, 143, 145, 164, 187, 209, 228
goldsmith's box 181, 181
gold thread see metal thread
Golestan, Hengamesh 248, 248
Granada: Alhambra 12, 13, 41, 124, 125, 134, 135; ceramics 123, 134, 135; horse bridle 135; gravestones and markers 23, 23, 26, 26, 37, 37, 82, 157, 194
Great Mongol Shahnama 221, 238
Greeks 156, 161

hadith 44, 46, 56
Hafiz 179, 186, 187
haft rangi see under ceramics
Haghe, Louis 22
Hajj 8, 56, 66, 125
al-Hajjaj ibn Yusuf 33
Hamadan 142
hammams 156, 170
Hamzanama 224, 225
Hand of Fatima 71, 71
Harar 212; alam 212, 212
al-Hariri 111
Harun al-Rashid 84
Hasan, Sultan 124
hatayi 160, 161, 163, 163; see also khata'i
Hayrettin Barbarossa 162
head-cloths 250, 251
Hebron 250
Hedwig beakers 113, 114, 114
Heraclius, Emperor 32, 32
heraldry 125
Herat 79, 137, 144; drawings 232; metalwork 89, 94, 94, 95, 96, 142, 145, 187, 187
hide see leather and hide
Hinduism 192, 193, 196, 197
hookahs see huqqas
house models 104, 104
Hülagü 49, 77
Humayun 154
huqqas 200, 201, 201
hurufiyya 243, 243
Husayn (grandson of the Prophet) 60, 60, 178
hyacinths 161
Hyderabad 194

Ibadis 60
Ibn Arabi 234
Ibn al-Athir 112

Ibn al-Bawwab 35
Ibn al-Muqaffa 44, 45
Ibn al-Tammar al-Wasiti 98, 99
Ibn Battutah 11
Ibn Fadlan 86
Ibn Jubayr 8
Ibn Khaldun 17, 125
Ibn Muqla 35, 37, 230
Ibn Rushd (Averroes) 44
Ibn Sa'id 113, 120
Ibn Yamin Fariyumadi 139
Ibn Zamrak 12
Ibrahim, Prophet see Abraham, Prophet
Ibrahim Adil Shah II 192, 192, 195, 195
Ibrahim Lodi 198
iconoclasm 46–7, 47
Idris, Prophet 72
Ilkhanids 77, 136, 137, 138–43, 146, 222
illustrated manuscripts see painting (manuscript)
ilm al-raml see geomancy
Imad al-Din Zangi 113, 115
incense burners 20, 20, 83, 119, 128
India 193–201; alams (standards) 61; albums 222, 222, 223; amulets 71; ceramics 83; chess 50; coins 49; daggers 204, 204; drawings 233; dress 175; glass 201, 201; jade 197, 197, 198, 198, 199, 199, 204, 204; jewellery 205, 205; gravestones 196, 196; metalwork 61, 71, 94, 96, 96, 200, 202–3, 202, 203; painting 40, 63, 155, 176, 192, 195, 221, 222, 224, 225, 234, 235, 239; pan and pandans 200; sitars 220; stone-carvings 194, 196, 199; tobacco and huqqas 200, 201, 201; tombs 13; trade 174, 196
indigo 209
Indonesia 208; batik 208, 209, 209; keris (kris) 208, 209, 209; manuscripts 208, 208; shadow puppets 208, 209, 209, 258, 258; textiles 210, 210, 211
inscriptions: amulets 56, 56, 71; architectural decoration 54, 107, 194; ceramics 21, 38, 39, 39, 43, 57, 57, 58, 71, 85, 89, 90, 91, 103, 103, 131, 131, 134, 134, 138, 138, 139, 140, 140, 160, 160, 161, 161, 169, 178, 178, 179, 179, 184, 184; glass 115, 127, 148; jade 198, 198; metalwork 34, 59, 73, 94, 97, 99, 100, 128, 129, 143, 143, 179, 179, 181; coins 32, 76; seals 86; stone 20, 20, 36, 36,

37, 37, 56, 56, 82, 107, 157, 196, 199; textiles 69, 110, 110, 156, 157, 167, 167, 187, 187, 209, 209; tiles 79, 138, 139; see also calligraphy; coins; scripts
Iran 89, 136–7, 147, 177, 190, 236, 248; albums 223; amulet 56; architectural ornament 29; bookbindings 229; bulla 83; calligraphy 231; carpets and rugs 61; celestial globe 49; ceramics 39, 41, 45, 47, 77, 79, 88, 89, 90–1, 91, 102, 102, 103, 104, 105, 112, 113, 122, 136, 138–41, 138, 139, 140, 141, 145, 146, 174, 178, 179, 180, 182, 183, 184, 185, 185, 236; chess pieces 51; costume albums 240, 240; dervish hat 69; drawings 185, 185, 229, 232, 233; dress 188–9, 188, 189; glass 31, 92–3, 92, 93; incense burner 83; ivory-carvings 51; jade 198; lacquer 177, 181, 186, 186; metalwork 28, 28, 29, 29, 49, 62, 94, 94, 95, 97, 98–9, 98, 99, 100–1, 100, 101, 142–3, 142, 143, 179, 181; mirrors 100–1, 100, 101; mosques 10; painting 20, 21, 45, 47, 68, 176, 177, 182, 183, 183, 222, 229, 235, 236, 237, 240; pavilions 182; photography 248; qibla indicator 49; rock crystal 92; Shia poster 60; stone-carvings 82, 136; textiles 69, 169, 177, 187, 187, 188–9, 188, 189, 190, 253; tiles 21, 21, 39, 47, 79, 136, 138, 138, 139, 179, 180, 180, 182, 182, 183, 236; trade 174, 177
Iraq 113; architectural ornament 29; astrolabe 48; calligraphy 55; ceramics 28, 38, 84, 85, 122, 123; doors 81; dress 175, 175; glass 31, 187; lutes 445; metalwork 29, 29, 48, 113, 120–1, 120, 121; mosques 80; painting (manuscript) 111, 136, 238; painting (wall) 81; photography 255; postcards 18; textiles 175, 175; tiles 31; wood-carvings 81
Isa ibn Ahmad ibn Muhammad 37
Isfahan 8, 11, 79, 152, 155, 177; albums 223; Ali Qapu 203; Chihil Sutun 177, 182; coffeehouses 172; drawings 185, 229; Hasht Bihisht 177, 182; Masjid-i Imam 10, 11; mosque of Shaykh Lutfallah 54; painting 68, 176, 222,

Note on transliteration

As this book is a general introduction, the transliteration of terms and phrases from their original source has been kept to a minimum. Most transliterations derive from the Arabic alphabet, with some variations (i.e., *v* vs *w* in Persian); in other cases, such as for Ottoman Turkish, the modern Turkish spelling in Latin script is used. Dates refer to the Gregorian calendar (AD) unless they are inscribed on the featured objects, in which case the Islamic calendar (AH) – which begins after the emigration, or *hijra*, of the Prophet Muhammad from Mecca to Medina – will also be given.

Key to authors' initials

AM: Amandine Mérat
FS: Fahmida Suleman
LA: Ladan Akbarnia
RWH: Rosalind Wade Haddon
SP: Seth Priestman
VP: Venetia Porter
WG: William Greenwood
ZKH: Zeina Klink-Hoppe

First published in 2018 in hardcover in the United States of America by Thames & Hudson Inc., 500 Fifth Avenue, New York, New York 10110

www.thamesandhudsonusa.com

Library of Congress Control Number 2018932601

ISBN 978-0-500-48040-3

Printed and bound in China by C & C Offset Printing Co. Ltd.